Michele
Walker
12/93

A Treasury of Needlecrafts

A Treasury of Needlecrafts

Home Sewing ~ Knitting
Crochet ~ Cross-Stitch ~ Quilting
Plastic Canvas

Jean Leinhauser, Rita Weiss, and the Editors of the American School of Needlework

Rodale Press, Emmaus, Pennsylvania

Our Mission

We publish books that empower people's lives.

RODALE BOOKS

Printed in the United States of America on acid-free ∞ paper

Produced for Rodale Press by American School of Needlework, Inc.

If you have any questions or comments concerning this book, please write:

Rodale Press
Book Readers' Service
33 East Minor Street
Emmaus, PA 18098

On the cover (clockwise from top left): Delphiniums and Roses, page 105; Razz Bearry, page 240; The Basket Quilt, page 221; Ribbons and Lace Jewelry Box, page 200; Romance Afghan, page 98; Our Neighborhood Afghan, page 98; Seashell Wall Vase, page 50; Time for Tea Doily, page 72.

ISBN 0–87596–592–X

2   4   6   8   10   9   7   5   3

Contents

Credits

American School of Needlework, Inc.
l455 Linda Vista Drive
San Marcos, CA 92069

Editorial Staff:
Jean Leinhauser, President
Rita Weiss, Executive Vice President
Roberta Matela, Vice President
Carol Wilson Mansfield, Art Director
Jane Cannon Meyers, Creative Director
Ann Harnden, Cross Stitch Editor
Carly Poggemeyer, Plastic Canvas Editor
Linda Causee, Quilting Editor
Mary Ann Frits, Sandra Scoville, Kathy Wesley,
   Knit and Crochet Editors
Meredith Montross, Associate Editor
Pat Hawes, Production Assistant
Candy Matthews, Administrative Assistant

Book Design:
Joyce Lerner, Graphic Solutions, Inc-Chicago

Cover Design:
Anita G. Patterson, Rodale Press, Inc.

Introduction

This book is truly a treasury — a trove of wonderful patterns in all of the most popular needlework skills.

The collection is from the archives of the American School of Needlework, Inc., a company dedicated to providing needlework instruction and patterns in printed form.

For each needlework skill — whether knitting, crocheting or counted cross stitch, we have provided easy to follow instructions for beginners (or as a refresher for the more experienced), followed by a collection of patterns.

The novice needleworker can sit down with this book and learn a variety of new skills: knitting, crocheting, crocheting with thread, counted cross stitch, needlepoint on plastic canvas, and home sewing.

The knitter will delight in patterns for traditional fisherman sweaters, beautiful afghans, baby clothes and fashion garments. The crocheter will enjoy making afghans, a gorgeous thread tablecloth, and lovely lacy pillows.

The cross stitcher will find designs for samplers, afghans, a table runner, towels and much more, all with easy to follow charts.

Plastic canvas devotees will enjoy making figural doorstops, Christmas decorations, baskets and mug mats.

The sewer will find a wealth of patterns: for nostalgic quilts, teddy bears, and table toppers and skirts.

We've enjoyed compiling this volume for you, and we hope you will have as much pleasure making the projects as we had creating them for you.

Jean Leinhauser

Rita Weiss

Knitting & Crocheting

Knitting & Crocheting

Knitting is one of the oldest needlework skills. Shepherds used to knit as they tended their flocks; knitted socks, sweaters, hats and gloves have warmed us for centuries. For many years knitting was done exclusively by men. In England, the knitting guilds would not admit women and the men jealously guarded their special techniques and patterns.

Today we knit fashion sweaters using beautiful yarns; warm and practical afghans with synthetic yarns that will withstand machine washing; and soft baby clothes with fine yarn. Nearly every baby arrives to a layette that includes at least one lovingly hand-knitted garment.

Crocheting is a newcomer on the block compared to knitting. Early records are unclear as to its origins, but we think fishermen may have carved bone hooks to use in working on their nets. Crochet came into its own as an imitation of fine lace, and reached its highest point with the magnificent pieces of Irish crochet produced in convents during the famines in Ireland in the 1800s.

Crocheting is quicker than knitting, and is easier to learn. It gives a bulkier fabric, and is thus not as often used for fashion garments. But for afghans, toys and accessories, it knows no equal. Today, with the great interest in things of the past, crocheters of all ages are using fine crochet cotton and steel hooks to produce doilies, bedspreads, tablecloths and accessory items.

Crocheting How-To

Chain (ch)

Crochet always starts with a basic chain stitch. To begin, make a slip loop knot on hook (**Fig 1**), leaving a 4" end of yarn.

Step 1: Take hook in right hand, holding it between thumb and third finger (**Fig 2**), and rest index finger near tip of hook.

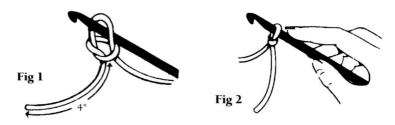

Fig 1   4"   Fig 2

Step 2: Take slip loop in thumb and index finger of left hand and bring yarn over third finger of left hand (**Fig 3a**), catching it loosely at left palm with remaining two fingers (**Fig 3b**).

Step 3: Bring yarn over hook from back to front (**Fig 4**) and draw through loop on hook: one chain stitch made. Repeat Step 3 for each additional chain desired, moving your left thumb and index finger up close to the hook after each stitch or two (**Fig 5**).

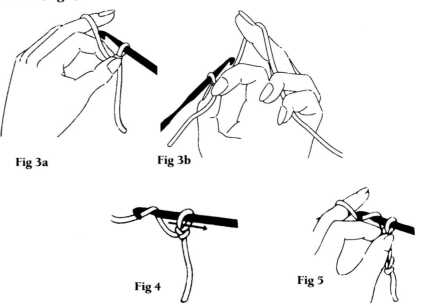

Fig 3a   Fig 3b

Fig 4   Fig 5

When counting number of chains, do not count the loop on the hook or the starting slip knot.

Single Crochet (sc)

First, make a chain to desired length.

Step 1: Insert hook in top loop of 2nd chain from hook (**Fig 6**); hook yarn (bring yarn over hook from back to front) and draw through (**Fig 7**).

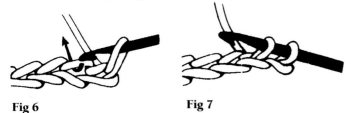

Fig 6   Fig 7

Step 2: Hook yarn and draw through 2 loops on hook (**Fig 8**): one single crochet made. Work a single crochet (repeat Steps 1 and 2) in each remaining chain.

Fig 8

To work additional rows, chain 1 and turn work counter-clockwise. Inserting hook under 2 loops of the stitch (**Fig 9**), work a single crochet (as before) in each stitch across.

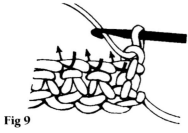

Fig 9

Double Crochet (dc)

Double crochet is a taller stitch than single crochet. Begin by making a chain to desired length.

Step 1: Bring yarn once over the hook; insert hook in the top loop of the 4th chain from hook (**Fig 10**). Hook yarn and draw through (**Fig 11**).

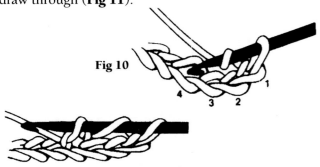

Fig 10

Fig 11

Step 2: Hook yarn and draw through first 2 loops on hook (**Fig 12**).

Fig 12

Step 3: Hook yarn and draw through last 2 loops on hook (**Fig 13**): one double crochet made. Work a double crochet (repeat Steps 1 through 3) in each remaining chain.

Fig 13

To work additional rows, make 3 chains and turn work counter-clockwise. Beginning in 2nd stitch (**Fig 14**) (3 chains count as first double crochet), work a double crochet (as before) in each stitch across (remember to insert hook under 2 top loops of stitch). At end of row, work last double crochet in the top chain of beginning chain-3 (**Fig 15**).

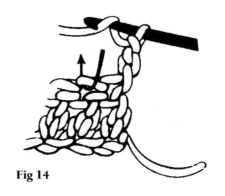

Fig 14

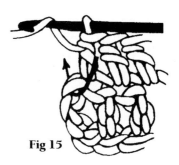

Fig 15

Half Double Crochet (hdc)

This stitch eliminates one step of double crochet - hence its name. It is taller than single crochet, but shorter than double crochet. Begin by making a chain to desired length.

Step 1: Bring yarn over hook; insert hook in top loop of 3rd chain from hook, hook yarn and draw through (3 loops now on hook).

Step 2: Hook yarn and draw through all 3 loops on hook (**Fig 16**): one half double crochet made. Work a half double crochet (repeat Steps 1 and 2) in each remaining chain.

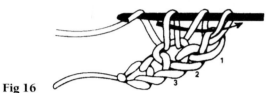

Fig 16

To work additional rows, make 2 chains and turn work counterclockwise. Beginning in 2nd stitch (2 chains count as first half double crochet), work a half double crochet (as before) in each stitch across. At end of row, work last half double crochet in the top chain of beginning chain-2.

Triple Crochet (trc)

Triple crochet is a tall stitch that works up quickly. First make a chain to desired length.

Step 1: Bring yarn twice over the hook, insert hook in 5th chain from hook (**Fig 17**); hook yarn and draw through (**Fig 18**).

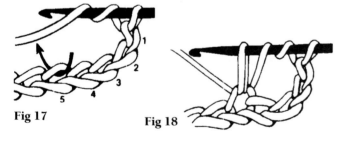

Fig 17   **Fig 18**

Step 2: Hook yarn and draw through first 2 loops on hook (**Fig 19**).

Step 3: Hook yarn and draw through next 2 loops on hook (**Fig 20**).

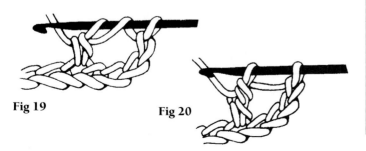

Fig 19   **Fig 20**

Step 4: Hook yarn and draw through remaining 2 loops on hook (**Fig 21**): one triple crochet made. Work a triple crochet (repeat Steps 1 through 4) in each remaining chain.

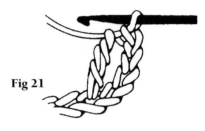

Fig 21

To work additional rows, make 4 chains and turn work counterclockwise. Beginning in 2nd stitch (4 chains count as first triple crochet), work a triple crochet (as before) in each stitch across. At end of row, work last triple crochet in the top chain of chain-4.

Slip Stitch (sl st)

This is the shortest of all crochet stitches, and usually is used to join work, or to move yarn across a group of stitches without adding height. To practice, make a chain to desired length; then work one row of double crochets.

Step 1: Insert hook in first st; hook yarn and draw through both stitch and loop on hook in one motion (**Fig 22**).

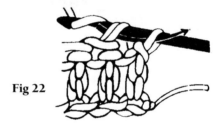

Fig 22

One slip stitch made. Work a slip stitch (repeat Step 1) in each stitch across.

Front Loop and Back Loop

Front Loop is the loop toward you at the top of the stitch.

Back Loop is the loop away from you at the top of the stitch.

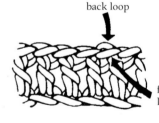

back loop

front loop

Overcast Stitch

To join two pieces together, *overcast stitch* is worked loosely.

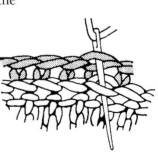

Crocheting with Thread and a Steel Hook

Don't be afraid to crochet with steel hooks and finer thread. You will be using exactly the same stitches you're familiar with, but at first it will feel clumsy and awkward. For an experienced crocheter, this is a bit of a surprise - suddenly feeling all thumbs again just as when you first learned to crochet. But this will pass in a few hours of crocheting, as you adjust your tension and working method to the new tools. Soon you will work much more by feel than when working with the heavier yarns. So be patient with any initial clumsiness and confusion - they won't be with you long.

Steel hooks range in size from 00 (large) to 14 (very fine), and are 5" long which is shorter than the aluminum or plastic hooks. Their shape is different from the other crochet hooks. There is the throat, then the shank, and after the shank the steel begins to widen again before it reaches the finger grip (**Fig 23**). When crocheting, it is important that the stitches do not slide beyond the shank as this will cause a loose tension and alter the gauge. If you find you are having difficulty at first, put a piece of cellophane tape around the hook to keep the stitches from sliding past the correct area. With practice, you will work in the right place automatically.

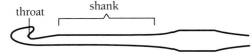

Fig 23

Washing

If your finished project should need washing, use warm water and a mild soap. Wash gently; do not rub, twist or wring. Rinse well, and gently press water out of piece. Roll piece up in a terry towel, then lay it out to dry as explained in the following blocking instructions.

Blocking

This simply means "setting" the finished piece into its final size and shape. To do this, spread the piece out on a flat padded surface (covered with terry toweling), having wrong side facing up. Be sure to shape piece to measurements given with the pattern, having picots, loops, scallops, etc. along the outside edges open and in correct alignment. If necessary, use rust-proof straight pins to hold the edges in place. If piece was not previously washed, dampen it thoroughly with a wet sponge or cloth, or spray it with a commercial spray starch - this will give a firmer shape but not stiff. Let dry completely before removing.

If further blocking is necessary, press through a damp cloth with a moderately hot iron on the wrong side (do not rest iron on any decorative raised stitch). When thoroughly dried, remove.

Starching

Starching Supplies

Before starting this procedure, assemble the following necessary supplies.

1. **Stiffening solution** - use one of the following:

(a) Equal amounts of water and commercial stiffening solution used to stiffen crocheted lace (available in your local craft or needlework store), thoroughly mixed

(b) Equal amounts of white craft glue and water, thoroughly mixed.

(c) Thick solution of commercial boilable starch (liquid or spray starches do not work)

2. **Plastic bag,** the type that locks across the top for mixing solution and soaking crocheted pieces

3. **Pinning board,** such as a sheet of Styrofoam (our preference), piece of cardboard or fabric cutting board, to block flat pieces to shape

4. **Rust-proof straight pins** to pin out and hold project in shape

5. **Plastic wrap** to cover blocking surface so stiffened project will slide off easily when dry

Starching Instructions

Once you have the supplies ready for starching and blocking, proceed as follows:

Step 1: Cover pinning board and blocking form with plastic wrap and secure in place.

Step 2: Pour stiffening solution into a plastic bag or bowl. Immerse project in solution and work into thread. Remove and press out extra stiffening solution. Do not squeeze - project should be very wet, but there should be no solution in the decorative holes (dab with a dry paper towel to correct this). Any excess stiffening solution can be stored in a locked plastic bag for as long as one week, mixing before next use.

Step 3: With right side up, shape stiffened project, being sure the design is properly aligned with all picots, lps, etc. open; using rust-proof pins, pin design in place as desired. Let project dry thoroughly before removing.

> **Hints:**
> 1. Keep hands clean throughout.
> 2. Keep spray water bottle handy to wet and re-shape.
> 3. Do not bend stiffened pieces unless slightly damp, as they may crack.

Knitting How-To

Casting On (CO)

Only one knitting needle is used with this method. First, measure off a length of yarn that allows about 1" for each stitch you are going to cast on. Make a slip knot on needle at this point as follows. Make a yarn loop, insert needle into loop and draw up yarn from free end to make a loop on needle (**Fig 24**). Pull yarn firmly, but not tightly, to form a slip knot on needle (**Fig 25**). This slip knot counts as your first stitch. Now work as follows:

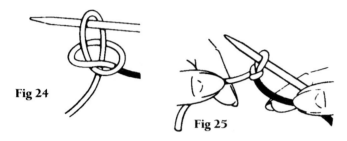

Fig 24

Fig 25

Step 1: Hold needle with slip knot in right hand, with yarn from skein to your right, and measured length of yarn to your left. With left hand, make a yarn loop (**Fig 26**) and insert needle into loop (**Fig 27**).

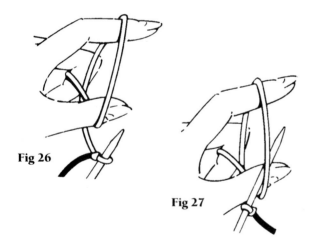

Fig 26

Fig 27

Step 2: Still holding loop in left hand; with right hand, pick up yarn from skein and bring it from back to front around the needle (**Fig 28**).

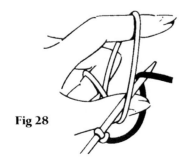

Fig 28

Step 3: Bring needle through loop and toward you; at the same time, pull gently on yarn end to tighten loop (**Fig 29**). Make it snug but not tight below needle.

Fig 29

You now have one cast-on stitch. Repeat Steps 1 through 3 for each additional stitch desired.

The Knit Stitch (K)

Step 1: Hold the needle with cast-on stitches in your left hand. Insert point of right needle in first stitch, from left of the stitch to the right, and under the left needle (**Fig 30**).

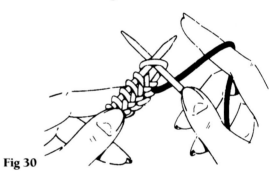

Fig 30

Step 2: With right index finger, bring yarn under and over point of right needle (**Fig 31**).

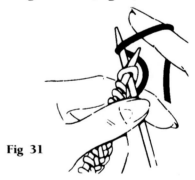

Fig 31

Step 3: Draw yarn through stitch with right needle point (**Fig 32**).

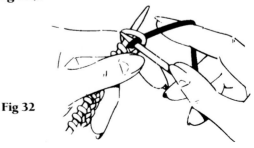

Fig 32

Step 4: Slip the loop on the left needle off, so the new stitch is entirely on the right needle (**Fig 33**).

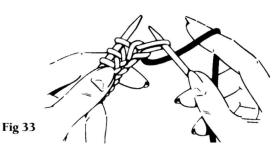

Fig 33

This completes one knit stitch. Repeat steps 1 through 3 for each knit stitch.

The Purl Stitch (P)

The reverse of the knit stitch is called the purl stitch. Instead of inserting the right needle point from left to right under the left needle (as you did for the knit stitch), you will now insert it from right to left, in front of the left needle.

Step 1: Insert right needle, from right to left, into first stitch, and in front of left needle (**Fig 34**).

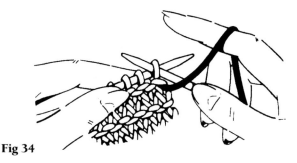

Fig 34

Step 2: Holding yarn in front of work (side toward you), bring it around right needle counterclockwise (**Fig 35**).

Fig 35

Step 3: With right needle, pull yarn back through stitch (**Fig 36**).

Fig 36

Slide stitch off left needle, leaving new stitch on right needle (**Fig 37**).

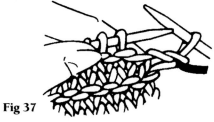

Fig 37

One purl stitch is now completed. Repeat steps 1 through 3 for each purl stitch.

Binding Off (BO)

To bind off on the knit side:

Step 1: Knit the first 2 stitches. Then insert left needle into the first of the 2 stitches (**Fig 38**), and pull it over the second stitch and completely off the needle (**Fig 39**). You have now bound off one stitch.

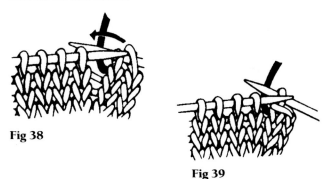

Fig 38

Fig 39

Step 2: Knit one more stitch; insert left needle into first stitch on right needle and pull it over the new stitch and completely off the needle (**Fig 40**). Another stitch is now bound off.

Fig 40

Repeat Step 2 until all sts are bound off and one loop remains on right-hand needle. "Finish off" or "end off" the yarn (cut yarn and draw end through last loop).

To bind off on the purl side:

Step 1: Purl the first 2 stitches. Now insert left needle into the first stitch on right needle, and pull it over the second stitch and completely off the needle. You have now bound off one stitch.

Step 2: Purl one more stitch; insert left needle into first stitch on right needle and pull it over the new stitch and completely off the needle. Another stitch is bound off.

Repeat Step 2 until all sts are bound off. "Finish off" or "end off" the yarn (cut yarn and draw end through last loop).

Yarn Over (YO)

To make a yarn over before a knit stitch, bring yarn to front of work as if you were going to purl, then take it over the right needle to the back into the position for knitting; then knit the next stitch (**Fig 41**).

Fig 41

To make a yarn over before a purl stitch, bring yarn around right needle from front to back, then back around into position for purling; purl the next stitch (**Fig 42**).

Fig 42

Color Changes

Always bring the new color from underneath the old to prevent holes in your knitting.

Blocking Sweaters

We prefer to allow sweaters to block themselves by carefully laying them out in the proper shape and size. Most yarns will respond. If, however, you find this is not satisfactory, we suggest the following:

Read the yarn labels, and follow the manufacturer's instructions. If there are no instructions on the labels, lay the sweater out to the proper shape and size. Cover with a damp, colorfast towel, and allow to dry thoroughly.

Use a steam iron only if absolutely necessary. Synthetic fibers may stretch when heat is applied. Wools and other natural fibers may shrink. Never touch an iron to the yarn.

Picking Up Stitches

To pick up a stitch, hold work with right side facing you. Hold yarn in your left hand behind the work, and a knitting needle in your right hand. Insert the needle into the work from front to back, one stitch from the edge; yarn over as if to knit, and draw the yarn through (**Fig 43**).

To space the stitches evenly, pick up 3 stitches in 3 consecutive edge stitches and then skip 1 edge stitch. Continue picking up stitches in this manner.

Fig 43

Gauge

It is essential to achieve the gauge - number of stitches and rows per inch - given in patt in order to make the correct size.

Before beginning your project, refer to the Gauge Note and make a gauge swatch using the hook or needle and yarn specified. Work several rows; finish off. Place work on a flat surface and measure sts in center of piece. If you have more sts to the inch than specified, use a larger size hook or needle. If you have fewer sts to the inch than specified, use a smaller size hook or needle. Then make another gauge swatch and check your gauge once again. Do not hesitate to change hook or needle size to obtain the specified gauge. Often you will not be able to achieve gauge with the size hook or needle recommended.

While working, continue to check your gauge. Select sts/rnds near the center of your work, using small safety pins or straight pins to identify the sts to be measured and always measure over two or more inches.

Fringe

Basic Instructions

Cut a piece of cardboard about 6" wide and half as long as specified in instructions for strands plus 1/2" for trimming allowance. Wind yarn loosely and evenly lengthwise around cardboard. When card is filled, cut yarn across one end. Do this several times, then begin fringing; you can wind additional strands as you need them.

Single Knot Fringe

Hold specified number of strands for one knot of fringe together, then fold in half. Hold project with right side facing you. Use crochet hook to draw folded end through space or stitch from right to wrong side (**Figs 44 and 45**); pull loose ends through folded section (**Fig 46**) and draw knot up firmly (**Fig 47**). Space knots as indicated in pattern instructions. Trim ends of fringe evenly.

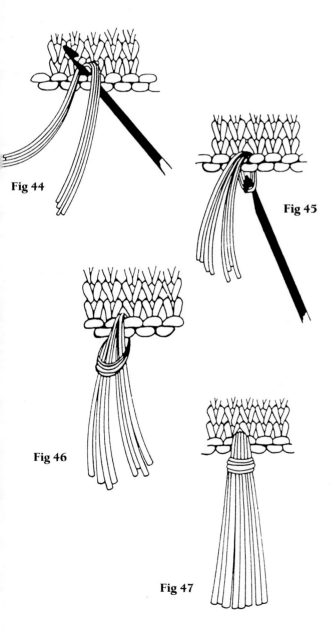

Fig 44

Fig 45

Fig 46

Fig 47

Spaghetti Fringe

Tie each knot with just one strand of yarn. Use same knotting method as Single Knot Fringe.

Double Knot Fringe

Begin by working Single Knot Fringe completely across one end of afghan. With right side facing you and working from left to right, take half the strands of one knot and half the strands in the knot next to it, and knot them together (**Fig 48**).

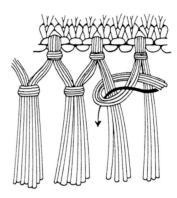

Fig 48

Triple Knot Fringe

First work Double Knot Fringe. Then working again on the right side from left to right, tie third row of knots (**Fig 49**).

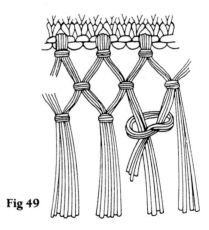

Fig 49

Abbreviations

beg	begin(ning)
bl(s)	back loop(s)
ch(s)	chain(s)
dc	double crochet(s)
dec	decrease (-ing)
fig	figure
hdc(s)	half double crochet(s)
inc	increase (-ing)
K	knit
lp(s)	loop(s)
P	purl
patt	pattern
prev	previous
PSSO	pass slip stitch over
rem	remain(ing)
rep	repeat(ing)
rnd(s)	round(s)
sc(s)	single crochet(s)
sk	skip
sl	slip
sl st(s)	slip stitch(es)
sp(s)	space(s)
st(s)	stitch(es)
stock st	stockinette stitch, knit 1 row, purl 1 row
tog	together
trc(s)	triple crochet(s)
YO	yarn over

Symbols

work even: This term in instructions means to continue working in the pattern as established, without increasing or decreasing.

* An asterisk is used to mark the beginning of a portion of instructions which will be worked more than once; thus, "rep from * twice" means after working the instructions once, repeat the instructions following the asterisk twice more (3 times in all).

† The dagger identifies a portion of instructions that will be repeated again later in the pattern.

: The number after a colon at the end of a row/rnd indicates the number of stitches you should have when the row/rnd has been completed.

() Parentheses are used to enclose instructions which should be worked the exact number of times specified immediately following the parentheses, such as: (K1, Pl) twice. They are also used to set off and clarify a group of sts that are to be worked all into the same sp or st, such as: (2 dc, ch 1, 2 dc) in corner sp.

[] Brackets and () parentheses are used to provide additional information to clarify instructions.

World's Easiest Knitted Sweater

designed by Carol Wilson Mansfield and Mary Thomas

This is just about the easiest knitted sweater we've ever seen – but it looks great with everything from jeans to a skirt. Done in a T-shape, it fits well and the finishing is very easy. We like the pretty stripes, but you can also make it in a solid color. This sweater is a perfect project for beginning knitters.

World's Easiest Knitted Sweater

Sizes

Body Bust:	32"	34"	36"	38"

Garment Measurements:

bust	34"	36"	38"	40"
length to underarm	13"	13"	13"	13"
sleeve length	8 1/2"	8 1/2"	8 1/2"	8 1/2"

Size Note: Instructions are written for body bust sizes as follows: 32(34-36-38).

Materials

Worsted weight yarn:
    11(12-13-14) oz beige (MC - main color);
    1 1/2 oz medium blue (C - contrasting color)
Sizes 6 and 8, 14" straight knitting needles (or size
    required for gauge)
6 stitch markers

Gauge

With larger size needles in stock st,
    9 sts = 2"; 12 rows = 2"

Instructions

Back

With smaller size needles and MC, cast on 77(81-87-91) sts. Work ribbing as follows:

Ribbing Row 1 (right side): * K1, P1; rep from * to last st; K1.

Ribbing Row 2: P1, * K1, P1; rep from * across. Rep last 2 rows until ribbing measures 2 1/2" from cast-on edge, ending by working Ribbing Row 2.

Change to larger size needles and work in pattern as follows:

Row 1 (marking row): K17(17-18-18), place marker, K3, place marker; * K17(19-21-23), place marker, K3, placemarker; rep from * once more; K17(17-18-18).

(**Note:** Sl markers on each following row.)

Row 2: Purl to first marker, K3; * purl to next marker, K3; rep from * once more; purl rem sts.

Row 3: * Knit.

Rep last 2 rows until work measures approx 13" from cast-on edge (or desired length to underarm), ending by working a wrong-side row. Use small safety pins or pieces of contrasting yarn and mark each end of last row for beg of armholes.

Continuing in patt as established (beg with Row 3, then rep

Rows 2 and 3) with MC, work 8(10-8-10) rows, then work striping pattern of 4 rows C, * 8(8-10-10) rows MC, 4 rows C; rep from * once more. When these last 28(28-32-32) rows of striping pattern are completed, finish off C and continue with MC only.

Next Row: Knit across, removing markers.

Continuing with same needle size, beg with Ribbing Row 2 and work in ribbing (same as for bottom ribbing) until armholes measure 8(8 1/4-8 1/2-9)" from markers, ending by working Ribbing Row 1 (right-side row). Bind off in knit.

Front

Work same as for back.

Sleeve (make 2)

With smaller size needles and MC, cast on 51(53-55-57) sts. Work in ribbing (rep Ribbing Rows 1 and 2 of Back) for 1", ending by working Ribbing Row 1.

Increase Row (wrong side): P1, (K1, P1) twice; * inc in next st (knit in front and back of same st), P1; rep from * to last 6(4-6-4) sts, (K1, P1) 3(2-3-2) times = 71(75-77-81) sts.

Change to larger size needles and work in pattern as follows:

Row 1 (marking row): K 34(36-37-39), place marker, K3; place marker, K 34(36-37-39). (**Note:** Sl markers on each following row.)

Row 2: Purl to marker, K3, purl rem sts. Change to C for stripe.

Row 3: With C, knit across.

Rows 4 through 6: Continuing with C, rep Rows 2 and 3 once, then rep Row 2 once more. Finish off C; change to MC.

Continuing with MC only, work in patt as established (beg with Row 3, then rep Rows 2 and 3) until sleeve measures approx 8 1/2" from cast-on edge (or desired length), ending by working a wrong-side row. Bind off loosely in knit.

Finishing

Sew shoulder seams, leaving about 9" center opening for neck. Sew top bound-off edge of each sleeve to armhole edge between markers, having center top of sleeve at shoulder seam. Sew side and sleeve seams. Weave in all ends. Block if necessary (see Blocking Sweaters, page 8).

Women's Fashion Vests

Nothing adds versatility to a wardrobe more than a vest. These two knitted charmers are a pleasure to make and fit beautifully.

Shawl-Collared Cable   **Nine to Five Vest**

Nine to Five Vest

designed by Sandy Scoville

This neat little knitted vest is great alone, or worn under a suit jacket or blazer. The vertical stripe is worked as a slip stitch, so no bobbins are required. If these aren't your colors, try black with red or rust with camel.

Sizes

Small (32-34)
Medium (36)
Large (38-40)
Finished chest measurement: About 36"(39", 42").
Instructions are written for size small (sm). Changes for
    size medium (med), and large (lg) are in
    parentheses ( ).

Materials

Worsted weight yarn:
    420(480, 540) yds, or 7(8, 9) oz navy;
    240(300, 360) yds, or 4(5, 6) oz green
Size 7 straight knitting needles, or size required for gauge
Size 5, 29" circular knitting needle
Stitch holder
3 buttons, 5/8" in diameter

Gauge

With larger needles, 5 sts = 1" in stock st

Pattern Stitch

Seed St
Row 1: * K1, P1, rep from * across.

Row 2: * P1, K1, rep from * across.

Rows 3 and 4: Rep Rows 1 and 2.

Instructions

Note: Vest is worked in alternating color stripes; when changing colors, drop the old color and carry it up the side, twisting it around the new color.

Back

With larger needles and green, cast on 76(86, 96) sts.

Row 1: Knit.

Row 2: Purl.

Row 3: Drop green, tie on navy; with navy, sl l; * K4, sl 1; rep from * across.

Row 4: Sl 1; * P4, sl 1; rep from * across.

Row 5: Sl 1; * K4, sl 1; rep from * across.

Row 6: Rep Row 4.

Row 7: With green, sl 1, K1, PSSO; knit across to last 2 sts; K2 tog.

Row 8: Purl.

Row 9: With navy, sl 1, K1, PSSO, K2; * sl 1, K4, rep from * to last 2 sts; K2 tog.

Row 10: P3, sl 1; * P4, sl 1, rep from * across, ending P3.

Continue in patt as established: 2 rows green, 4 rows navy, slipping every 5th st to maintain vertical green line. Inc 1 st each end on this and every 4th row 7(8, 8) times: 88(100, 110) sts. Work without inc until back measures 8" from beg, or desired length to underarm. End with a purl row.

Armhole Shaping
Row 1: Bind off 5(6, 8) sts, knit across in patt.
Row 2: Bind off 5(6, 8) sts, purl across in patt.
Row 3: Sl 1, K1, PSSO; knit in patt to last 2 sts; K2 tog.
Row 4: Purl across in patt.
Rep Rows 3 and 4, 3(4, 5) times more: 70(78, 82) sts. Continue in patt without dec until armhole measures 9" (9 1/2", 10"), ending with a purl row.

Shoulder and Neck Shaping
Note: Both shoulders will be worked at the same time with separate skeins of yarn.
Row 1: Work in patt over 27(30, 31) sts; tie on new skein; bind off next 16(18, 20) sts; continue in patt across.
Row 2: Purl in patt across both shoulders.
Row 3: Bind off 7(8, 9) sts; work in patt to last 2 sts on neck edge, K2 tog; drop first yarn, pick up second yarn; sl 1, K1, PSSO, work in patt across.
Row 4: Bind off 7(8, 9) sts; work in patt across both shoulders.
Rows 5 and 7: Rep Row 3.
Rows 6 and 8: Rep Row 4.
Bind off rem sts.

Right Front

With navy, cast on 2 sts (see Casting On, page 6); turn and P2.

Row 1: Inc (knit, leaving st on left-hand needle, then knit in bl of same st: inc made) in both sts: 4 sts.
Row 2: Purl.
Row 3: Tie on green; inc in first st, K2, inc in last st.
Row 4: Purl, cast on one st.

Row 5: With navy, inc, sl 1, K3; in next st K1, leaving st on left-hand needle; place right-hand needle behind left-hand needle, insert into back of same st, sl st onto right-hand needle; K1: 9 sts, 7 navy and 2 green.

Row 6: P1, sl 1 (green), P4, sl 1 (green), P2.

Row 7: Inc; K1, sl 1, K4, sl 1, K1; cast on 3 sts.

Row 8: (P4, sl 1) twice, P3.

Row 9: With green, inc; knit across; cast on 3 sts.

Row 10: Purl.

Row 11: With green, K1, leaving st on left-hand needle, place right-hand needle in back of left-hand needle; knit into back of same st with navy (inc made); K3; (sl 1, K4) twice; sl 1, K2, cast on 2 sts.

Row 12: (P4, sl 1 green) 4 times.

Row 13: With navy, K1 leaving st on left-hand needle; place right-hand needle behind left-hand needle, insert into back of same st, sl sts onto right-hand needle; (K4, sl 1) 3 times; K4.

Row 14: (P4, sl 1) 4 times; P1: 21 sts.

Row 15: With green, inc; knit across; cast on 6 sts: 28 sts.

Row 16: Purl across.

Row 17: With navy, inc, K1; (sl 1, K4) 5 times; sl 1; cast on 4 sts.

Row 18: (P4, sl 1) 6 times; P3.

Row 19: Inc, K2; (sl 1, K4) 6 times; cast on 5 sts: 39 sts.

Row 20: (P4, sl 1) 7 times; P4.

Note: The first sl st will be blue.

Row 21: With green, inc; knit across; cast on 0(5, 5) sts: 40(45, 45) sts.

Row 22: Purl.

Row 23: With navy, K1 leaving st on left-hand needle; place right-hand needle behind left-hand needle, insert into back of same st, sl st onto right-hand needle; knit in patt across; cast on 0(0, 5) sts: 41(46, 51) sts.

Row 24: Purl in patt.

Row 25: Inc; knit in patt across: 42(47, 52) sts.

Row 26: Purl in patt.

Row 27: With green, inc; knit across to last 2 sts; K2 tog.

Row 28: Purl.

Row 29: With navy, inc; knit in patt across to last 2 sts; K2 tog: 42(47, 52) sts.

Row 30: Purl in patt.

Row 31: Knit in patt to last st; inc in last st: 43(48, 53) sts.

Row 32: Purl in patt.

Row 33: With green, knit in patt.

Row 34: Purl.

Row 35: With navy, knit in patt.

Row 36: Purl in patt.

Row 37: Knit in patt across to last st; inc in st: 44(49, 54) sts.

Continuing in patt, work 5" without inc. Dec (sl 1, K1, PSSO) at center front edge every right-side row 4(6, 8) times, then every 4th row until 27(29, 30) sts rem.

At the same time . . .

Beg armhole shaping when front measures 8" from last cast-on row (side edge) and patt matches back.

Armhole Shaping

Row 1: Knit in patt.

Row 2: Bind off 5(6, 8) sts, purl across in patt.

Row 3: Knit in patt to last 2 sts; K2 tog.

Row 4: Purl in patt.

Rep Rows 3 and 4, 3(4, 5) times.

Continue in patt, dec as instructed on center front, until armhole measures 9"(91/2", 10") and patt matches back.

Shoulder and Neck Shaping

Row 1: Knit.

Row 2: Bind off 7(8, 8) sts; purl across.

Rows 3 and 5: Rep Row 1.

Rows 4 and 6: Rep Row 2.

Bind off rem 6(5, 6) sts.

Left Front

With navy, cast on 2 sts; turn and P2.

Row 1: Inc (knit, leaving st on left-hand needle, then knit in bl of same st: inc made) in both sts: 4 sts.

Row 2: Purl.

Row 3: Tie on green; inc in first st, K2, inc in last st.

Row 4: Purl, cast on 1 st; cut green.

Row 5: With navy, K1 leaving st on left-hand needle, place right-hand needle in back of left-hand needle, sl st (green) onto right-hand needle; K4, sl 1 green, inc in last st: 9 sts; 2 green, 7 navy.

Row 6: P2, sl 1 (green), P4, sl 1 (green), P1 ; cast on 3 sts.

Row 7: (K4, sl 1) twice; K1, inc: 13 sts.

Row 8: P3, (sl 1, P4) twice; cast on 3 sts.

Row 9: Tie on green, knit to last st; inc.

Row 10: Purl across; cast on 2 sts.

Row 11: With navy (K4, sl 1) 3 times; K3, K1 leaving st on left-hand needle; place right-hand needle behind left-hand needle, insert into back of same st, sl green st onto right-hand needle.

Row 12: (Sl 1, P4) 4 times; with green, cast on one st.

Row 13: Sl 1, (K4, sl 1) 4 times.

Row 14: (Sl 1, P4) 4 times; sl 1; with navy, cast on 6 sts.

Row 15: With green, knit in patt to last st; inc: 28 sts.

Row 16: Purl across; cast on 4 sts.

Row 17: With navy, K1, leaving st on left-hand needle; place right-hand needle behind left-hand needle, insert into back of same st, sl st onto right-hand needle; (K4, sl 1) 6 times; inc in last st.

Row 18: P2; (sl 1, P4) 6 times; sl 1, P1; with navy, cast on 4 sts.

Row 19: K5, (sl 1, K4) 6 times; sl 1, K1; inc in last st: 39 sts.

Row 20: P3; (sl 1, P4) 6 times; sl 1, P5; cast on 0 for sm size, 4 navy and 1 green for med and lg sizes: 39(44, 44) sts.

Row 21: With green, knit to last st; inc: 40(45, 45) sts.

Row 22: Purl across; cast on 0(0, 5) sts: 40(45, 50) sts.

Row 23: With navy, (sl 1, K4) 8(8, 9) times; sl 1, K3; K1 leaving st on left-hand needle; place right-hand needle behind left-hand needle, insert into back of same st, sl st onto right-hand needle: 41(46, 51) sts.

Row 24: Purl in patt.

Row 25: Knit in patt to last st; inc 42(47, 52) sts.

Row 26: Purl in patt.

Row 27: With green, K2 tog; knit to last st, inc.

Row 28: Purl.

Row 29: With navy, K2 tog; knit in patt to last st, inc: 42 (47, 52) sts.

Row 30: Purl in patt.

Row 31: Inc; knit in patt: 43(48, 53) sts.

Row 32: Purl in patt.

Row 33: With green, knit.

Row 34: Purl.

Row 35: With navy, knit in patt.

Row 36: Purl in patt.

Row 37: Inc; knit in patt: 44(49, 54) sts.

Mark this row for measuring later. Continuing in patt, work 5" without inc. Dec (K2 tog) at center front edge every right-side row 4(6, 8) times, then every 4th row until 27(29, 30) sts rem.

At the Same Time . . .

Continuing in patt, beg armhole shaping when front measures 8" from last cast-on row (side edge) and patt matches back.

Armhole Shaping

Note: If necessary, cut green, and rejoin to prevent carrying yarn across the bound off sts.

Row 1: Bind off 5(6, 8) sts, knit across.

Row 2: Purl.

Row 3: K2 tog, knit across.

Row 4: Purl.

Rep Rows 3 and 4, 3(4, 5) times. Continue in patt, dec as instructed on center front until armhole measures 9" (9 1/2", 10") and patt matches back.

Shoulder Shaping

Row 1: Bind off 7(8, 8) sts; knit across.

Row 2: Purl.

Rows 3 and 5: Rep Row 1.

Rows 4 and 6: Rep Row 2.

Bind off rem 6(5, 6) sts.

Finishing

Hold vest with right side facing you; with smaller needles and green, pick up an even number of sts along bottom edge of back. Work 4 rows seed st (see Pattern Stitch, page 14). Bind off loosely in patt.

Sew shoulder seams.

Armhole Edging

Hold vest with right side facing you; with smaller needles and green, pick up an even number of sts evenly spaced along one armhole; work 4 rows seed st (see Pattern Stitch, page 14). Bind off in patt.

Rep for second armhole.

Front Edging

Hold vest with right side facing you; with smaller needles and green, pick up an even number of sts evenly spaced around Left Front; work 4 rows seed st; bind off in patt.

Mark placement of 3 buttons.

Rep edging along Right Front, working buttonholes as follows:

On second row, work seed st to placement of first button; bind off 3 sts; work to placement of second button; bind off 3 sts; rep for 3rd buttonhole. On third row, cast on 3 sts for each buttonhole, replacing the bound off sts.

Sew side seams and center neck border sts. Sew on buttons. Block if necessary (see Blocking Sweaters, page 8).

Shawl-Collared Cable

designed by Sandy Scoville

Cables and seed stitch make this an interesting pattern. The shawl collar is easy to wear, and the front is accented with bright buttons. This knitted vest works well over either a skirt or pants, and is a good mate for jeans. You may want to make several in different colors.

Sizes

Small (32-34)
Med (36)
Lg (38-40)
Finished chest measurement: About 36"(39" 42")
Instructions are written for size small (sm); changes for size medium (med) and large (lg) are in parentheses ( ).

Materials

Worsted weight yarn:
    1000(1100, 1200) yds, or 14 (16, 18) oz rust
Size 7 straight knitting needles, or size required for gauge
Size 5 straight knitting needles
Cable needle
Stitch holder
10 markers
4 buttons, 7/8" in diameter

Gauge

With larger needles, 5 sts = 1" in stock st
With larger needles, 13 sts = 2" in K1, P1 ribbing

Pattern Stitches

Seed Stitch (over odd number of sts)
Row 1: * K, P1; rep from * across, ending K.
Row 2: Rep Row 1.
Rep these 2 rows for patt.

Seed Stitch (over even number of sts)
Row 1: * K1, P1; rep from * across.
Row 2: * P1, K1; rep from * across.
Rep these 2 rows for patt.

Cable Front (CF) (over 10 sts)
Row l: P2, K6, P2.
Row 2: K2, P6, K2.
Row 3: Rep Row 1.
Row 4: Rep Row 2.
Row 5: P2; sl 3 sts onto cable needle and hold in front, K3, K3 from cable needle; P2.
Row 6: Rep Row 2.

Row 7: Rep Row 1.
Row 8: Rep Row 2.

Cable Back (CB) (over 10 sts)
Row 1: P2, K6, P2.
Row 2: K2, P6, K2.
Row 3: Rep Row 1.
Row 4: Rep Row 2.
Row 5: P2; sl 3 sts onto cable needle and hold in back, K3, K3 from cable needle; P2 10 sts.
Row 6: Rep Row 2.
Row 7: Rep Row 1.
Row 8: Rep Row 2.

Instructions

Back

With larger needles, cast on 82(90, 98) sts; change to smaller needles.

Row 1 (right side)**:** * K1, P1; rep from * across.

Rep Row 1 until ribbing measures 3"(3", 3 1/2").

Purl one row, inc 6 sts evenly across 88(96, 104) sts.

Foundation Rows

Row l (right side): With larger needles, K1, P1, K1 (seed st); place marker; * P2, K6, P2: CF; place marker; (K1, P1) 3 times: seed st; rep from * once; place marker; K18(26, 34); place marker; ** (K1, P1) 3 times: seed st; place marker; P2, K6, P2: CB; place marker; rep from ** once; K1, P1, K1 (seed st).

Row 2: K1, P1, K1 (seed st); sl marker, * K2, P6, K2: CB; sl marker, (P1, K1) 3 times; rep from * once; P18(26, 34); ** (P1, K1) 3 times: seed st; K2, P6, K2: CF; rep from ** once; K1, P1, K1 (seed st).

Note: Markers may be removed when you are familiar with the patt as established.
Row 3: Rep Row 1.
Row 4: Rep Row 2.
Row 5: Rep Row 1, twisting cables as instructed in Pattern Stitches above.
Row 6: Rep Row 2.
Row 7: Rep Row 1.
Row 8: Rep Row 2.
Rep these 8 rows for patt until back measures 11" (11", 11 l/2") from beg, ending with a Row 8.

Armhole Shaping

Row 1: Bind off 5 sts; work in patt across.
Row 2: Bind off 5 sts; work in patt across.
Row 3: Sl 1, K1, PSSO; work in patt across to last 2 sts, K2 tog.
Row 4: Work in patt across.

Rows 5, 7, and 9: Rep Row 3.

Rows 6, 8, and l0: Rep Row 4 : 70(78, 86) sts. Continue in patt without dec until armhole measures about 7 1/2" (8", 8 l/2"), ending with a wrong-side row.

Neck Shaping

Note: Both shoulders will be worked at the same time using separate skeins of yarn.

Row 1: Work in patt across 22(24, 27) sts; join second skein, bind off center 26(30, 32) sts; work in patt across rem 22 (24, 27) sts.

Row 2: Work in patt across.

Row 3: Work in patt to last 2 sts (right shoulder); K2 tog; (left shoulder) sl 1, K1, PSSO, work in patt across.

Row 4: Work in patt across.

Row 5: Rep Row 3.

Row 6: Rep Row 4: 20(22, 25) sts on each shoulder.

Shoulder Shaping

Row 1: Bind off 10(11, 13) sts; work in patt across both shoulders.

Row 2: Bind off 10(11, 13) sts; work in patt across both shoulders.

Row 3: * Bind off 10(11,12) sts (right shoulder); work in patt across (left shoulder).

Row 4: Bind off rem 10(11, 12) sts.

Left Front

With larger needles, cast on 63(77, 85) sts; change to smaller needles.

Row 1: * K1, P1; rep from * across, ending K1.

Row 2: *P1, K1; rep from * across, ending P1.

Rep Rows 1 and 2 until ribbing measures same as back 3" (3", 3 1/2").

Rep Row 1 (wrong side).

FOUNDATION ROWS

Sm size only

Row 1 (right side): With larger needles, K1, P1, K1, place marker; P2, K6, P2, place marker; (K1, P1) 3 times, place marker; P2, K6, P2, place marker; (K1, P1) 17 times.

Row 2: (K1, P1) 17 times, sl marker; K2, P6, K2, sl marker; (P1, K1) 3 times; sl marker; K2, P6, K2, sl marker; K1, P1, K1.

Med size only

Row 1 (right side): With larger needles, K1, P1, K1, place marker; * P2, K6, P2, place marker; (K1, P1) 3 times; place marker; rep from * once; (K1, P1) 21 times.

Row 2: (K1, P1) 21 times; * sl marker; (P1, K1) 3 times; sl marker; K2, P6, K2; rep from * once; sl marker; K1, P1, K1.

Lg size only

Row 1 (right side): With larger needles, P1, * (K1, P1)

3 times, place marker; P2, K6, P2, place marker; rep from * once; (K1, P1) 3 times, place marker; (K1, P1) 23 times.

Row 2: (K1, P1) 23 times; sl marker; (P1, K1) 3 times, sl marker; * K2, P6, K2, sl marker; (P1, K1) 3 times; P1; rep from * once.

Note: Markers may be removed when you are familiar with the patt as established.

Row 3: Rep Row 1.

Row 4: Rep Row 2.

Row 5: Rep Row 1, twisting cables as instructed in Pattern Stitches, page 17.

Row 6: Rep Row 2.

Row 7: Rep Row 1.

Row 8: Rep Row 2.

Rep these 8 rows for patt until Left Front measures same as Back to armhole.

Armhole Shaping

Row 1: Bind off 5 sts, work in patt across.

Row 2: Work in patt across.

Sm size only

Row 3: Sl 1, K1, PSSO; K4, P2; (K1, P1) 3 times; P2, K6, P1, K2 tog, P1; (K1, P1) 16 times: 56 sts.

Med size only

Row 3: Sl 1, K1, PSSO, K4, P2, (K1, P1) 3 times; P2, K6, P2; (K1, P1) twice; K1, K2 tog, P1, (K1, P1) 20 times: 70 sts.

Lg size only

Row 3: Sl 1, K1, PSSO; P2, K6, P2; (K1, P1) 3 times; P2, K6, P2; (K1, P1) twice; K1, K2 tog, P1; (K1, P1) 22 times: 78 sts. Continue in patt, dec at beg of each right-side row 3 times more, and over last 2 sts before ribbing 1(3, 4) times more: 52(64, 71) sts.

Continue in patt without dec until armhole measures same as Back to Shoulder Shaping.

Shoulder Shaping

Row 1: Loosely bind off 9(11, 12) sts; work in patt across.

Row 2: Work in patt across.

Row 3: Loosely bind off 9(11, 13) sts 34(42, 46) collar sts rem on needle.

Continue in K1, P1 ribbing until collar measures 3 1/4" (3 1/2", 3 3/4") above shoulder.

Bind off.

Right Front

Work same as Left Front until ribbing measures 3/4", ending with a Row 1.

Buttonholes

Row 1: (P1, K1) 3 times; bind off next 3 sts; (P1, K1) 8(12, 14) times; bind off next 3 sts; work in patt across.

Row 2: * Work in patt across to bound off sts; cast on 3 sts (see Casting On, page 6); rep from * once; work in patt across. Continue ribbing as for Left Front, working Button-hole rows again immediately after working Foundation Rows.

FOUNDATION ROWS

Sm size only

Row 1 (right side): With larger needles, (P1, K1) 17 times, place marker; P2, K6, P2, place marker; (K1, P1) 3 times, place marker; P2, K6, P2, place marker; K1, P1, K1: 63 sts.

Row 2: K1, P1, K1, sl marker; K2, P6, K2, sl marker; (P1, K1) 3 times, sl marker; K2, P6, K2, sl marker; (P1, K1) 17 times.

Med size only

Row 1 (right side): (P1, K1) 21 times, place marker; * (K1, P1) 3 times, place marker; K2, P6, K2, place marker; rep from * once; K1, P1, K1: 77 sts.

Row 2: K1, P1 K1, sl marker; * K2, P6, K2, sl marker; (P1, K1) 3 times, sl marker; rep from * once; (K1, P1) 21 times.

Lg size only

Row 1 (right side): With larger needles, (P1, K1) 23 times, place marker; (K1, P1) 3 times, place marker; * P2, K6, P2, place marker; (K1, P1) 3 times, place marker; rep from * once; K1: 85 sts.

Row 2: K1, (P1, K1) 3 times, sl marker; * K2, P6, K2, sl marker; (P1, K1) 3 times, sl marker; rep from * once; (P1, K1) 23 times.

Note: Markers may be removed when you are familiar with the patt as established.

Row 3: Rep Row 1, working in buttonholes.
Row 4: Rep Row 2.
Row 5: Rep Row 1, twisting cables as instructed in Pattern Stitches, page 17.
Row 6: Rep Row 2.
Row 7: Rep Row 1.
Row 8: Rep Row 2.

Rep these 8 rows for patt until Right Front measures same as Back to Armhole.

Armhole Shaping

Row 1: Work in patt across.
Row 2: Bind off 5 sts; work in patt across.

Sm size only

Row 3: (P1, K1) 16 times; P1; sl 1, K1, PSSO; P1, K6, P2; (K1,P1) 3times; P2, K4, K2 tog: 56 sts.

Med size only

Row 3: (P1, K1) 20 times; P1; sl 1, K1, PSSO; P1; (K1, P1) twice; P2, K6, P2; (K1, P1) 3 times; P2, K4, K2 tog: 70 sts.

Lg size only

Row 3: (P1,K1) 22 times; P1; sl 1, K1, PSSO; P1 (K1, P1)

twice; P2, K6, P2; (K1, P1) 3 times; P2, K6, P2; K2 tog: 78 sts.

Continue in patt, dec after ribbing 1(3, 4) times more, and over last 2 sts 3 times more: 52(64, 71) sts.

Continue in patt without dec until armhole measures same as Back to Shoulder Shaping.

Shoulder Shaping

Row 1: Work in patt across.
Row 2: Bind off 9 (11, 12) sts; work in patt across.
Row 3: Work in patt across.
Row 4: Bind off 9 (11, 13) sts: 34(42, 46) collar sts rem on needle.

Continue in K1, P1 ribbing until collar measures 3 1/3"(3 1/2" 3 3/4") above shoulder. Bind off.

Sew shoulder seams. Sew collar ends tog; sew collar to back neck, easing sts to fit.

Armhole Edging

Hold right side facing you; with smaller needles, pick up an even number of sts evenly spaced around one armhole.

Row 1: * K1, P1; rep from * across.
Rows 2 through 4: Rep Row 1.

Bind off in ribbing. Rep for second armhole. Sew side seams. Sew buttons to Left Front. Block if necessary (see Blocking Sweaters, page 8).

America's Favorite Afghans

Afghans are just about the favorite projects of most knitters and crocheters. Here we've given you three classic favorite patterns: a fisherman knit, a crocheted ripple and a crocheted shell.

Summer Rose Shell

Sky Blue Rose Ripple

Fisherman's Afghan

Fisherman's Afghan

designed by Rita Weiss

The wonderful knitted textured patterns originally developed for use in sweaters worn by fishermen are beautifully adapted to this gorgeous afghan. The creamy, scoured wool of the sweaters resisted the sea mists; today we use synthetic yarns that will survive in our washing machines — but the look is just beautiful. A rich fringe provides the finishing touch.

Size

About 45" x 62" before fringing

Materials

Worsted weight yarn: 63 oz eggshell
Size 11, 14" straight knitting needles, or size required for gauge
Cable needle

Gauge

In garter st (knit every row), 7 sts = 2"

Pattern Stitches

Lattice (worked over 40 sts)
Row 1: * P2, K4, P2, K2, P8, CB [to work CB (cableback): sl next 2 sts onto cable needle and hold in BACK of work, K2, K2 from cable needle: CB made]; P8, K2, P2, K4, P2. (**Note:** for 80 st patt, rep from * once more on this and all following rows.)

Row 2: * K2, P4, K2, P2, K8; P4, K8, P2, K2, P4, K2.

Row 3: * P2, CF [to work CF (cable front): sl next 2 sts onto cable needle and hold in FRONT of work, K2, K2 from cable needle: CF made]; P2, † TL [to work TL (twist left): sl next 2 sts onto cable needle and hold in FRONT of work, P2, K2 from cable needle: TL made]; P4, TR [to work TR (twist right): sl next 2 sts onto cable needle and hold in BACK of work, K2, P2 from cable needle: TR made] †; rep from † to † once; P2, CB, P2.

Row 4: * K2, P4, K4, (P2, K4) 4 times, P4, K2.
Row 5: * P2, K4, P4, (TL, TR, P4) twice, K4, P2.
Row 6: * K2, P4, K6, P4, K8, P4, K6, P4, K2.
Row 7: * P2, K4, P6, CB, P3, PC [to work PC (popcorn): P1, K1, P1, K1 all in next st; sl 2nd, 3rd and 4th st on right-hand needle over first st (**Fig 1**): PC made] twice; P3, CB, P6, K4, P2.

Row 8: * K2, P4, K6, P4, K8, P4, K6, P4, K2.
Row 9: * P2, CF, P4, (TR, TL, P4) twice, CB, P2.

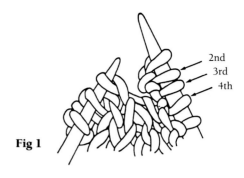

Fig 1

Row 10: * K2, P4, K4, (P2, K4) 4 times, P4, K2.
Row 11: * P2, K4, P2, (TR, P4, TL) twice, P2, K4, P2.
Row 12: * K2, P4, K2, P2, K8; P4, K8, P2, K2, P4, K2.
Row 13: * P2, K4, P2, K2, P3, (PC) twice; P3, CB, P3, (PC) twice; P3, K2, P2, K4, P2.
Rows 14 through 25: Rep Rows 2 through 13.

Diamonds (worked over 17 sts)
Row 1 (right side): * P6, sl 2 sts onto cable needle and hold in front of work, K2, P1, K2 from cable needle, P6. (**Note:** for 34 st patt, rep from * once more on this and all following rows.)

Row 2: * K6, P2, K1, P2, K6.

Row 3: * P5, BC [to work BC (back cross): sl 1 st onto cable needle and hold in BACK of work, K2, P1 from cable needle: BC made], K1, FC [to work FC (front cross): sl 2 sts onto cable needle and hold in FRONT of work, P1, K2 from cable needle: FC made], P5.

Row 4: * K5, P2, K1, P1, K1, P2, K5.
Row 5: * P4, BC, K1, P1, K1, FC, P4.
Row 6: * K4, P2, (K1, P1) twice; K1, P2, K4.
Row 7: * P3, BC, (K1, P1) twice; K1, FC, P3.
Row 8: * K3, P2, (K1, P1) 3 times; K1, P2, K3.

Row 9: * P2, BC, (K1, P1) 3 times; K1, FC, P2.
Row 10: * K2, P2, (K1, P1) 4 times; K1, P2, K2.
Row 11: * P1, BC, (K1, P1) 4 times; K1, FC, P1.
Row 12: * K1, P2, (K1, P1) 5 times; K1, P2, K1.
Row 13: * P1, FC, (P1, K1) 4 times; P1, BC, P1.

Row 14: * K2, P2, (K1, P1) 4 times; K1, P2, K2.
Row 15: * P2, FC, (P1, K1) 3 times; P1, BC, P2.
Row 16: * K3, P2, (K1, P1) 3 times; K1, P2, K3.
Row 17: * P3, FC, (P1, K1) twice; P1, BC, P3.
Row 18: * K4, P2, (K1, P1) twice, K1, P2, K4.

Row 19: * P4, FC, P1, K1, P1, BC, P4.
Row 20: * K5, P2, K1, P1, K1, P2, K5.
Row 21: * P5, FC, P1, BC, P5.
Row 22: * K6, P2, K1, P2, K6.

Rep Rows 1 through 22 for patt.

Honeycomb Rib (worked over 17 sts)

Row 1: * K3, sl next st onto cable needle and hold in BACK of work, K1, K1 from cable needle, sl next st onto cable and hold in FRONT of work, K1, K1 from cable needle; rep from * once; K3.

Row 2: Purl.

Row 3: * P3, sl next st onto cable needle and hold in FRONT of work, K1, K1 from cable needle, sl next st onto cable and hold in BACK of work, K1, K1 from cable needle; rep from * once; P3.

Row 4: Purl.

Rep Rows 1 through 4 for patt.

Afghan Instructions

Panel A (make one)

Cast on 80 sts loosely.

Work Rows 1 through 25 of Lattice patt.

Continuing in Lattice patt, rep Rows 2 through 25 in sequence, 11 times more.

Rep Rows 2 through 13 once; bind off loosely.

Panel B (make 2)

Cast on 34 sts loosely.

Work Rows 1 through 22 of Diamonds patt.

Continuing in Diamonds patt, rep Rows 1 through 22 in sequence, 14 times more; bind off loosely.

Panel C (make 2)

Cast on 17 sts loosely.

Work Rows 1 through 4 of Honeycomb Rib patt.

Rep Rows 1 through 4 in sequence, 81 times more; bind off loosely.

Assembling

Pin a Panel C and a Panel B with wrong sides tog; sew with overcast st, easing rows to fit. Following **Diagram A**, join rem panels in the same manner.

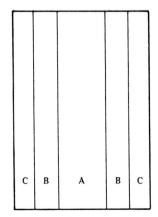

| C | B | A | B | C |

Diagram A

Fringe

Following Fringe instructions on page 9, make triple knot fringe. Cut 26" strands of yarn; use 8 strands for each knot. Tie knots evenly spaced (about every 5th st) across each short end of afghan. Then work double and triple knots per instructions. Trim ends evenly.

Sky Blue Rose Ripple

designed by Jean Leinhauser

Ripples — in both knit and crochet — are classic afghan favorites, and are fun to make. The zig-zag color patterns can be quite dramatic. This crochet ripple features added texture achieved by working in the back loops only of each stitch. We've done ours in muted shades of rose, blue and cream, but you may wish to use bright or dark colors to match your decor.

Size:

About 45" x 67"

Materials

Worsted weight yarn:
    8 oz lt blue;
    8 oz dk blue;
    12 oz blue ombre;
    12 oz dusty rose;
    11 oz off-white

Size J aluminum crochet hook, or size required for gauge

Gauge:

3 sc = 1"

Instructions

With lt blue, ch 219 loosely.

Foundation Row: Sc in 2nd ch from hook, sc in each of next 3 chs; * 3 sc in next ch, sc in next 4 chs, sk next 2 chs, sc in next 4 chs; rep from * 18 times more; 3 sc in next ch, sc in each of last 4 chs; ch 1, turn.

Row 1 (Ripple Patt Row): Working in bl only unless otherwise specified, sk first sc, * sc in each of next 4 sc, 3 sc in next sc; sc in each of next 4 sc, sk 2 sc; rep from * 18 times more; sc in each of next 4 sc, 3 sc in next sc; sc in next 3 sc, sk next sc, sc through both lps of last sc; ch 1, turn.

Rows 2 through 5: Rep Row 1. At end of Row 5, change to dusty rose (see Special Technique); ch 1, turn. Rep Ripple Patt Row (Row 1) in the following color sequence:

* 2 rows dusty rose

8 rows blue ombre

2 rows dusty rose

6 rows dk blue

4 rows dusty rose

8 rows off-white *

6 rows lt blue

Rep from * to * once: 72 rows completed (mid-point of afghan).

Continue to rep Ripple Patt Row in the following color sequence:

* 8 rows off-white

4 rows dusty rose

6 rows dk blue

2 rows dusty rose

8 rows blue ombre

2 rows dusty rose

6 rows lt blue

Rep from * once more.

Finish off and weave in all ends.

Summer Rose Shell

designed by Jean Leinhauser

A large hook and an open shell pattern make this crocheted afghan work up quickly. It's easy to make, and the understated pattern shows off the pretty color of the yarn you choose. The pattern has only three rows, so it's a great project for a beginner.

Size

About 41" x 63" before fringing

Materials

Worsted weight yarn: 47 oz rose
Size J aluminum crochet hook, or size required for gauge

Gauge

3 shells = 6"

Note: To check gauge, ch 21, work Rows 1 and 2 of patt. Finish off. Piece should measure 6" wide.

Instructions

Ch 153 loosely.

Row 1: In 6th ch from hook, work (2 dc, ch 1, 2 dc): shell made; * sk next 2 chs, dc in next ch, sk next 2 chs, shell in next ch; rep from * 23 times more; sk next 2 chs, dc in next ch: 25 shells; ch 3, turn.

Row 2: * Work shell in ch-1 sp of next shell, dc in next dc; rep from * 24 times more, working last dc in 6th ch at top of turning ch-6; ch 3, turn.

Row 3: * Work shell in ch-1 sp of next shell, dc in next dc; rep from * 24 times more, working last dc in top of turning ch-3; ch 3, turn.

Rep Row 3 until piece measures 63".

Finish off and weave in ends.

Fringe

Following Fringe instructions on page 9, make triple knot fringe. Cut 30" strands of yarn; use 6 strands for each knot of fringe. Tie knots in ch-1 sp of each shell and in each dc across each short end of afghan. Then work double and triple knots per instructions. Trim ends evenly.

Bulky Hat, Scarf & Mittens

designed by Mary Thomas

Let it snow, let it blow — this wonderful warm winter accessory set is quick to knit in doubled worsted weight yarn on large needles. Match the color to your coat; for an interesting tweed look, combine two colors of yarn — one strand of cream with one strand of brown; one of black with one of white; or red and black.

Sizes

Hat and mittens are designed to fit the average adult size head and hands. The scarf measures approx 7 1/2" wide x 72" long.

Materials

Worsted weight yarn: 20 oz wine heather

Size 10 1/2", 10" straight knitting needles (for mittens only)-or size required for gauge

Size 13, 14" straight knitting needles (for hat and scarf only)-or size required for gauge

> **Materials Note:**
> Yarn is used doubled throughout patt.

Gauge (for hat and scarf)

With larger size needles and 2 strands of yarn in patt st, 8 sts = 3"

Gauge (for mittens)

With smaller size needles and 2 strands of yarn in patt st, 3 sts = 1"

Hat Instructions

With larger size needles and 2 strands of yarn, cast on 53 sts. Work in patt st as follows:

Row 1 (right side): K1, * P2, K2; rep from * across.

Row 2: P1, * K2, P2; rep from * across.

Rep Rows 1 and 2 until work measures approx 10" from cast-on edge, ending by working Row 2.

Next Row: Sl 1 as to knit, * K2 tog; rep from * across: 27 sts.

Next Row: * P2 tog; rep from * to last st, P1: 14 sts. Cut yarn, leaving approx 24" ends. Thread ends into tapestry or yarn needle and weave through rem sts, removing knitting needle. Draw up tightly and fasten securely. Continue with same sewing length and sew side seam. Weave in all ends.

Scarf Instructions

With larger size needles and 2 strands of yarn, cast on 23 sts. Work in patt st as follows:

Row 1: * K2, P2; rep from * to last 3 sts, K2, P1.

Row 2: P2, * K2, P2; rep from * to last st, K1.

Rep Rows 1 and 2 until scarf measures approx 72" long. Bind off. Weave in all ends.

Mitten Instructions (make 2)

With smaller size needles and 2 strands of yarn, cast on 21 sts.

Work cuff as follows:

Ribbing Row 1: * K1, P1; rep from * to last st, K1.

Ribbing Row 2: P1, * K1, P1; rep from * across. Rep last 2 rows until cuff measures approx 2" from cast-on edge, ending by working Ribbing Row 2.

Now work patt st as follows:

Row 1 (right side): K1, * P2, K2; rep from * across.

Row 2: P1, * K2, P2; rep from * across.

Rep last two rows 3 times more (8 rows total from cuff).

Shape Thumb

Row 1 (dividing row): K1, (P2, K2) twice; K4, cast on 2 sts as follows: * With right hand, make a loop (**Fig 1**), turn loop clockwise and place on needle (**Fig 2**), pulling yarn to make st snug on needle (one cast-on st made); rep from * once more, leave rem 8 sts on left needle unworked.

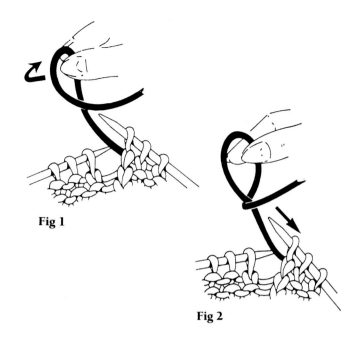

Fig 1

Fig 2

Row 2: Purl across both cast-on sts, P5, cast on one st (as before), leave rem 8 sts unworked.

Continuing on center 8 sts only, start with a knit row and work 8 rows in stock st, ending by working a purl row.

Next Row: * K2 tog; rep from * across: 4 sts. Cut yarn, leaving approx 12" ends. Thread ends into tapestry or yarn needle and weave through rem sts, removing knitting needle. Draw up tightly and fasten securely. Continue with same sewing length and sew thumb seam.

Shape Hand

Hold work with right side facing you and base of thumb at top. Join 2 strands of yarn at right of thumb next to sts on right needle.

Row 1 (joining row): Continuing with right needle (with 8 sts on it), pick up and knit 5 sts across base of thumb, then work (P2, K2) twice across sts on left needle: 21 sts.

Row 2: P1, * K2, P2; rep from * across.

Row 3: K1, * P2, K2; rep from * across.

Rep last two rows until mitten measures approx 7" from cuff, ending by working Row 2.

Next Row: Sl 1 as to knit, * K2 tog; rep from * across: 11 sts.

Next Row: * P2 tog; rep from * to last st, P1: 6 sts. Cut yarn, leaving approx 24" ends. Thread ends into tapestry or yarn needle and weave through rem sts, removing knitting needle. Draw up tightly and fasten securely. Continue with same sewing length and sew side seam. Weave in all ends.

Bright Lights Pullover

designed by Sandy Scoville

This bright, easy to knit and easy to wear tri-color sweater is done with slip stitch color changes so there's no need to join new yarn in the middle of a row. Have fun changing the color combinations; try a black background with red and white; or a camel background with dark brown and bright green.

Sizes

Sm (36-38)
Med (40-42)
Lg (44-46)
Instructions are written for size small (sm); changes for
   sizes medium (med), and large (lg) are in parentheses ( ).

Finished chest measurements

Sm (42")
Med (46")
Lg (50")

Materials

Worsted weight yarn: 13(13, 14) oz, or 680(680, 740)
   yds blue; 8(8, 9) oz, or 400(400,460) yds each red,
   grape, and mustard
Size 9 straight or 24" circular knitting needles (your
   preference), or size required for gauge
Size 7 straight or 24" circular knitting needle (your
   preference), or size required for gauge
Size 7, 16" circular knitting needle
Cable needle
Safety pins (optional)

> **Note:**
> When using circular needles, work back and forth
> in rows.

Gauge

With larger needles, 41/2 sts = 1" in stock st

Special Abbreviations

Yfwd . . . bring yarn from back to front between needles
Ybk . . . bring yarn from front to back between needles

Instructions

Note: Color is changed frequently. We recommend carrying the unused colors loosely up right side of your work by bringing the new color under those not in use. This will eliminate the need to weave in so many ends while finishing.

Back

With larger needles and blue, cast on 94(106, 112) sts; change to smaller needles.

Work K1, P1 ribbing in the following color sequence:

2 rows blue

2 rows mustard

2 rows blue

2 rows red

2 rows blue

2 rows mustard

2 rows blue

Change to larger needles.

Row 1: Continuing with blue, knit.

Row 2: Purl.

Rows 3 and 4: With mustard, knit.

Rows 5 and 6: Purl.

Row 7: With grape, * K2, sl 2 as if to purl, K2; rep from * 14(16, 17) times more; K2, sl 1 as if to purl; K1.

Row 8: P1, sl 1 as if to knit, P2; * P2, sl 2 as if to knit, P2; rep from * 14(16, 17) times more.

Row 9: * Sl 2 sts onto cable needle and hold in back, sl 1 as if to purl, K2 from cable needle; sl 1 st onto cable needle and hold in front, K2, sl 1 from cable needle as if to purl; rep from * 14(16, 17) times more; sl 2 sts onto cable needle and hold in back, sl 1 as if to purl, K2 from cable needle; K1.

continued on page 28

Row 10: P3, sl 1 as if to knit; * sl 1 as if to knit, P4, sl 1 as if to knit; rep from * 14(16, 17) times more.

Row 11: With mustard, knit.

Row 12: Purl.

Row 13: * With grape, sl 1 onto cable needle, hold in front, K2, sl 1 from cable needle as if to purl; sl 2 onto cable needle, hold in back, sl 1 as if to purl, K2 from cable needle; rep from * 14(16, 17) times more; sl 1 onto cable needle, hold in front, K2, sl 1 from cable needle as if to purl; K1.

Row 14: P1, sl 1 as if to knit, P2; * P2, sl 2 as if to knit, P2; rep from * 14(16, 17) times more.

Row 15: * K2, sl 2 as if to purl, K2; rep from * 14(16, 17) times more; K2, sl 1 as if to purl; K1.

Row 16: P1, sl 1 as if to knit, P2; * P2, sl 2 as if to knit, P2; rep from * 14(16, 17) times more.

Rows 17 and 18: With mustard, knit.

Rows 19 and 20: Purl, ending Row 20 with purl last 2 sts tog.

Row 21: With blue, knit.

Row 22: Purl.

Rows 23 and 24: Rep Rows 21 and 22.

Rows 25 and 26: With red, knit.

Row 27: With grape, K2(3, 1), sl 2 as if to purl; * K6, sl 2 as if to purl; rep from * 10(11, 12) times more; K1(4, 4).

Row 28: Purl, slipping the sl sts as you come to them.

Rows 29 and 30: With red, kni⁺

Row 31: With blue, knit.

Row 32: Purl.

Row 33: Knit.

Row 34: Purl .

Rows 35 and 36: With grape, knit.

Row 37: With red, K2(7, 5), sl 2 as if to purl; * K6, sl 2 as if to purl; rep from * 10(10, 11) times more; K1(8, 8).

Row 38: Purl, slipping the sl sts as you come to them.

Rows 39 and 40: With grape, knit.

Rows 41 through 54: Rep Rows 21 through 34.

Row 55: With mustard, * K1, yfwd, sl 1 as if to purl, ybk; rep from * across, ending K1.

Row 56: Purl.

Rows 57 through 72: Rep Rows 55 and 56 in the following color sequence:

2 rows red

2 rows mustard

2 rows blue

2 rows mustard

2 rows grape

2 rows mustard

2 rows red

2 rows mustard

Row 73: With blue, knit.

Row 74: Purl.

Row 75: Knit.

Row 76: Purl, inc in last st.

Rep Rows 3 through 72.

With blue, continue in stock st (knit one row, purl one row) until Back measures 24 1/2"(25", 25") from beg, ending by working a purl row.

Neck Shaping

Note: Both shoulders are worked at the same time with separate skeins of yarn.

Row 1: K28(34, 37); attach second skein of yarn, bind off center 37 sts; K28(34, 37).

Row 2: Purl across both shoulders.

Row 3: Knit to last 2 sts of first shoulder, K2 tog; on second shoulder, sl 1, K1, PSSO, knit across.

Row 4: Purl.

Bind off all sts.

Front

Work same as Back, working 8 rows fewer than Back to shoulder bind off.

Neck Shaping

Rows 1 through 4: Work same as for Back.

Rows 5 and 7: Rep Row 3.

Rows 6 and 8: Rep Row 4.

Bind off all sts.

Sleeves (make 2)

With larger needles and blue, cast on 42(46, 50) sts; change to smaller needles.

Work in K1, P1 ribbing in same color sequence as for Back, inc 10(12, 14) sts evenly spaced on last row: 52(58, 64) sts. Change to larger needles.

Row 1: Knit.

Row 2: Purl.

Rows 3 and 4: With mustard, knit.

Rows 5 and 6: Purl.

Row 7: With grape, * K2, sl 2 as if to purl, K2; rep from * 7 (8, 9) times more; K2, sl 1 as if to purl; K1.

Row 8: P1, sl 1 as if to knit, P2; * P2, sl 2 as if to knit, P2; rep from * 7(8, 9) times more.

Row 9: * Sl 2 onto cable needle and hold in back, sl 1 as if to purl, K2 from cable needle; sl 1 onto cable needle and hold in front, K2, sl 1 from cable needle as if to purl; rep from * 7(8, 9) times more; sl 2 onto cable needle and hold in back, sl 1 as if to purl, K2 from cable needle; K1.

Row 10: P3, sl 1 as if to knit; * sl 1 as if to knit, P4, sl 1 as if to knit; rep from * 7(8, 9) times more.

Row 11: With mustard, knit.

Row 12: Purl.

Row 13: * With grape, sl 1 onto cable needle, hold in front, K2, sl 1 from cable needle as if to purl; sl 2 onto cable needle, hold in back, sl 1 as if to purl, K2 from cable needle; rep from *7(8, 9) times more; sl 1 onto cable needle, hold in front, K2, sl 1 from cable needle as if to purl; K1.

Row 14: P1, sl 1 as if to knit, P2; * P2, sl 2 as if to knit, P2; rep from * 7(8, 9) times more.

Row 15: *K2, sl 2 as if to purl, K2; rep from *7 (8, 9) times more; K2, sl 1 as if to purl; K1.

Row 16: P1, sl 1 as if to knit, P2; *P2, sl 2 as if to knit, P2; rep from *7(8, 9) times more.

Rows 17 and 18: With mustard, knit.

Rows 19 and 20: Purl.

Row 21: With blue, knit, inc 1 st at each end of row: 54 (60, 66) sts.

Row 22: Purl.

Row 23: Knit.

Row 24: Purl.

Row 25: With red, knit, inc 1 st at each end of row: 56 (62, 68) sts

Row 26: Knit.

Row 27: With grape, K2(2, 4), sl 2 as if to purl; * K6, sl 2 as if to purl; rep from * 6(7, 7) times more, ending K4(2, 6).

Row 28: Purl, slipping the sl sts as you come to them.

Row 29: With red, knit, inc 1 st at each end of row: 58 (64, 70) sts.

Row 30: Knit.

Row 31: With blue, knit.

Row 32: Purl.

Row 33: Knit, inc 1 st at each end of row: 60(66, 72) sts.

Row 34: Purl.

Rows 35 and 36: With grape, knit.

Row 37: With red, K6(6, 2), sl 2 as if to purl; * K6, sl 2 as if to purl; rep from * across, ending K4(6, 4).

Row 38: Purl, slipping the sl sts as you come to them.

Row 39: With grape, knit, inc 1 st at each end of row: 62 (68, 74) sts.

Row 40: Knit.

Rows 41 through 46: Rep Rows 21 through 26 of Sleeve: 66(72, 78) sts.

Row 47: With grape, K4(4, 2), sl 2 as if to purl, * K6, sl 2 as if to purl; rep from * across, ending K4(2, 2).

Rows 48 through 54: Rep Rows 28 through 34, inc 1 st at end of Row 54: 71(77, 83) sts.

Row 55: With mustard, * K1, yfwd, sl 1 as if to purl, ybk; rep from * across, ending K1.

Row 56: Purl.

Rows 57 through 72: Rep Rows 55 and 56 in the same color sequence as for Back, inc 1 st at each end of Rows 61, 65, and 69: 77(87, 89) sts; adjust patt to increases.

Row 73: With blue, knit.

Row 74: Purl.

Row 75: Knit.

Row 76: Purl, inc in last st.

Rep patt, beg with Row 3 and ending with Row 54, eliminating all increases.

With blue, continue in stock st (knit one row, purl one row) until Sleeve measures 19"(20", 21"). Bind off loosely.

Finishing

Sew left shoulder seam.

With smaller needles and blue, pick up an even number of sts evenly spaced around neckline. Work in K1, P1 ribbing for 1 1/2" Bind off loosely in ribbing.

Sew right shoulder seam.

Mark sides of Front and Back with safety pins or thread for armholes 14" from beg. Holding right sides tog, sew sleeve to body between markers.

Sew side and sleeve seams, matching stripes.

Weave in all ends.

Block if necessary (see Blocking Sweaters, page 8).

Classic Fisherman

designed by Sandy Scoville

Deep dimension in traditional knitted cables highlights this finely crafted sweater. Based on the motifs originally created by fishermen's wives on the Aran Isles, off the coast of Scotland, this type of knitting is beloved throughout the world. This warm sweater is perfect for a walk in the woods, or anywhere there's a nip in the air.

Sizes

Small (36-38)
Med (40-42)
Lg (44-46)
Instructions are written for size small (sm); changes for sizes
    medium (med), and large (lg) are in parentheses ( ).

Finished chest measurements

Sm (42")
Med (46")
Lg (50")

Materials

Worsted weight yarn:
    40(42, 44) oz, or 1600(1700, 1800) yds off white
Size 9 straight or 24" circular knitting needles (your
    preference), or size required for gauge
Size 7 straight or 24" circular knitting needles (your
    preference, or size required for gauge
Size 7, 16" circular knitting needle
Markers
Cable needle
Safety pins (optional)

Note:
When using circular needles, work back and forth
in rows.

Gauge

With larger needles, 4 sts = 1" in seed st
With larger needles, 6 sts = 1 1/4" in cable patt

Pattern Stitches

Seed Stitch

Row 1 (foundation row): * P1, K1; rep from * across.

Row 2: Knit the knit sts, and purl the purl sts.

Row 3: Knit the purl sts, and purl the knit sts.

Row 4: Knit the knit sts, and purl the purl sts.

Rep Rows 3 and 4 for patt.

Double Cable (worked over 18 sts)
Note: Row 2 and all even numbered rows are worked by knitting the knit sts, and purling the purl sts.

Row 1: K1; sl next 3 sts onto cable needle, hold in front of work, K1, K3 from cable needle; (P1, K1) 4 times; sl next st onto cable needle, hold in back of work, K3, K1 from cable needle; K1.

Row 3: K2; sl next 3 sts onto cable needle, hold in front of work, K1, K3 from cable needle; (P1, K1) 3 times; sl next st onto cable needle, hold in back of work, K3, K1 from cable needle; K2.

Row 5: K3; sl next 3 sts onto cable needle, hold in front of work, K1, K3 from cable needle; (P1, K1) twice; sl next st onto cable needle, hold in back of work, K3, K1 from cable needle; K3.

Row 7: K4; sl next 3 sts onto cable needle, hold in front of work, K1, K3 from cable needle; P1, K1; sl next st onto cable needle, hold in back of work, K3, K1 from cable needle; K4.

Row 9: K5; sl next 3 sts onto cable needle, hold in front of work, K1, K3 from cable needle; sl next st onto cable needle, hold in back of work, K3, K1 from cable needle; K5.

Row 11: * Sl next 3 sts onto cable needle, hold in back of work, K3, K3 from cable needle *; sl next 3 sts onto cable needle, hold in front of work, K3, K3 from cable needle; rep from * to * once.

Row 13: K5; sl next st onto cable needle, hold in back of work, K3, K1 from cable needle; sl next 3 sts onto cable needle, hold in front of work, K1, K3 from cable needle; K5.

Row 15: K4; sl next st onto cable needle, hold in back of work, K3, K1 from cable needle; K1, P1; sl next 3 sts onto cable needle, hold in front of work, K1, K3 from cable needle; K4.

Row 17: K3; sl next st onto cable needle, hold in back of work, K3, K1 from cable needle; (K1, P1) twice; sl next 3 sts onto cable needle, hold in front of work, K1, K3 from cable needle; K3.

Row 19: K2; sl next st onto cable needle, hold in back of work, K3, K1 from cable needle; (K1, P1) 3 times; sl next 3 sts onto cable needle, hold in front of work, K1, K3 from cable needle; K2.

Row 21: K1; sl next st onto cable needle, hold in back of work, K3, K1 from cable needle; (K1, P1) 4 times; sl next 3 sts onto cable needle, hold in front of work, K1, K3 from cable needle; K1.

Rep Rows 1 through 22 for patt.

Cable Front (CF) over 6 sts

Rows 1 and 3: Knit.

Rows 2 and 4: Purl.

Row 5: Sl next 3 sts onto cable needle, hold in front of work, K3, K3 from cable needle.

Rows 6 and 8: Purl.

Row 7: Knit.

Cable Back (CB) over 6 sts

Rows 1 and 3: Knit.

Rows 2 and 4: Purl.

Row 5: Sl next 3 sts onto cable needle, hold in back of work, K3, K3 from cable needle.

Rows 6 and 8: Purl.

Row 7: Knit.

Instructions

Note: Markers are used to separate pattern stitches. They are set in place on the foundation row, and should be moved from the left-hand needle to the right-hand needle as you come to them. They may be removed when you are familiar with the pattern.

Back

With larger straight or circular needles, cast on 108(116, 124) sts; change to smaller straight or circular needles. Work in K1, P1 ribbing until Back measures 3" from beg; change to larger needles.

Note: When working foundation row, refer to Pattern Stitches, above.

Row 1 (foundation row): (P1, K1) twice (3, 5) times: Seed St; place marker; Double Cable patt over next 18 sts; place marker; (P1, K1) twice (3, 3) times: Seed St; place marker; P2; CF; place marker; P5, K1 in st below, P5, place marker; Double Cable patt over next 18 sts; place marker; P5, K1 in st below, P5; place marker; CB; place marker; P2; (P1, K1) twice (3, 3) times: Seed St; place marker; Double Cable patt over next 18 sts; place marker; (P1, K1) twice (3, 5) times: Seed St.

Row 2 (and all wrong-side rows): Keeping to patt on Seed St, knit all other knit sts and purl all other purl sts.

Rep Rows 1 and 2 referring to Pattern Stitches on pages 30 and 31 until Back measures 24 1/2"(25", 25") from beg.

Neck Shaping

Note: Both shoulders are worked at the same time with separate skeins of yarn.

Row 1: Work in patt across 39(43, 47) sts; join second skein of yarn; bind off center 30 sts; work in patt across.

Row 2: Work in patt across both shoulders.

Row 3: Work in patt to within 2 sts of neck edge, P2 tog; on second shoulder, sl 1, P1, PSSO, work in patt across.

Row 4: Rep Row 2.

Bind off all sts.

Front

Work same as for Back, working 6 rows fewer than Back to shoulder bind-off.

Neck Shaping

Rows 1 through 4: Work same as for Back Neck Shaping.

Rows 5 and 6: Rep Rows 3 and 4.

Bind off all rem sts.

Sleeves (make 2)

With larger straight or circular needles, cast on 46(50,54) sts; change to smaller needles. Work in K1, P1 ribbing until Sleeve measures 3" from beg; inc 22 sts evenly on last (wrong-side) row: 68(72, 76) sts; change to larger needles.

Row 1 (foundation row): (K1, P1) 3(4, 5) times: Seed St; P2, CF over next 6 sts; P5, K1 in st below, P5; Double Cable patt over next 18 sts; P5, K1 in st below, P5; CB over next 6 sts; P2, (K1, P1) 3(4,5) times: Seed St.

Row 2 (and all wrong-side rows): Keeping to patt on Seed St, knit all other knit sts, and purl all other purl sts.

Rep Rows 1 and 2, inc at each end of every 4th right-side row, keeping inc sts in Seed St patt, until there are 108(116, 124) sts on needle, and Sleeve measures 18"(19", 20") from beg. Bind off.

Finishing

Sew shoulder seams.

Neckband

With 16" circular needle, pick up sts evenly spaced around neck, beg at center back. Knit in rnds until neckband measures 2". Bind off loosely.

Fold neckband to inside and sew bound-off edge to inside of row where sts were picked up. Sew sleeves in place from marker to marker. Sew side and sleeve seams. Block if necessary (see Blocking Sweaters, page 8).

Quick and Easy Classics

Crocheters love quick and easy projects, and these afghans fill the bill. In addition, their fresh and pretty colors provide the perfect home accent.

Just Peachy Granny

Mile-A-Minute

Mile-A-Minute

designed by Jean Leinhauser

Mile-A-Minute crocheted afghans have taken their place as favorites alongside grannies and ripples. They are fun and quick to do, are worked in strips that are then sewn or crocheted together. Thus they are easy to carry along for trips to the doctor's office or long car rides. Each strip begins with a long piece just one shell wide; decorative borders are then worked around this center shell strip. For a nice color change, try off white for the center shell strip, then medium and dark rose for the two borders.

Size
About 48" x 64"

Materials
Worsted weight yarn:
   16 oz lt teal;
   9 oz med teal;
   18 oz med peach
Size I aluminum crochet hook, or size required for gauge

Gauge
3 dc = 1"
One completed strip = 5 1/2" wide

Instructions

Panel (make 9)

Center Shell
With lt teal, ch 6; join to form a ring.
Row 1 (right side): Ch 3 for side, in ring work (3 dc, ch 2, 3 dc): shell made; dc in ring for side; ch 3, turn.

Row 2: In ch-2 sp of shell, work shell; dc in top of ch-3 sp; ch 3, turn.

Rep Row 2 until piece measures 54" long, ending by working a right side row. Finish off lt teal.

Note: Each Panel should have the exact same number of rows.

First Border
Rnd 1: Hold Panel with right side facing you; join med peach in ring formed by beg ch-6 of Row 1; ch 1, work 7 sc in same sp; working across side, work 3 sc in each side dc-sp or ch-3 lp to top of Panel; sc in next 3 dc, 7 sc in ch-2 sp at top of Panel, sc in next 3 dc; 3 sc in each side dc-sp or ch-3 lp on opposite side; join to beg ch-1; do not turn.

Rnd 2: Sl st in next sc; ch 3 (counts as a dc), dc in next 2 sc, in next sc work (dc, ch 7, dc), dc in each of next 3 sc, dc in each sc along side to center sc of 7-sc group at top of piece; in center sc work (dc, ch 7, dc), dc in each sc across next side; join in top of beg ch-3. Finish off med peach.

Second Border
With right side facing you, join med teal in ch-7 lp at top of Panel; ch 3, in same sp work (4 dc, ch 5, 5 dc); * ch 1, sk next dc, dc in next dc; rep from * to next ch-7 lp (**Note:** adjust placement of sts as needed so that dc before ch-7 lp is skipped); in ch-7 lp work (5 dc, ch 5, 5 dc); ** ch 1, sk next dc, dc in next dc; rep from ** to beg of rnd; sk last dc; join to top of beg ch-3. Finish off and weave in all ends.

Assembly

Join strips along sides, leaving open from point where Panel starts to curve at top and bottom. To join, hold strips with right sides tog and sew with overcast st through outer lps only.

Just Peachy Granny

designed by Jean Leinhauser

This crocheted afghan is an updated version of the traditional granny, one of the most popular afghan patterns of all time. This version has accents of popcorn stitches in the corners of each square, adding an interesting dimensional touch. For a feminine color change try two shades of lavender with off white, and a soft green replacing the teal.

Size
About 45" x 60"

Materials
Worsted weight yarn:
   16 oz dk peach;
   11 oz med peach;
   19 oz cream;
   7 oz dk teal
Size J aluminum crochet hook, or size required for gauge

Gauge
3 dc = 1"
1 square = 8 1/2"

Pattern Stitch

Popcorn (PC)
Working loosely, * YO, insert hook from front to back to front around post of next dc, pull up a 1/2" lp; rep from * twice in same dc; YO, pull yarn through first 6 lps on hook, YO, pull yarn through last 2 lps on hook: PC made.

Instructions

Granny Square (make 35)

With med peach, ch 4; join to form a ring.

Rnd 1: Ch 3 (counts as a dc in this and all following rnds), 2 dc in ring; (ch 2, 3 dc in ring) 3 times; ch 2; join in top of beg ch-3.

Rnd 2: Sl st in next 2 dc; sl st in next ch-2 corner sp; ch 3, in same sp work (2 dc, ch 2, 3 dc); * in next corner sp work (3 dc, ch 2, 3 dc); rep from * twice more; join in top of beg ch-3.

Rnd 3: Sl st in next 2 dc and in next ch-2 corner sp; ch 3, in same sp work (2 dc, ch 2, 3 dc); * 3 dc in sp between next two 3-dc groups for side; in next corner sp work (3 dc, ch 2, 3 dc); rep from * twice more; 3 dc in sp between next two 3-dc groups; join in top of beg ch-3. Finish off and weave in ends.

Rnd 4: Join dk teal in any ch-2 corner sp; ch 3, in same sp work (2 dc, ch 2, 3 dc); * 3 dc in sp between each pair of dc groups along side; in next corner sp work (3 dc, ch 2, 3 dc); rep from * twice more; 3 dc in sp between each pair of dc groups along last side; join in top of beg ch-3; finish off dk teal.

Rnd 5: Join cream in any ch-2 corner sp; work as for Rnd 4; do not finish off.

Rnd 6: Sl st in next 2 dc and in next ch-2 sp; ch 3, 4 dc in same sp; * dc in next 15 dc, 5 dc in next ch-2 corner sp; rep from * twice more; dc in last 15 dc; join in top of beg ch-3. Finish off cream.

Rnd 7: Join dk peach in 3rd dc of any 5-dc corner group; in same dc work (sc, hdc, sc): corner made; sc in next dc, PC in next dc; * sc in next 15 dc, PC in next dc, sc in next dc, in next dc work (sc, hdc, sc): corner made; sc in next dc, PC in next dc; rep from * twice more; sc in next 15 sc, PC in next sc, sc in last sc; join in beg sc. Finish off and weave in all ends.

Joining

Join squares in 7 rows of 5 squares. To join squares, hold two squares with right sides tog. Carefully matching sts on both squares and with dk peach, sew with overcast st in bls only (see page 4) across side, beg and ending with one corner st.

Join squares in rows; then sew rows tog in same manner, being sure that all four-corner junctions are firmly joined.

Edging

With right side of afghan facing you, join dk peach in hdc of upper right-hand corner.

Rnd 1: Ch 3 (counts as a dc on this and following rnds), 2 dc in same hdc: corner made; along each side of afghan, work dc in each st and trc in each joining; in each rem corner hdc of afghan work 3 dc: corner made; join in 3rd ch of beg ch-3.

Rnd 2: Ch 3, 3 dc in next dc: corner made; dc in each dc along each side, working 3 dc in each center dc of each rem outer corner; join in 3rd ch of beg ch-3.

Rnd 3: Ch 3, dc in next dc, 5 dc in next dc: corner made; dc in each dc along each side, working 5 dc in each center dc of each rem outer corner; join in 3rd ch of beg ch-3. Finish off and weave in ends.

Oh-So-Sweet Baby Jacket

designed by Mary Thomas

Lucky the baby who is welcomed to the world with this soft and sweet knitted jacket. The Traveling Leaf pattern stitch which adds delicacy is made with YOs and is easy and fun to do. The jacket has a little collar which adds a dressy look.

Sizes

	birth-3 months	4-5 months
body chest	17"	18"
garment chest (buttoned)	18"	19"

Size Note: Instructions are written for smallest size with changes in parentheses for larger size.

Materials

Baby weight yarn: 4 1/2(5) oz pink
Size 3 straight knitting needles, or size required for gauge
3 buttons 3/8" diameter

Gauge

In stock st, 7 sts = 1"; 9 rows = 1"

Lace Pattern Stitch-traveling leaf (See photo)

(multiple of 12 sts + 5)
Row 1 (right side): K2, * K1, YO, K3, K2 tog; K1, sl 1 (as to knit), K1, PSSO; K3, YO; rep from * to last 3 sts, K3. (**Note:** Throughout patt, each YO counts as one st.)
Rows 2,4 and 6: Purl.
Row 3: Rep Row 1.
Row 5: K2, * K1, sl 1, K1, PSSO; K3, YO, K1, YO, K3, K2 tog; rep from * to last 3 sts; K3.
Row 7: Rep Row 5.
Row 8: Purl.
Rep Rows 1 through 8 for patt.

Instructions

Back

Cast on 113(125) sts. Knit 9 rows (for garter st border). Now work in Lace Patt St until piece measures 5 3/4"(6 1/4") from cast-on edge, ending by working a purl row.

Next Row (dec row - right side): K10(8); * K2 tog; rep from * to last 11(9) sts; knit rem 11(9) sts: 67(71) sts.

Knit next 3 rows (for garter st band at beg of yoke).

Shape Armholes

Starting with a knit row, work in stock st and at the same time bind off 3 sts at beg of next 2 rows, then dec one st at each end of every other row until 53(55) sts rem on needle. Work even until armholes measure 3 1/4"(3 1/2"), ending by working a purl row.

Shape Shoulders

Bind off 5 sts at beg of next 6 rows, then bind off rem 23(25) sts (for back of neck).

Left Front

Cast on 59(71) sts. Knit 9 rows (for garter st border). Now work in Lace Patt St as follows:

Row 1 (right side): Work Row 1 of Lace Patt St across to last 6 sts, K6 (for garter st front band).
Row 2: K6, purl rem sts.
Keeping 6 sts of front band in garter st and rem sts in Lace Patt St as established, work even until piece measures 5 3/4"(6 1/4") from cast-on edge, ending by working a wrong side row.
Next Row (dec row - right side): K9(1), * K2 tog; rep from * to last 6 sts, K6: 37(39) sts.
Knit next 3 rows (for garter st band at beg of yoke).

Shape Armhole

Bind off 3 sts, knit rem sts: 34(36) sts.

Next Row: K6, purl rem sts.

Keeping 6 sts of front band in garter st and rem sts in stock st, dec one st at armhole edge on next row and then on every other row until 30(31) sts rem on needle. Work even until armhole measures 2 1/4"(2 1/2"), ending at front edge.

Shape Neck

Bind off first 10(11) sts, purl rem sts: 20 sts. Continuing in stock st, dec one st at neck edge on every row 5 times (15 sts). Work even until armhole measures same as back, ending at armhole edge.

continued on page 38

Shape Shoulder

Bind off 5 sts at beg of next row and following alternate row. Work one row even. Bind off rem 5 sts.

Right Front

Cast on 59(71) sts. Knit 9 rows. Now work in Lace Patt St as follows:

Row 1 (right side): K6 (for garter st front band), work Row 1 of Lace Patt St over rem sts.

Row 2: Purl (Row 2 of Lace Patt St) to last 6 sts, K6.

Keeping 6 sts of front band in garter st and rem sts in Lace Patt St as established, work even until piece measures 5 3/4"(6 1/4") from cast-on edge, ending by working a wrong side row.

Next Row (dec row - right side): K6, * K2 tog; rep from * to last 9(1) st(s), knit rem 9(1) st(s): 37(39) sts.

Next Row: Knit.

Next Row (buttonhole row): K2, bind off next 2 sts, knit rem sts.

Next Row: Knit across to bound-off sts of buttonhole, cast on 2 sts, knit rem sts: 37(39) sts.

Next Row: Knit.

Work 2 more buttonholes evenly spaced up to neck edge in this same manner and at the same time work shaping as follows:

Shape Armhole

Bind off first 3 sts, purl across to last 6 sts, K6. Keeping 6 sts of front band in garter st and rem sts in stock st, dec one st at armhole edge on next row and then on every other row until 30(31) sts rem on needle. Work even until armhole measures 2 1/4"(2 1/2"), ending at front edge.

Shape Neck

Bind off 10(11) sts, knit rem sts: 20 sts. Continuing in stock st, dec one st at neck edge on every row 5 times: 15 sts. Work even until armhole measures same as back, ending at armhole edge.

Shape Shoulder

Bind off 5 sts at beg of next row and following alternate row. Work one row even. Bind off rem 5 sts.

Sleeve (make 2)

Cast on 34(36) sts. Work in K1, P1 ribbing for 1".

Next Row (inc row - wrong side): P3(4), * inc in next st (to inc, purl in front and back of same st), P1; rep from * to last 3(4) sts, inc in next st, P2(3): 49(51) sts.

Now work in Lace Patt St as follows:

Row 1 (right side): K0(1), * K1, YO, K3, K2 tog; K1, sl 1, K1, PSSO; K3, YO; rep from * to last 1(2) st(s); K1(2).

Rows 2, 4 and 6: Purl.

Row 3: Rep Row 1.

Row 5: K0(1), * K1, sl 1, K1, PSSO; K3, YO, K1; YO, K3, K2 tog; rep from to last 1(2) st (s); K1(2).

Row 7: Rep Row 5.

Row 8: Purl.

Rep last 8 rows until sleeve measures 6"(61/2") from cast-on edge, ending by working a purl row.

Shape Cap

Keeping patt correct, bind off 3 sts at beg of next 2 rows, then dec one st at each end of next row and then on every other row until 15 sts rem on needle. Bind off.

Finishing

Sew shoulder seams. Sew side and sleeve seams. Sew sleeves into armholes.

Collar

With inside of jacket facing you, start in 3rd st of left front band and pick up 21(23) sts across left front neck edge to shoulder seam, pick up 23(25) sts across back neck edge and pick up 21(23) sts across right front neck edge, ending in 3rd st of front band: 65(71) sts.

Row 2: Knit (forms a turning ridge).

Row 3 (inc row): K8, * inc in next st (to inc, knit in front and back of same st), K2; rep from * to last 9 sts; inc in next st, K8: 82(90) sts.

Row 4: K6, purl to last 6 sts; K6.

Row 5: Knit.

Rep last 2 rows until collar measures 1" from neck edge, ending by working a knit row.

Knit 4 more rows (for garter st border). Bind off in knit. Weave in ends. Sew on buttons.

Glistening Galaxy Tablecloth

The rich look of crochet cotton is showcased in this lovely crocheted square or rectangular traditional tablecloth, adapted from a very old pattern. Because the cloth is made from squares which are then joined, you can make it any size to fit any table.

Sizes

Square   52 1/2" x 52 1/2" (10 motifs x 10 motifs)
Small oblong   52 1/2" x 73 1/2" (10 motifs x 14 motifs)
Medium oblong 63" x 84" (12 motifs x 16 motifs)
Large oblong   63" x 105" (12 motifs x 20 motifs)

Size Note: To change sizes, add or subtract motifs for desired measurements, and remember to adjust thread amounts accordingly (approx 40 yds of thread are required to make one motif).

Materials

Bedspread-weight crochet cotton, ecru:

    Square size: 4200 yds
    Small oblong size: 5800 yds
    Medium oblong size: 7950 yds
    Large oblong size: 9900 yds

Size 7 steel crochet hook (or size required for gauge)

Gauge

One motif = 5 1/4" square

Instructions

First Motif

Note: All rnds are worked on right side - do not turn at beg of rnds.

Ch 8, join with a sl st to form a ring.

Rnd 1: Ch 4, work beg CL (beginning cluster stitch) in ring as follows: Keeping last lp of each st on hook, work 2 trc in ring (3 lps now on hook), YO hook and draw through all 3 lps on hook (beg CL made). * Ch 5, work CL (cluster stitch) in ring as follows: Keeping last lp of each st on hook, work 3 trc in ring (4 lps now on hook), YO hook and draw through all 4 lps on hook (CL made); rep from * 6 times more, ch 5, join with a sl st in top of beg CL: 8 CL with ch-5 sp between each CL.

Rnd 2: Ch 1, sc in same st (st where prev rnd was just joined); * work 5 sc in next ch-5 sp, sc in top of next CL; rep

from * 6 times more, work 5 sc in last ch-5 sp; join with a sl st in beg sc: 48 sc.

Rnd 3: Ch 1, sc in same st; * ch 6, sk next 2 sc, sc in next sc; rep from * 14 times more, ch 3, sk last 2 sc, join with a dc in beg sc (this completes last lp and brings thread into position to start next rnd):16 lps.

Rnd 4: * Ch 6, sc in next sp; rep from * 14 times more, ch 6, sk next 3 chs of next lp, then join with a sl st in top of next dc of same lp (st used to join prev rnd):16 lps.

Rnd 5: Sl st into next sp, ch 4 (counts as first trc of rnd), work 7 trc in same sp; * ch 2, sc in next sp; ch 2, work 8 trc in next sp; rep from * 6 times more, ch 2, sc in last sp; * ch 2, join with a sl st in top of beg ch-4: eight 8-trc groups with two ch-2 sps between each group.

Rnd 6: Ch 4 (first 3 chs count as first dc of rnd), dc in next trc of same 8-trc group, work (ch 1, dc in next trc of same 8-trc group) 6 times; * † ch 1, sk next ch-2 sp, trc in next sc; ch 1, sk next ch-2 sp, dc in first trc of next 8-trc group, work (ch 1, dc in next trc of same 8-trc group) 7 times; ch 1, sk next ch-2 sp, work (trc, ch 5, trc) in next sc (for corner) †; ch 1, sk next ch-2 sp, dc in first trc of next 8-trc group, work (ch 1, dc in next trc of same 8-trc group) 7 times; rep from * twice more, then rep from † to † once; ch 1, sk last ch-2 sp, join with a sl st in 3rd ch of beg ch-4.

Rnd 7: Sl st in next ch and in next dc; ch 4, sk next ch-1 sp, dc in next dc, work (ch 1, sk next ch-1 sp, dc in next dc) 4 times, * † ch 4; sk next ch-1 sp, dc, and next ch-1 sp; sc in next trc, ch 4; sk next ch-1 sp, dc, and next ch-1 sp; dc in next dc, work (ch 1, sk next ch-1 sp, dc in next dc) 5 times, ch 4; sk next ch-l sp, dc, ch-1 sp, and next trc; work (trc, ch 5, trc) in next ch-5 corner sp †, ch 4; sk next trc, ch-1 sp, dc, and next ch-1 sp; dc in next dc, work (ch 1, sk next ch-1 sp, dc in next dc) 5 times; rep from * twice more, then rep from † to † once; ch 4, sk last ch-1 sp, join with a sl st in 3rd ch of beg ch-4.

Rnd 8: Sl st in next ch and in next dc; ch 4, sk next ch-1 sp, dc in next dc, work (ch 1, sk next ch-1 sp, dc in next dc) twice; † ch 4, sk next ch-1 sp and dc, sc in next ch-4 sp; ch 5, sc in next ch-4 sp; ch 4, sk next dc and ch-1 sp, dc in next dc, work (ch 1, sk next ch-1 sp, dc in next dc) 3 times, ch 4; sk next ch-1 sp, dc and next ch-4 sp; work 4 trc with ch 3 between each trc in next ch-5 corner sp †, ch 4; sk next ch-4 sp, dc and next ch-1 sp; dc in next dc, work (ch 1, sk next ch-1 sp, dc in next dc) 3 times; rep from * twice more, then rep from † to † once; ch 4, sk last ch-4 sp, join with a sl st in 3rd ch of beg ch-4.

Rnd 9: Ch 3, dec over next 3 dc (sk ch-1 sp between each dc) as follows: keeping last lp of each st on hook, work dc in each of next 3 dc (4 lps now on hook), YO hook and draw through all 4 lps on hook (dec made); * † work (ch 5, dc) in each of next 3 sps, ch 5, dec over next 4 dc (sk ch-1 sp between each dc) as follows: keeping last lp on each st on hook, work dc in each of next 4 dc (5 lps now on hook), YO hook and draw through all 5 lps on hook (dec made); work (ch 5, sk next sp, trc in next trc) twice; ch 5; work (CL, ch 7, CL) in next sp at corner (to work CL, see instructions in Rnd 1); ch 5, trc in next trc; ch 5, sk next sp, trc in next trc †; ch 5, sk next sp, dec over next 4 dc; rep from * twice more, then rep from † to † once; ch 5, sk next sp and beg ch-3, then join with a sl st in top of next st (dec st). Finish off and weave in ends.

2nd Motif

Work same as First Motif until first 8 rnds are completed, then work next (9th) rnd, joining motif to prev motif along one side as follows:

Rnd 9 (joining rnd)**:** Work same as for First Motif around to sp at 2nd corner, then join to prev motif along next side as follows: ch 5, work CL in corner sp on working motif; ch 3, sl st in center ch of corresponding corner lp on prev motif; ch 3, work one more CL in same corner sp on working motif; ch 2, sl st in next sp on prev motif; ch 2, trc in next trc on working motif; ch 2, sl st in next sp on prev motif; ch 2, sk next sp on working motif, then work trc in next trc on working motif; ch 5, sk next sp on working motif, dec over next 4 dc on working motif; ch 2, sk next sp on prev motif, sl st in next sp on prev motif; ch 2, dc in next sp on working

motif; † ch 2, sl st in next sp on prev motif; ch 2, dc in next sp on working motif †; rep from † to † once more; ch 2, sl st in next sp on prev motif; ch 2, dec over next 4 dc on working motif; ch 5, sk next sp on working motif, trc in next trc on working motif; ch 2, sk next sp on prev motif, sl st in next sp on prev motif; ch 2, sk next sp on working motif, trc in next trc on working motif; ch 2, sl st in next sp on prev motif; ch 2, work CL in next sp at corner on working motif; ch 3, sl st in center ch of next corner lp on prev motif; ch 3, work one more CL in same corner sp on working motif (motifs now joined along one side). Complete rnd on working motif in same manner as for First Motif. Finish off and weave in ends.

Following Motifs

Work in same manner as for 2nd Motif, joining side(s) as required, until there are:

for square size, 10 joined rows with 10 motifs in each row

for small oblong size, 10 joined rows with 14 motifs in each row

for medium oblong size, 12 joined rows with 16 motifs in each row

for large oblong size, 12 joined rows with 20 motifs in each row.

Edging

With right side facing you, join thread with a sl st in any outer corner sp, ch 4, work beg CL in same sp. Work picot lp as follows: Ch 6, sl st in 4th ch from hook, ch 2 (picot lp made). Work CL in same sp, work picot lp, work (CL, picot lp, CL) in next sp; * ch 3, sc in next sp; work picot lp, sc in next sp; ch 3, work (CL, picot lp, CL) in next sp; rep from * to next outer corner sp, work picot lp, work (CL, picot lp, CL) in outer corner sp. Work edging around rem sides and corners in same manner, ending by working picot lp, join with a sl st in top of beg CL. Finish off and weave in ends.

Block tablecloth to measurements following blocking instructions, page 5.

V–Neck Baby Jacket

designed by Mary Thomas

Easy to work cluster stitches form an interesting block pattern on this crocheted jacket that is perfect for either a boy or a girl. Accent the jacket with cute buttons — we used bunnies.

Sizes

	3 months	6 months	1 year
body chest	18"	19"	20"
garment chest (buttoned)	19"	20"	21"

Size Note: Instructions are written for smallest size with changes in parentheses for larger sizes.

Materials

Baby weight yarn: 4(4 1/2, 5) oz baby blue
Sizes F and G aluminum crochet hooks (or size required for gauge)
2 buttons (1/2" diameter)

Gauge

With smaller size hook in patt, 7 CL = 3"; (sc row + CL row) 5 times = 3"

Instructions

Back and Fronts

Starting at bottom edge with larger size hook, ch 88 (94, 100).

Row 1 (wrong side)**:** Sc in 2nd ch from hook and in each ch across: 87(93, 99) sc. Change to smaller size hook. Ch 3, turn.

Row 2: Work CL (cluster) in next sc as follows: Keeping last lp of each st on hook, work 3 dc in next sc (4 lps now on hook), YO and draw through all 4 lps on hook : CL made; * ch 1 loosely (will make it easier to work into ch on next row), sk next sc, CL in next sc; rep from * to last sc; do not ch 1, dc in last sc: 43(46, 49) CLs; ch 1, turn.

Row 3: Sc in first dc; * sc in next CL and in next ch; rep from * to last CL; sc in CL and in top of ch-3: 87(93, 99) sc; ch 3, turn.

Rep Rows 2 and 3 until piece measures 6 1/2" (6 1/2", 7") from beg edge, ending by working Row 2.

Now shape left front as follows:

Row 1: Sc in first dc, sk next CL, sc in next ch; * sc in next CL and in next ch; rep from * 8(9, 10) times more; leave rem sts unworked: 20(22, 24) sc; ch 3, turn.

Row 2: CL in next sc; * ch 1, sk next sc, CL in next sc; rep from * to last 2 sc; do not ch 1, dc in last 2 sc: 9(10, 11) CLs; ch 1, turn.

Row 3: Sc in first dc, sk next dc; * sc in next CL and in next ch; rep from * to last CL; sc in CL and in top of ch-3: 19(21, 23) sc; ch 3, turn.

Row 4: CL in next sc; * ch 1, sk next sc, CL in next sc; rep from * to last sc; do not ch 1, dc in last sc: 9(10, 11) CLs; ch 1, turn.

Row 5: Sc in first dc, sk CL, sc in next ch; * sc in next CL and in next ch; rep from * to last CL; sc in CL and in top of ch-3: 18(20, 22) sc; ch 3, turn.

Rep Rows 2 through 5, 1(2, 2) time(s), then rep Rows 2 and 3, 1(0,1) time. At end of last row, you should have 15(16,17) sc. Finish off.

Shape Back

Sk next CL from left front shaping just completed, then with smaller size hook, join yarn with a sl st in next ch.

Row 1: Ch 1, sc in same st; * sc in next CL and in next ch; rep from * 20(21, 22) times more, leave rem sts unworked: 43(45, 47) sc; ch 3, turn.

Row 2: CL in next sc; * ch 1, sk next sc, CL in next sc; rep from * to last sc; do not ch 1, dc in last sc: 21(22, 23) CLs; ch 1, turn.

Row 3: Sc in first dc; * sc in next CL and in next ch; rep from * to last CL; sc in CL and in top of ch-3: 43(45, 47) sc; ch 3, turn.

Rep Rows 2 and 3, 4(5, 6) times. At end of last row, finish off.

Shape Right Front

Sk next CL from back shaping just completed, then with smaller size hook, join yarn with a sl st in next ch.

Row 1: Ch 1, sc in same st; * sc in next CL and in next ch; rep from * to last CL; sk CL, sc in top of ch-3: 20(22, 24) sc; ch 3, turn.

Row 2: Dc in next sc, CL in next sc; * ch 1, sk next sc, CL in next sc; rep from * to last sc; do not ch 1, dc in last sc: 9(10, 11) CLs; ch 1, turn.

Row 3: Sc in first dc; * sc in next CL and in next ch; rep from * to last CL; sc in CL, sk dc, sc in top of ch-3: 19(21, 23) sc; ch 3, turn.

Row 4: CL in next sc; * ch 1, sk next sc, CL in next sc; rep from * to last sc; do not ch 1, dc in last sc: 9(10, 11) CLs; ch 1, turn.

Row 5: Sc in first dc; * sc in next CL and in next ch; rep from * to last CL; sk CL, sc in top of ch-3: 18(20, 22) sc; ch 3, turn.

Rep Rows 2 through 5, 1(2, 2) time(s), then rep Rows 2 and 3, 1(0, 1) time. At end of last row, you should have 15(16, 17) sc. Finish off.

Sleeve (make 2)

With smaller size hook, ch 34(38, 42).

Row 1 (wrong side): Sc in 2nd ch from hook and in each ch across: 33(37, 41) sc; ch 3, turn.

Row 2: CL in next sc; * ch 1, sk next sc, CL in next sc; rep from * to last sc; do not ch 1, dc in last sc: 16(18, 20) CLs; ch 1, turn.

Row 3: Sc in first dc; * sc in next CL and in next ch; rep from * to last CL; sc in CL and in top of ch-3: 33(37, 41) sc; ch 3, turn.

Rep Rows 2 and 3 until sleeve measures 5 1/2"(6", 7") long, ending by working Row 2.

Next Row: Change to larger size hook, and rep Row 3. Finish off.

Finishing

Sew shoulder seams. Sew sleeve seams, then sew sleeves into armholes, having last row worked on sleeves matched with armhole edges.

Sleeve Edging (make 2)

With right side facing you and smaller size hook, join yarn with a sl st at seam.

Rnd 1: Ch 1, sc in each st around sleeve edge; join with a sl st in beg sc; ch 1, turn.

Rnd 2 (wrong side): Sl st in each st around; join with a sl st in beg st. Finish off and weave in ends.

Front, Neck and Bottom Edging

With right side facing you and smaller size hook, join yarn with a sl st at neck edge at right shoulder seam.

Rnd 1: Ch 1, sc in each st across back edge, work in sc evenly spaced down left front edge (about 3 sc in every 2 rows), work 3 sc in st at bottom corner; sc in each st across bottom edge, 3 sc in st at bottom corner; work in sc evenly spaced up right front edge to correspond to sts on left front edge; join with a sl st in beg sc; ch 1, turn.

Before working next rnd, mark front edge (left front for boys or right front for girls) for 2 button lps, having first lp at start of v-neck shaping and the other lp about 5 or 6 sts down from first lp.

Rnd 2 (wrong side): * Sl st in each st to marker for button lp, ch 4, sk next sc, sl st in next sc; rep from * once more; sl st in each rem sc around; join with a sl st in beg st. Finish off and weave in ends.

Sew on buttons.

Crayons Baby Afghan

designed by Rita Weiss

Babies are attracted to bright primary colors, and will love this cheery crocheted afghan. The colors are fun to work with, and the pattern is easy to make. Making this is as much fun as a coloring book!

Size

About 36" x 47"

Materials

Sport weight yarn:

    11 oz yellow;

    3 oz red;

    3 oz green;

    3 oz blue;

    3 oz orange

Size G aluminum crochet hook, or size required for

    gauge

Gauge

4 dc = 1"

Special Technique

To change colors: Work dc until 2 lps rem on hook, finish off color used, leaving 4" end for weaving in later. With new color (leave 4" end), YO and draw through 2 lps on hook: color changed.

Instructions

With yellow, ch 186 loosely.

Row 1: Sc in 2nd ch from hook and in each rem ch:185 sc; ch 3, turn.

Row 2: Sk first 3 sc, (3 dc in next sc, sk 2 sc) 3 times; in next sc work (3 dc, ch 3, 3 dc); * (sk 2 sc, 3 dc in next sc) twice; sk 2 sc, (YO, insert hook in st and draw up a lp, YO and draw through 2 lps on hook) 3 times; YO and draw through all 4 lps on hook: cluster made; sk 4 sc, cluster in next sc, (sk 2 sc, 3 dc in next sc) twice; sk 2 sc, in next sc work (3 dc, ch 3, 3 dc); rep from * 6 times more; sk 2 sc, (3 dc in next sc, sk 2 sc) 3 times; dc in last sc; ch 3, turn.

Row 3 (patt row): Sk first sp (between first dc and 3-dc group); work 3 dc in each of next 3 sps (between each pair of 3-dc groups); (3 dc, ch 3, 3 dc) in ch-3 sp at point; * 3 dc in each of next 2 sps; cluster in next sp, sk sp between clusters, cluster in next sp; work 3 dc in each of next 2 sps, (3 dc, ch 3, 3 dc) in ch-3 sp at point; rep from * 7 times more; work 3 dc in each of next 3 sps, dc in last sp (between last 3-dc group and ch-3); ch 3, turn.

Rows 4 through 7: Rep Row 3. At the end of Row 7, change to red in last dc (see Special Technique); ch 3, turn.

Rep Patt Row (Row 3) using the following 24-row sequence:

3 rows red

3 rows green

6 rows yellow

3 rows blue

3 rows orange

6 rows yellow

Rep 24-row sequence twice more: 79 rows. Finish off and weave in ends.

Lullaby Baby Afghan

designed by Rita Weiss

Lullaby and goodnight . . . baby will surely sleep soundly under this sweet crocheted coverlet. Grandma can start this afghan before the baby arrives, as its combination of blue and pink makes it perfect for either a girl or a boy.

Size

About 40" x 40"

Materials

Sport weight yarn:
    7 oz white;
    5 oz pink;
    5 oz blue
Size F aluminum crochet hook, or size required for
    gauge

Gauge

4 sc = 1"

Gauge note: To test gauge and determine correct hook size, ch 17; sc in 2nd ch from hook and in each rem ch across. Work even in sc on 16 sts for 17 more rows. Your swatch should measure 4" square.

Instructions

With blue, ch 174 loosely.

Foundation Row (wrong side): Sc in 2nd ch from hook and in each of next 4 chs; 3 sc in next ch; * sc in each of next 3 chs, sk 2 chs; sc in each of next 3 chs, 3 sc in next ch; rep from * across to last 5 chs; sc in each of rem 5 chs; ch 1, turn.

Row 1: Working in bls only (see page 4) of each st across, dec over first 2 sts as follows: draw up a lp in each of next 2 sts, YO and draw through all 3 lps now on hook: dec made; sc in each of next 4 sts, 3 sc in next st; * sc in each of next 3 sts, sk 2 sts, sc in each of next 3 sts, 3 sc in next st; rep from * across to last 6 sts; sc in each of next 4 sts, dec over last 2 sts; ch 1, turn.

Rows 2 through 4: Rep Row 1. At end of Row 4, join pink by drawing lp through; finish off blue; ch 1, turn.

Row 5: Working through both lps, sl st loosely in each sc of prev row; join white by drawing lp through; finish off pink; ch 1, turn.

Row 6: Leaving pink sl sts unworked and working in bl only of each sc of Row 4, rep Row 1.

Rows 7 through 10: Rep Row 1. At end of Row 10, join blue as above; finish off white; ch 1, turn.

Row 11: Working through both lps, sl st loosely in each sc of prev row; join pink as above; finish off blue; ch 1, turn.

Row 12: Leaving blue sl sts unworked and working in bl only of each sc of Row 10, rep Row 1.

Rows 13 through 16: Rep Row 1. At end of Row 16, join blue as above; finish off pink; ch 1, turn.

Row 17: Rep Row 11, changing to white at end of row.

Row 18: Leaving blue sl sts unworked and working in bl only of each sc of Row 16, rep Row 1.

Rows 19 through 22: Rep Row 1. At end of Row 22, join pink as above; finish off white; ch 1, turn.

Row 23: Rep Row 5, changing to blue at end of row.

Row 24: Leaving pink sl sts unworked and working in bl only of each sc of Row 22, rep Row 1.

Rows 25 through 28: Rep Row 1. At end of Row 28, join pink as above; finish off blue; ch 1, turn.

Rep 29: Rep Row 5.

Rep Rows 6 through 29 four times.

Rep Rows 6 through 28 once. Finish off and weave in ends.

Heart Box

designed by Kathy Wesley

Crisply starched and filled with silk flowers, this little thread crocheted box captures the heart with its charm. Use it as a table or dresser decoration, or fill it with candy as a Valentine's Day Gift.

Finished Size
About 5 1/2" x 5 1/2" x 2" high

Materials
Bedspread-weight crochet cotton, one 225-yd ball white
Size 7 steel crochet hook, or size required for gauge

Trimmings
starching supplies (see page 5)
6" square of Styrofoam®, 2" thick
1 yd 1/4"-wide picot-edge lt peach satin ribbon
one 1/2" diameter peach ribbon rose
assorted dried flowers
assorted silk flowers
hot glue or tacky craft glue

Gauge
9 dc = 1"

Instructions

Ch 6, join to form a ring.

Rnd 1 (right side): Ch 4 (counts as a dc and a ch-1 sp), * dc in ring, ch 1; rep from * 6 times more; join in 3rd ch of beg ch-4: 8 dc.

Rnd 2: Sl st in next ch-1 sp; ch 3, in same sp work (dc, ch 1, 2 dc): beg shell made; * in next sp work (2 dc, ch 1, 2 dc): shell made; rep from * 6 times more; join in 3rd ch of beg ch-3: 8 shells.

Rnd 3: Sl st in next dc and in next ch-1 sp; in same sp work beg shell; ch 3, * in ch-1 sp of next shell work shell: shell in shell made; ch 3; rep from * 6 times more; join in 3rd ch of beg ch-3.

Rnd 4: Sl st in next dc and in next ch-1 sp; in same sp work beg shell; ch 1, 3 dc in next ch-3 lp, ch 1, * shell in next shell; ch 1, 3 dc in next ch-3 lp, ch 1; rep from * 6 times more; join in 3rd ch of beg ch-3.

Rnd 5: Sl st in next dc and in next ch-1 sp; in same sp work beg shell; ch 1, 2 dc in next dc, dc in next dc, 2 dc in next dc, ch 1, * shell in next shell; ch 1, 2 dc in next dc, dc in next dc, 2 dc in next dc, ch 1; rep from * 6 times more; join in 3rd ch of beg ch-3.

Rnd 6: Sl st in next dc and in next ch-1 sp; in same sp work beg shell; * † ch 1, 2 dc in next dc, dc in next 3 dc, 2 dc in next dc, ch 1 †, shell in next shell; rep from * 6 times more, then rep from † to † once; join in 3rd ch of beg ch-3.

Rnd 7: Sl st in next dc and in next ch-1 sp; in same sp work beg shell; * † ch 1, dc in next 7 dc, ch 1 †, shell in next shell; rep from * 6 times more, then rep from † to † once; join in 3rd ch of beg ch-3.

Rnd 8: Sl st in next dc and in next ch-1 sp; in same sp work (dc, ch 1, 2 dc, ch 1, 2 dc); * † ch 1, sk next dc, dc in next 5 dc, ch 1 †, in ch-1 sp of next shell work (2 dc, ch 1) 3 times; rep from * 6 times more, then rep from † to † once; join in 3rd ch of beg ch-3.

Rnd 9: Sl st in next dc and in next ch-1 sp; in same sp work beg shell; ch 3, in next ch-1 sp work shell; * † ch 1, sk next ch-1 sp and next dc, dc in next 3 dc, ch 1 †, sk next ch-1 sp, in next ch-1 sp work shell; ch 3, in next ch-1 sp work shell; rep from * 6 times more, then rep from † to † once; join in 3rd ch of beg ch-3.

Rnd 10: Sl st in next dc and in next ch-1 sp; in same sp work beg shell; * † ch 1, in next ch-3 lp work (dc, ch 1, dc): V-st made; ch 1, shell in next shell; ch 1, dc in 2nd dc of next 3-dc group, ch 1 †, shell in next shell; rep from * 6 times more, then rep from † to † once; join in 3rd ch of beg ch-3.

Rnd 11: Sl st in next dc and in next ch-1 sp; in same sp work beg shell; ch 1, shell in ch-1 sp of next V-st; ch 1, shell in next shell; ch 2, * sk next dc, shell in next shell; ch 1, shell in ch-1 sp of next V-st; ch 1, shell in next shell; ch 2; rep from * around; join in 3rd ch of beg ch-3.

Rnd 12: Sl st in next dc and in next ch-1 sp; in same sp work beg shell; ch 1, * † (dc in next dc, ch 1) twice; dc in next ch-1 sp, ch 1, (dc in next dc, ch 1) twice; shell in next shell; ch 2 †, shell in next shell; ch 1; rep from * 6 times more, then rep from † to † once; join in 3rd ch of beg ch-3.

Rnd 13: Sl st in next dc and in next ch-1 sp; in same sp work beg shell; ch 1, * † sk next ch-1 sp, (dc in next ch-1 sp, ch 1) 4 times; shell in next shell; ch 2 †, shell in next shell; ch 1; rep from * 6 times more, then rep from † to † once; join in 3rd ch of beg ch-3.

Rnd 14: Sl st in next dc and in next ch-1 sp; in same sp work beg shell; ch 1, * † sk next ch-1 sp, (dc in next ch-1 sp, ch 1) 3 times; shell in next shell; ch 2 †, shell in next shell; ch 1; rep from * 6 times more, then rep from † to † once; join in 3rd ch of beg ch-3.

Rnd 15: Sl st in next dc and in next ch-1 sp; in same sp work beg shell; ch 1, * † sk next ch-1 sp, (dc in next ch-1 sp, ch 1) twice; shell in next shell; ch 2 †, shell in next shell; ch 1; rep from * 6 times more, then rep from † to † once; join in 3rd ch of beg ch-3.

Rnd 16: Sl st in next dc and in next ch-1 sp; in same sp work beg shell; ch 1, * † sk next ch-1 sp, shell in next ch-1 sp †, ch 1, (shell in next shell, ch 1) twice; rep from * 6 times more, then rep from † to † once; shell in next shell; ch 1; join in 3rd ch of beg ch-3.

Rnd 17: Sl st in next dc and in next ch-1 sp; ch 3, in same sp work 4 dc; sc in next ch-1 sp, * 5 dc in next ch 1 sp, sc in next ch-1 sp; rep from * around; join in 3rd ch of beg ch-3.

Rnd 18: Sl st in next 2 dc; ch 3, in same dc work (2 dc, ch 1, 3 dc); ch 2, * in 3rd dc of next 5-dc group work (3 dc, ch 1, 3 dc); ch 2; rep from * around; join in 3rd ch of beg ch-3. Finish off and weave in all ends.

Finishing

Starching and Blocking Instructions
Step 1: Trace heart pattern; place on Styrofoam® square and cut heart form.

Step 2: Following Starching and Blocking Instructions on page 5, place saturated crocheted piece on form. Pin at indentation at top of Heart and as necessary along sides. As Heart dries, shape edge.

Trimming Instructions
Step 1: Arrange dried and silk flowers inside Heart in a pleasing manner; glue in place.

Step 2: Cut an 18" length of ribbon and tie bow

with 1 1/2" loops; glue to point of Heart. With remaining ribbon, tie bow with 1" loops; glue on top of first bow. Glue ribbon rose on top of bows.

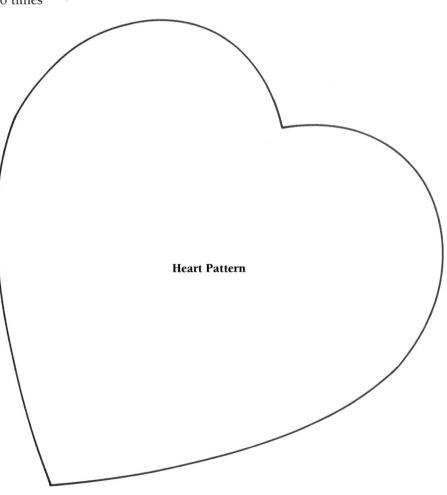

Heart Pattern

Seashell Wall Vase

designed by Kathy Wesley

Shaped like a graceful seashell, this pretty thread crochet vase can hold dried or silk flowers to provide a feminine accent. Starch it to shape and trim it with ribbon for an unusual accessory.

Finished Size

About 6" x 3" x 4" high

Materials

Bedspread-weight crochet cotton, one 225-yd ball cream
Size 7 steel crochet hook, or size required for gauge

Trimmings

starching supplies (see page 5)
1/3 yd 1/4"-wide picot-edge mauve satin ribbon
assorted dried flowers
small amount Spanish moss
hot glue or tacky craft glue

Gauge

9 dc = 1"

Instructions

Ch 5, join to form a ring.

Rnd 1 (right side): Ch 5 (counts as a dc and a ch-2 sp), * dc in ring, ch 2; rep from * 4 times more; join in 3rd ch of beg ch-5: 6 dc.

Rnd 2: Sl st in next ch-2 sp; ch 3, in same sp work (dc, ch 1, 2 dc): beg shell made; * ch 1, in next ch-2 sp work (2 dc, ch 1, 2 dc): shell made; rep from * 4 times more; ch 1; join in 3rd ch of beg ch-3: 6 shells.

Rnd 3: Sl st in next dc and in next ch-1 sp; in same sp work beg shell; * ch 2, sk next ch-1 sp, in ch-1 sp of next shell work shell: shell in shell made; rep from * 4 times more; ch 2; join in 3rd ch of beg ch-3.

Rnd 4: Sl st in next dc and in next ch-1 sp; in same sp work beg shell; * ch 2, dc in next ch-2 sp, ch 2, shell in next shell; rep from * 5 times more, ending last rep without working shell; join in 3rd ch of beg ch-3.

Rnd 5: Sl st in next dc and in next ch-1 sp; in same sp work beg shell; * ch 2, 2 dc in next dc, ch 2, shell in next shell; rep from * 5 times more, ending last rep without working shell; join in 3rd ch of beg ch-3.

Rnd 6: Sl st in next dc and in next ch-1 sp; in same sp work beg shell; * ch 2, 2 dc in each of next 2 dc, ch 2, shell in next shell; rep from * 5 times more, ending last rep without working shell; join in 3rd ch of beg ch-3.

Rnd 7: Sl st in next dc and in next ch-1 sp; in same sp work (dc, ch 1, 2 dc, ch 1, 2 dc); * † ch 2, 2 dc in next dc, dc in next 2 dc, 2 dc in next dc, ch 2 †; in next shell work (2 dc, ch 1, 2 dc, ch 1, 2 dc); rep from * 4 times more, then rep from † to † once; join in 3rd ch of beg ch-3.

Rnd 8: Sl st in next dc and in next ch-1 sp; in same sp work beg shell; ch 2, in next ch-1 sp work shell; * † ch 2, dc in next 4 dc, ch 2 †; in next ch-1 sp work shell, ch 2, in next ch-1 sp work shell; rep from * 4 times more, then rep from † to † once; join in 3rd ch of beg ch-3.

Rnd 9: Sl st in next dc and in next ch-1 sp; in same sp work beg shell; * † ch 2, dc in next ch-2 sp, ch 2, shell in next shell; ch 2, sk next ch-2 sp and next dc, dc in next 2 dc, ch 2 †; in next ch-1 sp work shell; rep from * 4 times more, then rep from † to † once; join in 3rd ch of beg ch-3.

Rnd 10: Sl st in next dc and in next ch-1 sp; in same sp work beg shell; ch 2, * † 2 dc in next dc, ch 2, shell in next shell; ch 2, sk next ch-2 sp, dc between next 2 dc, ch 2 †; shell in next shell; rep from * 4 times more; then rep from † to † once; join in 3rd ch of beg ch-3.

Rnd 11: Sl st in next dc and in next ch-1 sp; in same sp work beg shell; ch 2, * † in next dc work (dc, ch 1, dc), ch 1, in next dc work (dc, ch 1, dc), ch 2 †; (shell in next shell, ch 2) twice; rep from * 4 times more, then rep from † to † once; shell in next shell; ch 2; join in 3rd ch of beg ch-3.

Rnd 12: Sl st in next dc and in next ch-1 sp; in same sp work

beg shell; * † ch 2, sk next ch-2 sp, (2 dc in next dc, ch 1) 3 times; 2 dc in next dc, ch 2, shell in next shell; ch 1 †; shell in next shell; rep from * 4 times more, then rep from † to † once; join in 3rd ch of beg ch-3.

Rnd 13: Sl st in next dc and in next ch-1 sp; in same sp work beg shell; * † ch 2, (2 dc in each of next 2 dc, ch 1) 3 times; 2 dc in each of next 2 dc, ch 2 †; shell in each of next 2 shells; rep from * 4 times more, then rep from † to † once; shell in next shell; join in 3rd ch of beg ch-3.

Rnd 14: Ch 1, sc in each dc and in each ch around; join in first sc.

Rnd 15: Ch 3, sc in next sc, * ch 2, sc in next sc; rep from * around; join in first ch of beg ch-3. Finish off and weave in all ends.

Finishing

Starching and Blocking Instructions
Following starching and blocking instructions on page 5, fold saturated crocheted piece in half, placing crumpled plastic wrap in between sides to keep separated. As piece dries shape top edge to ruffle.

Trimming Instructions
Place moss inside Vase. Arrange flowers in Vase in a pleasing manner and glue in place. Tie bow with 1 1/2" loops; glue to front of Vase.

Doily Wall Pocket

This easy thread crochet doily is starched into an interesting cone shape that can be hung or placed flat on a table. Accent it with a silk and dried flower posy for a soft-color accessory.

Finished Size
Cone shape, about 10" long x 7" wide at top

Materials
Bedspread-weight crochet cotton, one 225-yd ball cream
Size 7 steel crochet hook, or size required for gauge

Trimmings
starching supplies (see page 5)
1/3 yd 1/4"-wide picot-edge mauve satin ribbon
small amount Spanish moss
assorted dried flowers
hot glue or tacky craft glue

Gauge
9 dc = 1"

Instructions

Ch 8, join to form a ring.

Rnd 1 (right side): Ch 3 (counts as a dc on this and following rnds), 23 dc in ring; join in 3rd ch of beg ch-3: 24 dc.

Rnd 2: Ch 3, keeping last lp of each dc on hook, dc in next 3 dc; YO and draw through all 4 lps on hook; ch 5, * keeping last lp of each dc on hook, dc in next 4 dc; YO and draw through all 5 lps on hook; ch 5; rep from * 4 times more; join in 3rd ch of beg ch-3: 6 ch-5 lps.

Rnd 3: Sl st in next lp; ch 3, 7 dc in same lp; 8 dc in each rem lp; join in 3rd ch of beg ch-3: 48 dc.

Rnd 4: Ch 4 (counts as an sc and a ch-3 lp on this and following rnds), * sk next dc, sc in next dc, ch 3; rep from * around; join in first ch of beg ch-4: 24 lps.

Rnd 5: Sl st in next lp; ch 4, * sc in next lp, ch 3; rep from * around; join in first ch of beg ch-4.

Rnd 6: Sl st in next lp; ch 3, 4 dc in same lp; 5 dc in each rem lp; join in 3rd ch of beg ch-3: 120 dc.

Rnd 7: Sl st in next 2 dc; ch 4, * sc in 3rd dc of next 5-dc group, ch 3; rep from * around; join in first ch of beg ch-4: 24 lps.

Rnd 8: Sl st in next lp; ch 4, * sc in next lp, ch 3; rep from * around; join in first ch of beg ch-4.

Rnd 9: Sl st in next lp; ch 3, 6 dc in same lp; 3 sc in next lp, * 7 dc in next lp, 3 sc in next lp; rep from * around; join in 3rd ch of beg ch-3.

Rnd 10: Sl st in next 3 dc; ch 6 (counts as an sc and ch-5 lp), sc in 2nd sc of next 3-sc group, ch 5, * sc in 4th dc of next 7-dc group, ch 5, sc in 2nd sc of next 3-sc group, ch 5; rep from * around; join in first ch of beg ch-6: 24 lps.

Rnd 11: Sl st in next 2 chs, sl st in same ch-5 lp; ch 1, sc in same lp; ch 6, * sc in next lp, ch 5; rep from * around; join in first ch of beg ch-6.

Rnd 12: Sl st in next 2 chs, sl st in same ch-5 lp; ch 1, in same lp work (sc, ch 3, 3 dc); in each rem lp work (sc, ch 3, 3 dc); join in first sc.

Rnd 13: Sl st in next 2 chs, sl st in same ch-3 lp; ch 4, dc in same lp; ch 3, * in next ch-3 lp work (dc, ch 1, dc); ch 3; rep from * around; join in 3rd ch of beg ch-4.

Rnd 14: Sl st in next ch-1 sp; ch 6, sc in next ch-3 lp, ch 5, * sc in next ch-1 sp, ch 5, sc in next ch-3 lp, ch 5; rep from * around; join in first ch of beg ch-6: 48 lps.

Rnd 15: Sl st in next 2 chs, sl st in same ch-5 lp; ch 6, * sc in next ch-5 lp, ch 5; rep from * around; join in first ch of beg ch-6.

Rnds 16 and 17: Rep Rnd 15.

Rnd 18: Sl st in next 2 chs, sl st in same ch-5 lp; ch 3, 7 dc in same lp, * (sc in next ch-5 lp, ch 5) 4 times; sc in next ch-5 lp, 8 dc in next ch-5 lp; rep from * 7 times more, ending last rep without working last 8 dc; join in 3rd ch of beg ch-3: 8 8-dc groups.

Rnd 19: Ch 4, (dc in next dc, ch 1) 7 times; (sc in next

ch-5 lp, ch 5) 3 times; sc in next ch-5 lp, ch 1, * (dc in next dc, ch 1) 8 times; (sc in next ch-5 lp, ch 5) 3 times; sc in next ch-5 lp, ch 1; rep from * around; join in 3rd ch of beg ch-4.

Rnd 20: Sl st in next ch-1 sp; ch 3, 2 dc in same sp; 3 dc in each of next 8 ch-1 sps, * † (sc in next ch-5 lp, ch 5) twice; sc in next ch-5 lp †, 3 dc in each of next 9 ch-1 sps; rep from * 7 times more, then rep from † to † once; 3 dc in next ch-1 sp; join in 3rd ch of beg ch-3.

Rnd 21: Sl st in next dc; ch 4, (sk next dc, dc in next dc, ch 1) 11 times; dc in next ch-5 lp, ch 3, dc in next ch-5 lp, ch 1, * (dc in next dc, ch 1, sk next dc) 13 times; dc in next dc, ch 1, dc in next ch-5 lp, ch 3, dc in next ch-5 lp, ch 1; rep from * 6 times more; (dc in next dc, ch 1) twice; join in 3rd ch of beg ch-4. Finish off and weave in all ends.

Finishing

Starching and Blocking Instructions
Following starching and blocking instructions on page 5, pin crocheted piece flat on pinning board. Let dry. Spray with water until sides can be rounded as shown in photo; let dry.

Trimming Instructions
Place moss inside tip of Doily Wall Pocket. Arrange flowers inside Pocket in a pleasing manner; glue in place. Tie bow with 1" loops; glue to front of Doily Wall Pocket.

Ribbons and Lace Pillows

Make an elegant thread crocheted motif, following the step-by-step instructions. Then stitch it to a satiny fabric, add lace ruffles, satin ribbon roses and bows, a string of pearls or two, and you've created a boudoir accessory that adds a luscious accent to any room.

General Directions for Creating a Lacy Pillow

There are several basic techniques and information on materials that will help you in creating Lacy Pillows using our crocheted motifs. We have included this information here. We suggest that you read through these General Directions carefully before beginning your pillow.

Materials for Trimmed Pillows

Fabrics such as satin, moire and faille are wonderful for pillow top and back. For making a pillow form, muslin or similar weight cotton fabric is suitable. Amounts of fabric needed are given with the materials list for each pillow.

Ribbons are woven through many of the crocheted motifs, as well as used for bows and streamers. Amounts, widths and type of ribbon used for our pillows are given with the materials list for each pillow. You may vary the widths of ribbon specified for bows, but not if ribbon is to be woven through crocheted motif.

Ribbon roses are now readily available pre-made in satin ribbon with little green leaves. They are approximately 1/2" or 3/4" in diameter.

Lace, and lots of it, is what makes these pillows so special. The amount and width of ivory lace used is given with the materials list. If the lace you like is not the exact width, you may feel confident that it will still work up into a wonderful pillow. Even though the lace is purchased pre-gathered, gathering it more will result in a prettier pillow. Generally it is gathered one-and-one half times the measurement of the area where it will be stitched. All lace ruffles are machine-stitched in place.

Pearls can be either sewn or glued to the pillow. Strands of pearls that come with the pearls fused to the string are easier to use. If using pearls that come off the string, you may want to re-string them onto a stronger double thread before sewing them onto the pillow. Strands of pearls are sewn on to pillow top by taking small hand stitches between pearls.

Special Techniques for Trimmed Pillows

Bunny Bow

Make two loops (**Fig 1**). Cross right loop over left loop and then down through circle (**Fig 2**); holding only the loops, pull tight. Adjust loops for a nice, even bow (**Fig 3**). This bow can also be made with two lengths of ribbon, treating them as one, for a Double Bunny Bow.

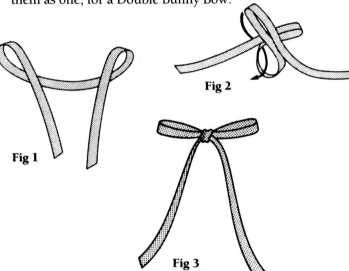

Fig 1   Fig 2   Fig 3

Pinched Bow

Using length of ribbon specified in the project, make two loops (one on each side), holding center of bow pinched between thumb and forefinger (**Fig 4**). With needle and double thread, take a stitch through center gathers and then wrap thread tightly around center (**Fig 5**). Take a couple of small stitches to secure center.

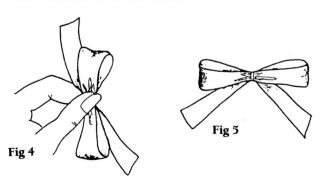

Fig 4   Fig 5

Flowering Fan

Ring of Roses

Making Lace-Edged Pillows

Measurements given for pillow fabric allow for 1/2" seam allowances. The Pillow Instructions will indicate at what point to add the lace ruffle to the outer edge of the pillow top. Before starting, make sure to pin all trims already on pillow top toward the center so they won't get caught in seams.

Step 1: After gathering lace ruffle to fit around pillow top, pin it with straight edge overlapping the 1/2" seam allowance and ruffled edge toward center (**Fig 6**). Overlap ends of lace about 1" and make sure you have pinned extra gathers at each corner. Machine or hand baste ruffle along 1/2" seam allowance.

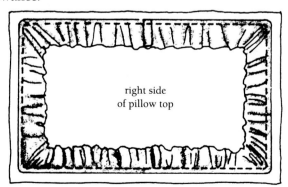

right side
of pillow top

Fig 6

Step 2: Place back piece and top piece right sides together and pin. Check that all trims are toward inside and won't get caught in seam. Machine-stitch together using basting stitches as a guide and leaving an opening for inserting pillow form.

Step 3: Trim and clip corners. Turn to right side.

Making Pillow Forms

Pillow forms should be 1" wider in both length and width than the sewn pillow cover. The measurements given for pillow form muslin allows for 1 1/2" seam allowances and will give you a form that fits snugly inside the cover. This is the secret of attractive pillows.

Step 1: Sew top and back pieces, right sides together along 1/2" seam allowance, leaving an opening for turning.

Step 2: Trim and clip corners; turn right side out.

Step 3: Stuff firmly with polyester fiberfill, paying special attention to corners. Slip-stitch opening closed.

Step 4: Insert form into pillow cover. Form can be folded in half to insert it more easily. Slip-stitch opening closed.

Flowering Fan

Frilly and feminine, this fan-shaped pillow is a wonderful accent for a boudoir. You follow the shape of the crocheted piece to custom cut the pillow fabric. Then trim it with lots of lace, ribbons and ribbon roses.

Size

Motif, 7" x 13"
Finished pillow, about 10" x 15 1/2" (without lace)

Materials for Crocheted Motif

Bedspread-weight crochet cotton
Size 7 steel crochet hook, or size required for gauge

Gauge

8 sc = 1"

Crochet Instructions

Starting at bottom of fan, ch 10, join with a sl st to form a ring.

Row 1: Ch 3 (counts as a dc), 23 dc in ring; join with a sl st in 3rd ch of beg ch-3: 24 dc. Do not turn.

Row 2: (Ch 5, sk 1 dc, sc in next dc) 5 times: 5 ch-5 lps; ch 2, sk 1 dc, dc in next dc; ch 7, turn.

Row 3: Sc in next ch-5 lp; (ch 7, sc in next ch-5 lp) 4 times: 5 ch-7 lps; ch 3, turn.

Row 4: Sl st in ch-7 lp; ch 3 (counts as a dc), in same lp work (2 dc, ch 3, 3 dc): shell made; * ch 1, in next ch-7 lp work (3 dc, ch 3, 3 dc): shell made; rep from * 3 times more: 5 shells; ch 3, turn.

Row 5: Holding back last lp of each dc on hook, dc in next 3 dc, YO and draw through all 4 lps on hook: cluster made; in ch-3 sp of shell work (3 dc, ch 3, 3 dc): shell made; holding back last lp of each dc on hook, dc in next 3 dc, YO and draw through all 4 lps on hook: cluster made; * ch 1, in next 3 dc work cluster; in ch-3 sp of next shell, work shell; in next 3 dc work cluster; rep from * 3 times more: 5 shells; ch 3, turn.

Row 6: * In next 3 dc work cluster, ch 1; shell in shell, ch 1; in next 3 dc work cluster, ch 2; rep from * 4 times more, ending last rep without working last ch 2: 5 shells and 4 ch-2 sps; ch 3, turn.

Row 7: * In next 3 dc work cluster, ch 3; shell in shell, ch 3; in next 3 dc work cluster: cluster-shell-cluster made for rib of Fan; ch 3, rep from * 4 times more, ending last rep without working last ch 3: 5 cluster-shell-clusters (which will continue as ribs of Fan until Row 17, but not be counted); 1 ch-3 sp between each rib; ch 3, turn.

Row 8: * Work cluster-shell-cluster as before; ch 1, in ch-3 sp between ribs work (trc, ch 2, trc), ch 1; rep from * 3 times more; work cluster-shell-cluster: (ch-1 sp, ch-2 sp, ch-1 sp) between each rib; ch 3, turn.

Row 9: * Work cluster-shell-cluster; ch 3, sk ch-1 sp, in ch-2 sp work (trc, ch 3, trc), ch 3; rep from * 3 times more; work cluster-shell-cluster: 3 ch-3 sps between each rib; ch 3, turn.

Row 10: * Work cluster-shell-cluster; ch 1, sk 1 ch-3 sp, (in center ch-3 sp work trc, ch 2) 3 times; trc in same sp, ch 1; rep from * 3 times more; work cluster-shell-cluster: (ch-1 sp, 3 ch-3 sps, ch-1 sp) between each rib; ch 3, turn.

Row 11: * Work cluster-shell-cluster; ch 2, holding back last lp on hook, work 3 trc in next ch-2 sp, YO and draw through all 4 lps on hook: trc cluster made; ch 2, in center ch-2 sp work (trc, ch 2, trc); ch 2, in next ch-2 sp work trc cluster; ch 2; rep from * 3 times more; work cluster-shell-cluster: (ch-2 sp, trc cluster, 3 ch-2 sps, trc cluster, ch-2 sp) between each rib; ch 3, turn.

Row 12: * Work cluster-shell-cluster; ch 2, sk 1 ch-2 sp, in next ch-2 sp work trc cluster; ch 2, in center ch-2 sp work (trc, ch 2) 3 times; trc in same sp; ch 2, in next ch-2 sp work trc cluster; ch 2; rep from * 3 times more; work cluster-shell-cluster: (ch-2 sp, trc cluster, 5 ch-2 sps, trc cluster, ch-2 sp) between each rib; ch 3, turn.

Row 13: * Work cluster-shell-cluster; ch 2, sk 1 ch-2 sp, in next ch-2 sp work trc cluster; ch 2, trc in next ch-2 sp; ch 2, in center ch-2 sp work (trc, ch 2, trc); ch 2, trc in next ch-2 sp; ch 2, in next ch-2 sp work trc cluster; ch 2; rep from * 3 times more; work cluster-shell-cluster: (ch-2 sp, trc cluster, 5 ch-2 sps, trc cluster, ch-2 sp) between each rib; ch 3, turn.

Row 14: * Work cluster-shell-cluster; ch 2, sk 1 ch-2 sp, in next ch-2 sp work trc cluster; ch 2, † in next ch-2 sp work (trc, ch 2, trc); ch 2 † rep from † to † twice more; in next ch-2 sp work trc cluster; ch 2; rep from * 3 times more; work cluster-shell-cluster: (ch-2 sp, trc cluster, 7 ch-2 sps, trc cluster, ch-2 sp) between each rib; ch 3, turn.

Row 15: * Work cluster-shell-cluster; ch 2, sk 1 ch-2 sp; † in next ch-2 sp work trc cluster, ch 2; trc in next ch-2 sp, ch 2; in next ch-2 sp work trc cluster, ch 2 † in center ch-2 sp work (trc, ch 2, trc); ch 2; rep from † to † once more; rep from * 3 times more; work cluster-shell-cluster: 9 ch-2 sps (4 trc cluster) between each rib; ch 3, turn.

Row 16: * Work cluster-shell-cluster; ch 2, sk 1 ch-2 sp; † in next ch-2 sp work trc cluster, ch 2; in next ch-2 sp work (trc, ch 2, trc), ch 2 †; rep from † to † twice more; in next ch-2 sp work trc cluster, ch 2; rep from * 3 times more; work cluster-shell-cluster: 11 ch-2 sps (4 trc clusters) between each rib; ch 3, turn.

Row 17: * † In next 3 dc work cluster; ch 4, in ch-3 sp of next shell work trc cluster; ch 4, in next 3 dc work cluster †; (ch 3, trc cluster in next ch-2 sp) 9 times; ch 3; rep from * 3 times more; rep from † to † once more: 10 ch-3 sps between ribs, 2 ch-4 sps over tip of ribs; turn.

Row 18: * (5 sc in next ch-4 sp) twice; (4 sc in next ch-3 sp) 10 times; rep from * 3 times more; (5 sc in next ch-4 sp) twice; finish off and weave in ends.

Pillow Instructions

Materials for Trimmed Pillow

blue satin fabric, two pieces about 11" x 18"
lightweight paper to make pillow pattern
2 3/4 yds 1/4" wide blue satin ribbon
1 1/8 yds 1 1/2" wide blue satin ribbon
2 yds 3/8" wide blue picot-edge ribbon
eleven 1/2" diameter lt blue ribbon roses
three 3/4" diameter antique blue ribbon roses
2 3/8 yds 2" wide ivory pre-gathered lace

1 3/4 yds 1" wide ivory lace gathered to 1/2" wide flat lace (If not available, buy each width separately and make your own.)
1 3/8 yds 4 mm ivory pearls
muslin for pillow form, two pieces about 12" x 19"
polyester fiberfill for stuffing

Step 1: Read General Directions on page 54 for special finishing techniques and hints.

Step 2: To make pillow pattern, place crocheted fan motif flat on paper; measure 2" out from fan on all sides and mark (**Fig 1**). Use this pattern to cut out pillow top and back.

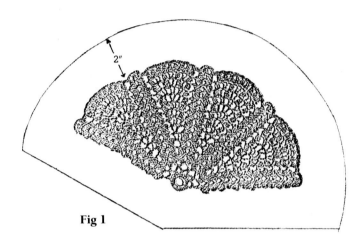

Fig 1

Step 3: Weave 1/4" wide ribbon through spaces in each V-shaped section of fan (see photo) letting ends of ribbon extend past ends of fan.

Step 4: Pin fan in center of pillow top; stitch around all edges catching in ends of ribbon.

Step 5: Cut 30" piece of 1" wide lace; gather it to fit to top edge of fan (about 20"). Pin along edge of fan folding under ends of lace; stitch in place. Cut a 33" piece of 1" wide lace and gather to about 22" long; pin about 1/2" outside the first row of lace and stitch in place.

Step 6: Stitch rows of pearls between each V-shaped section and along inner row of lace as shown in photo.

Step 7: Cut a 22" piece of 1 1/2" wide ribbon and run gathering stitches down the center. Pull up gathers to fit along outside of pillow; pin center gathers about 3/4" from outer row of lace. Stitch through center of ribbon to attach to pillow.

Step 8: Cut eight 6" pieces of 1/4" wide ribbon; make a Bunny Bow (see General Directions, page 54) with each piece. Tack one bow and one small ribbon rose at outer end of each woven ribbon piece, referring to photo for placement.

Step 9: Measure distance around all edges of pillow top, and cut a length of 2" wide lace one-and-one-half times this distance. Gather lace to fit around pillow. Make pillow as in Making Lace-Edged Pillows, page 55, leaving an opening in one straight side for inserting pillow form.

Step 10: Cut fabric for pillow form using pillow pattern but cutting fabric 1/2" larger on all sides. Make pillow form as in Making Pillow Forms, page 55. Insert form into pillow and slip-stitch opening closed.

Step 11: Cut a 16" piece of 1 1/2" wide ribbon; with a double strand of sewing thread, run gathering stitches along one long end; pull thread so that ribbon forms a circular pouf. Turn under ends of ribbon and slip-stitch folded ends together; set aside.

Step 12: Repeat Step 11 using 2" wide lace to form pouf. With two 36" pieces of 3/8" wide picot-edge ribbon, make a Double Bunny Bow (see General Directions, page 54). To assemble ribbon rose bouquet at lower point of fan: tack bow to center of lace pouf; tack ribbon pouf to center of bow; tack three 3/4" ribbon roses and three 1/2" ribbon roses to center of ribbon pouf. Position bouquet at lower point of fan and hand-stitch in place.

Ring of Roses

Make an easy satin-covered pillow, center it with this lovely round doily, lavish it with lace, ribbons and Irish crochet roses and you have the perfect pillow for a ring bearer or to accent a frilly bed. If you make it for a wedding accessory, do it in all white or match the pillow satin to the bridesmaids' gowns.

Size

Motif, center circle, 6 1/2" across; roses, 2" across
Finished pillow, about 9" x 9" (without lace)

Materials for Crocheted Motif

Bedspread-weight crochet cotton
Size 7 steel crochet hook, or size required for gauge

Gauge

8 sc = 1"

Crochet Instructions

Center Circle

Ch 5, join with a sl st to form a ring.

Rnd 1: (Ch 4, sc in ring) 5 times: 5 ch-4 lps. Do not turn; work in rnds.

Rnd 2: * (Sc, 3 dc, sc) in next ch-5 lp: petal made; rep from * 4 times more; join with a sl st in back of beg sc: 5 petals.

Rnd 3: * Ch 5, sc in back of work between next 2 petals: ch-5 lp made; rep from * 4 times more, ending last rep without working last sc; join with a sl st in sl st of prev rnd: 5 ch-5 lps.

Rnd 4: Ch 1, * (sc, 5 dc, sc) in next ch-5 lp: petal made; rep from * 4 times more; join with a sl st in back of beg ch-l: 5 petals.

Rnd 5: (**Note:** On this rnd, make all sl sts in back of work.) * Ch 4, sl st in base of center dc of next petal: ch-4 lp made; ch 4, sl st between next 2 petals: ch-4 lp made; rep from * 4 times more, ending last rep with a sl st in sl st of prev rnd: 10 ch-4 lps.

Rnd 6: Ch 1, * (sc, 5 dc, sc) in next ch-4 lp: petal made; rep from * 9 times more; join with a sl st in back of beg ch-1: 10 petals.

Rnd 7: Ch 7, sc in top of center dc on next petal; * ch 4, trc between next 2 petals; ch 4, trc in top of center dc of next petal; rep from * 8 times more; ch 2, dc in 3rd ch of beg ch-7 (counts as a ch-4 lp): 20 ch-4 lps.

Rnd 8: (Ch 6, sc in next ch-4 lp) 19 times; ch 3, dc in next ch-4 lp (counts as a ch-6 lp): 20 ch-6 lps.

Rnd 9: (Ch 4, sc in next ch-6 lp) 19 times; ch 4, sl st in top of dc of last rnd (counts as a ch-4 lp): 20 ch-4 lps.

Rnd 10: Ch 1, (6 sc in next ch-4 lp) 20 times; join with a sl st in beg ch-1: 120 sc.

Rnd 11: Ch 5 (counts as a trc and ch-1 sp); (sk next sc, trc in next sc, ch 1) 59 times; join with a sl st in 4th ch of beg ch-5: 60 ch-1 sps.

Rnd 12: Sl st in next ch-1 sp; ch 5 (counts as a trc and ch-2 sp); (trc in next ch-1 sp, ch 2) 59 times; join with a sl st in 4th ch of beg ch-5: 60 ch-2 sps.

Rnd 13: * Ch 7, sk next ch-2 sp, sc in next ch-2 sp; ch 7, sk next ch-2 sp, sc in next trc; rep from * 19 times more, ending last rep without working last sc; join with a sl st in joining sl st of prev rnd: 40 ch-7 sps.

Rnd 14: Sl st in next 3 chs, sc in same ch-7 lp; * ch 5, sl st in top of sc; ch 7, sl st in top of same sc; ch 5, sl st in top of same sc: picot group made; (ch 4, sc in next ch-7 lp) twice; rep from * 19 times more, ending last rep without working last sc; join with a sl st in beg sc: 20 picot groups. Finish off and weave in ends.

Roses (make 4)

Rep Rnds 1 through 6 of Center Circle. Finish off and weave in ends.

Pillow Instructions

Materials for Trimmed Pillow

blue satin fabric, two pieces 10" x 10"

4 1/2 yds 1/4" wide blue satin ribbon

ten 1/2" diameter ribbon roses (5 lt blue and 5 antique blue)

3 3/4 yds 2 1/4" wide ivory pre-gathered lace

1 3/8 yds 4 mm ivory pearls

3/8 yd 2 mm ivory pearls

fourteen 8 mm ivory pearls

muslin for pillow form, two pieces 11" x 11"

polyester fiberfill for stuffing

tacky craft glue or hot glue

Step 1: Read General Directions, pages 54 and 55, for special finishing techniques and hints.

Step 2: Weave 1/4" wide ribbon through outer circle of spaces on center circle crocheted motif; slip-stitch ends together.

Step 3: Pin center circle in center of pillow top; stitch around all edges leaving picot groups free at outer edge.

Step 4: On pillow top, mark center point of each side 1" in from edge. Cut a 36" piece of pre-gathered lace and run gathering stitches along straight edge. Gather lace to fit from side mark to side mark forming a diamond on pillow top; pin and stitch in place.

Step 5: Stitch 4 mm pearls in place at inner edge of ribbon and at base of gathered lace.

Step 6: Tack ribbon roses around outer edge of motif at every other picot group, alternating lt blue and antique blue roses.

Step 7: Glue 8 mm pearls as follows: one between each ribbon rose, six on center flower, referring to photo for placement, and one in center of each of the four small flower motifs.

Step 8: Cut 2 mm pearls into five 2" pieces. Form each piece into a loop and glue ends around center flower as in photo.

Step 9: Gather lace to fit around pillow top. Make pillow as in Making Lace-Edged Pillows, page 55, leaving an opening in one side for inserting pillow form.

Step 10: Make pillow form as in Making Pillow Forms, page 55. Insert form into pillow and slip-stitch opening closed.

Step 11: Cut four 10" pieces of lace for poufs. With a double strand of sewing thread, run gathering stitches along straight edge of lace piece; pull thread tight, forming a circular pouf; slip-stitch ends together. Repeat for each remaining pouf.

Step 12: Cut four 36" pieces of ribbon; with each piece, make a Pinched Bow (see General Directions, page 54) with two 2" loops on each side. Tack a bow to center of each lace pouf; tack a crocheted rose to center of each bow. Tack completed poufs to center of each pillow side as in photo.

Trailing Roses, Filet Edging

Lovers of filet crochet will enjoy making this floral edging. We show it here as a towel edging, but it can be used on sheets or pillowcases. It's easy to make it the exact length you want. The easy pattern is a good choice for a beginner at filet.

Size

Fits standard towel widths 11 1/4", 16", or 24"
Size Note: Instructions are written for 11 1/4"-wide towel. Changes for 16" and 24" towels are in parentheses ( ).

Material

Bedspread-weight crochet cotton:
    one (one, two) 225-yd ball(s) white
Size 7 steel crochet hook, or size required for gauge

Trimmings

3/4 yd (1 yd, 1 1/2 yds) 1/2"-wide white braid trim
sewing needle and matching thread

Gauge

9 dc= 1"

Crochet Instructions

Edging (make 2)

Note: Edging is reversible.

Ch 56.

Row 1: Dc in 8th ch from hook (7 skipped chs count as a ch-2 sp, a dc, and a ch-2), * ch 2, sk next 2 chs, dc in next ch; rep from * 5 times more; dc in next 3 chs, (ch 2, sk next 2 chs, dc in next ch) 7 times; dc in next 6 chs; ch 5, turn.

Row 2: Dc in 4th and 5th chs from hook (3 skipped chs count as a dc on this and following rows), dc in next 4 dc, ch 2, sk next 2 dc, dc in next dc, (ch 2, sk next sp, dc in next dc) 5 times; (2 dc in next sp, dc in next dc) twice; ch 2, sk next 2 dc, dc in next dc, (ch 2, sk next sp, dc in next dc) 7 times; ch 5 (counts as first dc and a ch-2 sp on following rows), turn.

Row 3: Sk next sp, dc in next dc, (ch 2, sk next sp, dc in next dc) 6 times; 2 dc in next sp; dc in next dc, (ch 2, sk next 2 dc, dc in next dc) twice; (2 dc in next sp, dc in next dc) twice; (ch 2, sk next sp, dc in next dc) 4 times; dc in next 6 dc; ch 5, turn.

Row 4: Dc in 4th and 5th chs from hook, dc in next 4 dc, ch 2, sk next 2 dc, dc in next dc, (ch 2, sk next sp, dc in next dc) 3 times; 2 dc in next sp; dc in next 7 dc, 2 dc in next sp; dc in next dc, ch 2, sk next sp, dc in next 4 dc, (ch 2, sk next sp, dc in next dc) 4 times; 2 dc in next sp; dc in next dc, (ch 2, sk next sp, dc in next dc) twice; ch 5, turn.

Row 5: Sk next sp, dc in next dc, ch 2, sk next sp, dc in next 4 dc, 2 dc in next sp; (dc in next dc, ch 2, sk next sp) 3 times; dc in next 4 dc, ch 2, sk next sp, dc in next 10 dc; ch 2, sk next 2 dc, dc in next dc, 2 dc in next sp; dc in next dc, (ch 2, sk next sp, dc in next dc) 3 times; dc in next 6 dc; turn.

Row 6: Sl sl in next 4 dc; ch 3, dc in next 3 dc, 2 dc in next sp; dc in next dc, (ch 2, sk next sp, dc in next dc) twice; dc in next 3 dc, ch 2, sk next sp, dc in next dc, ch 2, sk next 2 dc, dc in next 4 dc; ch 2, sk next 2 dc, dc in next dc, ch 2, sk next sp, dc in next 4 dc; ch 2, sk next sp, (dc in next dc, 2 dc in next sp) twice; dc in next 4 dc, ch 2, sk next 2 dc, dc in next dc, (ch 2, sk next sp, dc in next dc) twice; ch 5, turn.

Row 7: Sk next sp, dc in next dc, ch 2, sk next sp, dc in next dc, 2 dc in next sp; dc in next 10 dc; 2 dc in next sp; dc in next dc, ch 2, sk next 2 dc, dc in next dc, (ch 2, sk next sp, dc in next dc) twice; ch 2, sk next 2 dc, (dc in next dc, 2 dc in next sp) twice; dc in next 4 dc, (ch 2, sk next sp, dc in next dc) twice; dc in next 6 dc; turn.

Row 8: Sl st in next 4 dc; ch 3, dc in next 3 dc, 2 dc in next sp; dc in next dc, ch 2, sk next sp, dc in next dc, (ch 2, sk next 2 dc, dc in next dc) 3 times; (ch 2, sk next sp, dc in next dc) 3 times; 2 dc in next sp; dc in next dc, (ch 2, sk next 2 dc, dc in next dc) 5 times; (ch 2, sk next sp, dc in next dc) twice; ch 5, turn.

Row 9: Sk next sp, dc in next dc, (ch 2, sk next sp, dc in next dc) 5 times; 2 dc in next sp; dc in next dc, ch 2, sk next 2 dc, dc in next dc, (2 dc in next sp, dc in next dc) 5 times; (ch 2, sk next sp, dc in next dc) twice; dc in next 6 dc; turn.

Row 10: Sl st in next 4 dc; ch 3, dc in next 3 dc, 2 dc in next sp; dc in next dc, ch 2, sk next sp, dc in next dc, ch 2, sk next 2 dc, dc in next 10 dc; ch 2, sk next 2 dc, dc in next dc,

ch 2, sk next sp, dc in next 4 dc, (ch 2, sk next sp, dc in next dc) 6 times; ch 5, turn.

Row 11: Sk next sp, dc in next dc, (ch 2, sk next sp, dc in next dc) 5 times; dc in next 3 dc, (ch 2, sk next sp, dc in next dc) twice; (ch 2, sk next 2 dc, dc in next dc) twice; dc in next 3 dc, 2 dc in next sp; dc in next dc, ch 2, sk next sp, dc in next 7 dc; ch 5, turn.

Row 12: Dc in 4th ch and 5th ch from hook, dc in next 4 dc, ch 2, sk next 2 dc, dc in next dc, ch 2, sk next sp, dc in next 4 dc, ch 2, sk next 2 dc, dc in next dc, (ch 2, sk next sp, dc in next dc) 4 times; dc in next 3 dc, (ch 2, sk next sp, dc in next dc) 6 times; ch 5, turn.

Row 13: Sk next sp, dc in next dc, (ch 2, sk next sp, dc in next dc) 5 times; ch 2, sk next 2 dc, dc in next dc, 2 dc in next sp, dc in next dc, (ch 2, sk next sp, dc in next dc) 4 times; ch 2, sk next 2 dc, dc in next dc, (ch 2, sk next sp, dc in next dc) twice; dc in next 6 dc; ch 5, turn.

Rep Rows 2 through 13, 3 (4, 7) times. At end of last row, do not ch 5. Finish off and weave in ends.

Finishing

Step 1: Referring to photo for placement, sew short ends of Edging to sides of towel, turning edges under.

Step 2: Cut braid trim in half; sew one length to top edge of Edging, turning ends under.

A Blizzard of Snowflakes

designed by Mary Thomas

Crocheting snowflakes is like eating peanuts: you can't stop with just one! This collection gives you a variety of pure white, lacy designs to hang on a tree, decorate gifts, or sprinkle around on tables. We've given you a variety of sizes.

Snowflake No. 1

Finished Size

About 3" diameter

Materials

Bedspread-weight crochet cotton: 8 yds white
Size 7 steel crochet hook
Starching and blocking supplies (see page 5)

Instructions

Note: Work all rnds on right side (do not turn at beg of rnds).

Ch 6, join with a sl st to form a ring.

Rnd 1: Ch 1, work 12 sc in ring, join with a sl st in beg sc.

Rnd 2: Ch 1, sc in same st (st where prev rnd was just joined); * ch 5, sk next sc, sc in next sc; rep from * 4 times more, ch 5, sk last sc, join with a sl st in beg sc: 6 ch-5 sps.

Rnd 3: Ch 1, sc in same st; * ch 5, work cluster st (abbreviated CL) in next ch-5 sp as follows: keeping last lp of each st on hook, work 3 trc in next ch-5 sp (4 lps now on hook), YO hook and draw through all 4 lps on hook (**Fig 1** - CL made); ch 5, sc in next sc; rep from * 4 times more, ch 5, work CL in last ch-5 sp; ch 5, join with a sl st in beg sc.

Rnd 4: Ch 1, * work 5 sc over next ch-5 lp; ch 5, sc in 5th ch from hook (picot made) †; rep from to † twice more (3 picots now made); sc in ch at base of 3rd picot from hook (**Fig 2**); work 5 sc over next ch-5 lp; rep from * around, join

with a sl st in beg sc. Finish off and weave in ends.

Starch and block snowflake out to size following General Instructions on page 5.

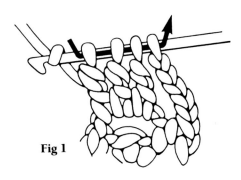

Fig 1

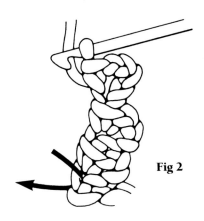

Fig 2

Snowflake No. 2

Finished Size

About 3 1/2" diameter

Materials

Bedspread-weight crochet cotton: 7 yds white
Size 7 steel crochet hook

Instructions

Note: Work all rnds on right side (do not turn at beg of rnds).

Ch 8, join with a sl st to form a ring.

Rnd 1: Ch 3, dc in ring; * ch 3, work 2 dc in ring; rep from * 4 times more, ch 3, join with a sl st in top of beg ch-3: six 2-dc groups with ch-3 sp between each group.

Rnd 2: Ch 1, sc in same st (st where, prev rnd was just joined), ch 3, sc in next dc; * ch 12, sl st in 7th ch from hook (picot lp made); ch 5, sk next ch-3 sp, sc in next dc; ch 3, sc in next dc; rep from * 4 times more, ch 12, sl st in 7th ch from hook (last picot lp made); ch 5, sk last ch-3 sp, join with a sl st in beg sc.

Rnd 3: Sl st into next ch-3 sp, ch 1, sc in same sp; * † ch 5, sk next ch-5 lp of point, work (sc, ch 3, sc, ch 6, sc, ch 3, sc) all in next picot lp (at top of point) †; ch 5, sk next ch-5 lp of same point, sc in next ch-3 sp (between points); rep from * 4 times more, then rep from † to † once; ch 5, sk next ch-5 lp of same point, join with a sl st in beg sc. Finish off and weave in ends.

Starch and block snowflake out to size following General Instructions on page 5.

Snowflake No. 3

Finished Size:

About 4 1/2" diameter

Materials

Bedspread-weight crochet cotton: 14 yds white
Size 7 steel crochet hook

Instructions

Note: Work all rnds on right side (do not turn at beg of rnds).

Ch 8, join with a sl st to form a ring.

Rnd 1: Ch 4, work beg cluster st (abbreviated beg CL) in ring as follows: keeping last lp of each st on hook, work 2 trc in ring (3 lps now on hook), YO hook and draw through all 3 lps on hook (**Fig 1** - beg CL made). * Ch 5, work CL in

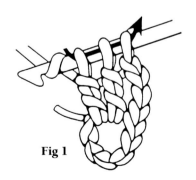

Fig 1

ring as follows: keeping last lp of each st on hook, work 3 trc in ring (4 lps now on hook), YO hook and draw through all 4 lps on hook (CL made); rep from * 4 times more, ch 5, join with a sl st in top of beg CL: 6 CL with ch-5 sp between each CL.

Rnd 2: Ch 1, sc in same st (st where prev rnd was just joined); * work 2 sc in beg of next ch-5 sp, ch 12 (for point), now work sc in 2nd ch from hook and in each of rem 10 chs of point; work 2 more sc in same ch-5 sp on working rnd, sc in top of next CL; rep from * around, ending last rep without working last sc, join with a sl st in beg sc.

Rnd 3: Sl st in each of next 2 sc; * working up side of next point, ch 3, sl st in next ch; ch 7, sk next ch, sl st in next ch; ch 9, sk next ch, sl st in next ch; ch 7, sk next ch, sl st in next ch; ch 5, sk next ch, sl st in next ch; ch 3, sk next ch, sl st in next ch (at top); now working down other side of same point, ch 7, sl st in first sc; ch 3, sk next sc, sl st in next sc; ch 5, sk next sc, sl st in next sc; ch 7, sk next sc, sl st in next sc; ch 9, sk next sc, sl st in next sc; ch 7, sk next sc, sl st in next sc (at bottom); ch 3, sl st in each of next 5 sc between points on working rnd; rep from * around, ending last rep by working a sl st in each of last 2 sc (instead of next 5 sc), do not join. Finish off and weave in ends.

Starch and block snowflake out to size following General Instructions on page 5.

Snowflake No. 4

Finished Size
About 5" diameter

Materials
Bedspread-weight crochet cotton: 14 yds white
Size 7 steel crochet hook

Instructions

Note: Work all rnds on right side (do not turn at beg of rnds).

Ch 5, join with a sl st to form a ring.

Rnd 1: Ch 6, dc in ring; * ch 3, dc in ring; rep from * 3 times more, ch 3, join with a sl st in 3rd ch of beg ch-6: 6 ch-3 sps.

Rnd 2: Ch 1, sc in same st (st where prev rnd was just joined); * work (sc, hdc, dc, hdc, sc) all in next ch-3 sp (for scallop), sc in next dc; rep from * 4 times more, work (sc, hdc, dc, hdc, sc) in last ch-3 sp (for last scallop), join with a sl st in beg sc.

Rnd 3: Ch 3, work (dc, ch 3, 2 dc) in same st (beg shell made); * ch 3, sc in center st of next scallop; ch 3, sk next 2 sts of same scallop, work (2 dc, ch 3, 2 dc) in next sc (between scallops - shell made); rep from * 4 times more, ch 3, sc in center st of last scallop; ch 3, sk next 2 sts of same scallop, join with a sl st in top of beg ch-3.

Rnd 4: Sl st in next dc and then into sp of beg shell, ch 3, dc in same sp. * Work long point as follows: † ch 5, sl st in 4th ch from hook (picot made) †; rep from † to † twice more

(3 picots now made); ch 10, sl st in 9th ch from hook (for lp at tip of point); rep from † to † 3 times (3 more picots made); ch 1, work 2 more dc in sp of same shell on working rnd (long point completed). Sk next ch-3 sp, work 2 dc in next sc. Work short point as follows: rep from † to † once, ch 10, sl st in 9th ch from hook; rep from † to † once, ch 1, work 2 more dc in same sc on working rnd (short point completed). Sk next ch-3 sp, work 2 dc in sp of next shell; rep from * around, ending last rep without working last 2 dc, join with a sl st in top of beg ch-3. Finish off and weave in ends.

Starch and block snowflake out to size following General Instructions on page 5.

Snowflake No. 5

Finished Size

About 4 1/2" diameter

Materials

Bedspread-weight crochet cotton: 18 yds white
Size 7 steel crochet hook

Instructions

Note: Work all rnds on right side (do not turn at beg of rnds).

Ch 8, join with a sl st to form a ring.

Rnd 1: Ch 1, work 12 sc in ring; join with a sl st in beg sc.

Rnd 2: Ch 1, sc in same st (st where prev rnd was just joined); * ch 5, sk next sc, sc in next sc; rep from * 4 times more, ch 5, sk last sc, join with a sl st in beg sc: 6 ch-5 sps.

Rnd 3: Ch 1, work (3 sc, ch 3 - for picot, 3 sc) in each ch-5 sp around; join with a sl st in beg sc.

Rnd 4: Sl st in each of next 2 sc and then into next picot, ch 1, sc in same picot; * ch 9, sk next 6 sc, sc in next picot; rep from * 4 times more, ch 9, sk last 3 sc and next 3 sc (where sl sts were worked), join with a sl st in beg sc.

Rnd 5: Ch 1; in each ch-9 sp around, work four 3-sc groups with ch 3 (for picot) between each group; join with a sl st in beg sc.

Rnd 6: Sl st in next sc, ch 1, sc in same st; * ch 5, sc in center sc of next 3-sc group; ch 15, sc in center sc of next 3-sc group; ch 5, sc in center sc of next 3-sc group, sc in center sc of next 3-sc group; rep from * around, ending last rep without working last sc, join with a sl st in beg sc.

Rnd 7: Ch 1, * work (3 sc, ch 3, 3 sc) in next ch-5 sp; work (3 sc, ch 3, 3 sc, ch 3, sc, hdc, dc) in first half of next ch-15 sp; ch 3, sc in 3rd ch from hook (for picot at tip of point); work (dc, hdc, sc, ch 3, 3 sc, ch 3, 3 sc) in last half of same ch-15 sp; work (3 sc, ch 3, 3 sc) in next ch-5 sp; rep from * around, join with a sl st in beg sc. Finish off and weave in ends.

Starch and block snowflake out to size following General Instructions on page 5.

Snowflake No. 6

Finished Size

About 4 3/4" diameter

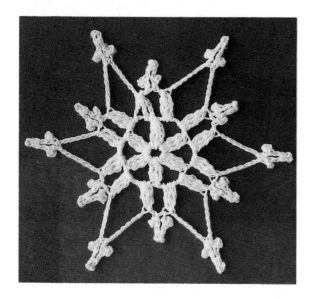

Materials

Bedspread-weight crochet cotton: 10 yds white
Size 7 steel crochet hook

Instructions

Note: Work all rnds on right side (do not turn at beg of rnds).

Ch 8, join with a sl st to form a ring.

Rnd 1: Ch 4, work beg cluster st (abbreviated beg CL) in ring as follows: keeping last lp of each st on hook, work 2 trc in ring (3 lps now on hook), YO hook and draw through all 3 lps on hook (**Fig 1** - beg CL made); * Ch 5, work CL in ring

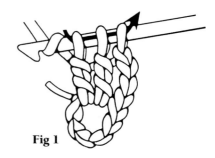

Fig 1

as follows: keeping last lp of each st on hook, work 3 trc in ring (4 lps now on hook), YO hook and draw through all 4 lps on hook (CL made); rep from * 4 times more, ch 5, join with a sl st in top of beg CL: 6 CL with ch-5 sp between each CL.

Rnd 2: Sl st into next ch-5 sp, ch 4, work beg CL in same sp; * ch 11, sc in 4th ch from hook (picot made); † ch 5, sc in 4th ch from hook (another picot made) †; rep from † to † once more (3 picots now made), sc in ch at base of 3rd picot from hook (**Fig 2**); ch 7, work CL in same ch-5 sp (where prev CL was worked); rep from † to † 3 times (3 picots now made), sc in ch at base of 3rd picot from hook, work CL in

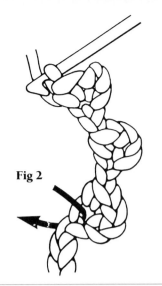

Fig 2

next ch-5 sp; rep from * around, ending last rep without working last CL, join with a sl st in top of beg CL. Finish off and weave in ends.

Starch and block snowflake out to size following General Instructions on page 5.

Snowflake No. 7

Finished Size
About 5" diameter

Materials
Bedspread-weight crochet cotton: 15 yds white
Size 7 steel crochet hook

Instructions

Note: Work all rnds on right side (do not turn at beg of rnds).

Ch 12, join with a sl st to form a ring.

Rnd 1: Ch 1, sc in ring; * ch 2, dc in ring; ch 2, sc in ring; rep from * 4 times more, ch 2, dc in ring; ch 2, join with a sl st in beg sc: 12 ch-2 sps.

Rnd 2: Sl st into next ch-2 sp, ch 1, sc in same sp; * ch 6, sc in next ch-2 sp; ch 3, sc in next ch-2 sp; rep from * 4 times more, ch 6, sc in last ch-2 sp; ch 3, join with a sl st in beg sc.

Rnd 3: Sl st into next ch-6 sp, ch 4, work 4 trc in same sp; * ch 5, sc in next ch-3 sp; ch 5, work 5 trc in next ch-6 sp; rep from * 4 times more, ch 5, sc in last ch-3 sp; ch 5, join with a sl st in top of beg ch-4.

Rnd 4: Ch 4, work beg cluster st (abbreviated beg CL) over next 4 trc as follows: keeping last lp of each st on hook, work trc in each of next 4 trc (5 lps now on hook), YO hook and draw through all 5 lps on hook (**Fig 1** - beg CL made);

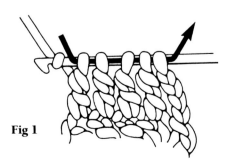

Fig 1

* Ch 7, sc in next ch-5 sp; ch 3, sc in next ch-5 sp; ch 7, work CL over next 5 trc as follows: keeping last lp of each st on hook, work trc in each of next 5 trc (6 lps now on hook), YO hook and draw through all 6 lps on hook (CL made); rep from * 4 times more, ch 7, sc in next ch-5 sp; ch 3, sc in last ch-5 sp; ch 7, join with a sl st in top of beg CL.

Rnd 5: Ch 1, work (sc, ch 5, sc) in top of beg CL (where prev rnd was just joined); * † ch 4, sk next ch-7 sp, trc in next ch-3 sp; ch 5, sc in 5th ch from hook (picot made); work (ch 9, sc in 5th ch from hook - for picot) twice (3 picots now made), work one more trc in same ch-3 sp on working rnd †; ch 4, sk next ch-7 sp, work (sc, ch 5, sc) in top of next CL; rep from * 4 times more, then rep from † to † once, ch 4, sk last ch-7 sp, join with a sl st in beg sc. Finish off and weave in ends.

Starch and block snowflake out to size following General Instructions on page 5.

Santa Stocking

designed by Miriam Dow

It's big enough to hold wonderful things — and can be made in any color yarn. Our cheerful crocheted stocking is decorated two different ways, or you can create your own. The stocking's top is pretty and furry, and can also be used without added decorations.

Size
About 20" long

Materials
Worsted weight yarn: 7 oz red or green
2 oz white
six 1" gold bells or 14" of 3/4"- wide white ball fringe
white sewing thread
Sizes J and K aluminum crochet hooks, or size required for gauge

Gauge
With size K hook: 3 sc = 1"

Instructions

Cuff
Starting at lower edge with white and size J hook, ch 44.

Row 1: sc in 2nd ch from hook and in each rem ch: 43 sc; ch 1, turn.

Row 2 (wrong side)**:** Working in BLs only (see page 4), * sc in next sc; ch 2, sl st in top of last sc (picot made); ch 1; rep from * 42 times more; sc in same st as last sc: 43 picots; ch 1, turn.

Row 3: Working in unused lps of Row 1, sc in each sc: 43 sc; ch 1, turn.

Rows 4 through 8: Rep Rows 2 and 3; ending last row with ch 10 (for hanging lp); sc in same last sc; finish off.

Leg
Row 1: With right side of Cuff facing you and with size K hook, join red yarn with a sl st in first ch of beg-ch of Cuff; ch 1, sc in same st and in each rem ch: 43 sc; ch 1, turn.

Row 2: Sc across row; ch 1, turn.

Rep Row 2 until Leg is 9 1/2" long.

Heel Shaping
First Side

Row 1: Sc in next 4 sc, sl st in next sc: 5 sts; do not ch, turn.

Row 2: Sk sl st, sl st in next sc; sc in next 3 sc: 4 sts; ch 1, turn.

Row 3: Sc in next 4 sts; sc in same st as sl st of Row 1; sc in next sc; sl st in next sc: 7 sts; ch 1, turn.

Row 4: Sk sl st, sl st in next sc; sc in next 5 sc: 6 sts; ch 1, turn.

Row 5: Sc in next 6 sts; sl st in same st as sl st of Row 3; sc in next sc, sl st in next sc: 9 sts; do not ch, turn.

Row 6: Sk sl st, sl st in next sc; sc in next 7 sts: 8 sts; ch 1, turn.

Row 7: Sc in next 8 sts; sc in same st as sl st of Row 5; sc in next sc, sl st in next sc: 11 sts; do not ch, turn.

Row 8: Sk sl st, sl st in next sc; sc in next 9 sc: 10 sts; ch 1, turn.

Row 9: Sc in next 10 sts; sc in same st as sl st of Row 7; sc in next sc, sl st in next sc: 13 sts; do not ch, turn.

Row 10: Sk sl st, sl st in next sc; sc in next 11 sc: 12 sts; ch 1, turn.

Row 11: Sc in next 10 sc, sl st in next sc: 11 sts; do not ch, turn.

Row 12: Sk sl st, sl st in next sc; sc in next 9 sc: 10 sts; ch 1, turn.

Row 13: Sc in next 8 sc, sl st in next st: 9 sts; do not ch, turn.

Row 14: Sk sl st, sl st in next sc; sc in next 7 sc: 8 sts; ch 1, turn.

Row 15: Sc in next 6 sc, sl st in next st: 7 sts; do not ch, turn.

Row 16: Sk sl st, sl st in next sc; sc in next 5 sc: 6 sts; ch 1, turn.

Row 17: Sc in next 6 sts, hdc in sl st of Row 15; sc in next st, hdc in sl st of Row 13; sc in next st, hdc in sl st of Row 11; sc in next st, hdc in sl st of Row 9; draw up a lp in each of next

2 sts, YO and draw through 3 lps on hoop (dec made); sc in rem 28 sc: 42 sts; ch 1, turn.

Second Side
Rep Rows 1 through 17 of First Side of Heel Shaping, ending with sc in rem 27 sc: 41 sts; ch 1, turn.

Foot

Row 1: Sc across row: 41 sc; ch 1, turn.

Rep Row 1 until foot measures 5 1/2", ending with a wrong side row.

Toe Shaping
Front Side
Row 1 (right side): Sc in next 29 sc, draw up a lp in each of next 2 sts, YO and draw through 3 lps on hook (dec made): 30 sts; ch 1, turn.

Row 2: Sc in next 18 sc; dec in next 2 sc: 19 sts; ch 1, turn.

Row 3: Sc in next 17 sc; dec in next 2 sc: 18 sts; ch 1, turn.

Rows 4 through 9: Rep Row 3, having 12 sts at end of Row 9; finish off.

Back Side
Sew seam along back of foot section, carefully matching rows. (**Note:** Do not sew back of leg section.)

Row 1: With right side of stocking facing you, join red yarn with sl st in sc that is next to last sc (dec st) of Row 1 of Front Side of Toe Shaping; ch 1, sc in same sc; sc in next 9 sc; sc in seam; sc in next 8 sc; dec in next 2 sc: 20 sts; ch 1, turn.

Rep Rows 2 through 9 of Front Side of Toe Shaping; finish off and weave in all ends.

Finishing

Sew seam for toe. Sew remainder of back seam from foot through Cuff. For red stocking, sew ball fringe to beg-ch row of Cuff. For green stocking, with white yarn, attach bells to beg-ch row of Cuff.

Tiny Hat

designed by Mary Thomas

Just a few rounds of thread crochet, a few minutes of time, and a little bit of trim, and you have produced a "tiny treasure" to hang on your Christmas tree or use as a package decoration. What a charming way to accent a beautifully wrapped gift!

Size

About 5" diameter before blocking, and 4" diameter
  after blocking

Materials

Bedspread-weight crochet cotton, 30 yds white or ecru
Size 7 steel crochet hook (or size required for gauge)
Starching and blocking supplies (see page 5)
1 1/2" diameter plastic or foam ball

Gauge

First 4 rnds of hat = 2" diameter

Instructions

Note: Work all rnds on right side (do not turn at beg of rnds).

Ch 7, join with a sl st to form a ring.

Rnd 1: Ch 5, dc in ring; * ch 2, dc in ring; rep from * 5 times more, ch 2, join with a sl st in 3rd ch of beg ch-5: 8 ch-2 sps.

Rnd 2: Ch 1, sc in same st (st where prev rnd was just joined); * work 3 sc in next ch-2 sp, sc in next dc; rep from * around to last ch-2 sp, work 3 sc in last ch-2 sp, join with a sl st in beg sc: 32 sc.

Rnd 3: Ch 3, * sk next sc, dc in next sc; ch 3, work 5 dc over last dc just made (for scallop); sk next sc on working rnd, dc in next sc; rep from * around to last 3 sc, sk next sc, dc in next sc; ch 3, work 5 dc over last dc just made (for last scallop); sk next sc on working rnd, join with a sl st in top of beg ch-3: 8 scallops.

Rnd 4: Ch 8, sc in first dc of next scallop; * ch 5, sk next 4 dc of same scallop, dc in next dc (st between scallops); ch 5, sc in first dc of next scallop; rep from * around, ch 2, join with a dc in 3rd ch of beg ch-8 (this completes last lp and brings thread into position to start next rnd).

Rnd 5: * Ch 5, sc in next ch-5 sp; rep from * 14 times more,

ch 5, sk first 2 chs of next lp, then join with a sl st in top of next dc (st that joined prev rnd).

Rnd 6: Ch 3, * dc in next ch-5 sp; ch 3, work 5 dc over last dc just worked (for scallop), dc in next sc on working rnd; rep from * around to last ch-5 sp, dc in last ch-5 sp; ch 3, work 5 dc over last dc just worked (for last scallop), join with a sl st in top of beg ch-3: 16 scallops.

Rnd 7: Rep Rnd 4.

Rnd 8: * Ch 6, sc in next ch-5 sp; rep from * 30 times more, ch 3, sk next 2 chs of next lp, then join with a dc in top of next dc (st that joined prev rnd).

Rnd 9: * † Ch 5, work 2 dc in next ch-6 sp; ch 3, sl st in top of last dc just worked (for picot), work one more dc in same sp †; ch 5, sc in next ch-6 sp; rep from * to last ch-6 sp, rep from † to † once, ch 5, sk next 3 chs of next lp, then join with a sl st in top of next dc (st that joined prev rnd). Finish off and weave in ends.

Finishing

The final and very important step in making a lace hat is the starching and blocking.

Step 1: Follow laundering, starching and blocking instructions on page 5, shaping crown of hat over half of a 1 1/2" diameter plastic or foam ball.

Step 2: Trim as desired, using artificial flowers, lace, and ribbon.

Frame-up

designed by Kathy Wesley

Frame a loving couple, or a favorite person or pet, in this lacy thread crochet frame trimmed with romantic ribbon. To make your chosen picture fit, you can have an old photo — or a new one — enlarged or reduced at a photocopy shop.

Finished Size
About 6" x 6 1/2"

Materials:
Bedspread-weight crochet cotton, one 225-yd ball cream
Size 7 steel crochet hook, or size required for gauge

Trimmings
starching supplies (see page 5)
2/3 yd 1/4"-wide picot-edge lt peach satin ribbon
one 3/8" peach porcelain rose
4" square lightweight cardboard
picture to fit opening
hot glue or tacky craft glue

Gauge
9 dc = 1"

Instructions

Ch 78, join to form a ring, being careful not to twist ch.

Rnd 1 (right side): Ch 6 (counts as a dc and a ch-3 lp), sk next ch, dc in next ch, (ch 3, sk next ch, dc in next ch) 36 times; ch 1, sk next 3 chs; join in 3rd ch of beg ch-6: 38 ch-3 lps.

Rnd 2: Sl st in next 3 chs, in next dc, and in next ch-3 lp; ch 3, in same ch-3 lp as last sl st made work (dc, ch 1, 2 dc): beg shell made; * ch 1, dc in next ch-3 lp, ch 1, in next ch-3 lp work (2 dc, ch 1, 2 dc): shell made; ch 1, rep from * 17 times more; ch 1, sk next ch-3 lp and next dc, sc in next ch-1 sp, ch 1, sk next dc and next ch-3 lp; join in 3rd ch of beg ch-3: 18 shells made.

Rnd 3: Sl st in next dc and in next ch-1 sp; in same sp work beg shell; † [ch 1, in next dc work (dc, ch 1, dc): V-st made; ch 1, in ch-1 sp of next shell work shell: shell in shell made] 8 times †; shell in next dc, in ch-1 sp of next shell work shell: shell in shell made; rep from † to † once; ch 1, sc in next sc, ch 1; join in 3rd ch of beg ch-3.

Rnd 4: Sl st in next dc and in next ch-1 sp; in same sp work beg shell; in ch-1 sp of next V-st work V-st; shell in next shell, shell in ch-1 sp of next V-st; † [shell in next shell, in ch-1 sp of next V-st work V-st] 6 times †; shell in each of next 2 shells; rep from † to † once; shell in next shell; shell in ch-1 sp of next V-st, shell in next shell; in ch-1 sp of next V-st work V-st; shell in next shell; ch 1, sc in next sc, ch 1; join in 3rd ch of beg ch-3.

Rnd 5: Sl st in next dc and in next ch-1 sp; ch 3, 5 dc in same sp; 6 dc in ch-1 sp of each V-st and each shell around; join in 3rd ch of beg ch-3. Finish off and weave in all ends.

Finishing

Starching and Blocking Instructions
Following starching and blocking instructions on page 5; place saturated crocheted piece on pinning board and shape into a heart. Pin in place and let dry.

Trimming Instructions
Step 1: Starting and ending at top of opening, weave ribbon through Rnd 1 of Frame; tie bow with 1" loops. Glue rose on bow. Referring to photo for placement, glue ends of ribbon to Frame beside bow loops.

Step 2: Cut piece of lightweight cardboard the size of Frame opening to outer edge of ribbon.

Step 3: Center picture in opening and cut to size of cardboard. Glue edges of wrong side of picture to cardboard; then glue right side of edges of picture to ribbon on wrong side of frame.

Time For Tea Doily

This adaptation of a traditional pattern is a useful, large size that can double as a table topper. In pure white crochet cotton and freshly starched, it will be a wonderful accent for your home.

Size

About 18" in diameter

Materials

Bedspread-weight crochet cotton:
    250 yds (two 225-yd balls) white
Size 7 steel crochet hook, or size required for gauge

Gauge

8 dc = 1"

Instructions

Ch 6, join to form a ring.

Rnd 1: Ch 3 (counts as first dc), 11 dc in ring; join in 3rd ch of beg ch-3: 12 dc.

Rnd 2: Ch 3, dc in same ch as joining, 2 dc in each of next 11 dc; join in 3rd ch of beg ch-3: 24 dc.

Rnd 3: Ch 7, sk next dc, dc in next dc, (ch 4, sk next dc, dc in next dc) 10 times; ch 4; join in 3rd ch of beg ch-7.

Rnd 4: Sl st in next lp; ch 3 (counts as a dc in this and following rnds), in same lp work (dc, ch 2, 2 dc): beg shell made; * ch 2, in next lp work (dc, ch 1, dc), ch 2, in next lp work (2 dc, ch 2, 2 dc): shell made; rep from * 5 times more, ending last rep without working last shell; 30 in in 3rd ch of beg ch-3: 6 shells made.

Rnd 5: Sl st in next dc and in next ch-2 sp; ch 3, in same sp work beg shell, * ch 3, sc in next ch-2 sp, ch 3, in next ch-1 sp work (dc, ch 1, dc), ch 3, sc in next ch-2 sp, ch 3, in ch-2 sp of next shell work shell: shell in shell made; rep from * 5 times more, ending last rep without working last shell; join in 3rd ch of beg ch-3.

Rnd 6: Sl st in next dc and in next ch-2 sp; ch 3, in same sp work beg shell, * ch 5, sk next 2 lps, in next ch-1 sp work (dc, ch 1, dc), ch 5, sk next 2 lps, shell in next shell; rep from * 5 times more, ending last rep without working last shell; join in 3rd ch of beg ch-3.

Rnd 7: Ch 3, dc in next dc, * 2 dc in next ch-2 sp, dc in next 2 dc, 5 dc in next ch-5 lp, dc in next dc, dc in next ch-1 sp, dc in next dc, 5 dc in next ch-5 lp, dc in next 2 dc; rep from * 5 times more, ending last rep without working last 2 dc; join in 3rd ch of beg ch-3: 114 dc.

Rnd 8: Ch 3, dc in next 17 dc, 2 dc in next dc, (dc in next 18 dc, 2 dc in next dc) 5 times; join in 3rd ch of beg ch-3: 120 dc.

Rnd 9: Ch 8 (counts as a dc and ch-5 lp), sk next 3 dc, dc in next dc, * ch 5, sk next 3 dc, dc in next dc; rep from * around, ending last rep without working last dc; join in 3rd ch of beg ch-8: 30 dc.

Rnd 10: Sl st in next lp; ch 3, in same lp work beg shell, * ch 3, in next ch-5 lp work (dc, ch 1, dc), ch 3, in next ch-5 lp work shell; rep from * 14 times more, ending last rep without working last shell; join in 3rd ch of beg ch-3.

Rnd 11: Sl st in next dc and in next ch-2 sp; ch 3, in same sp work beg shell, * ch 3, in next ch-1 sp work (dc, ch 1, dc), ch 3, shell in next shell; rep from * 14 times more, ending last rep without working last shell; join in 3rd ch of beg ch-3.

Rnd 12: Rep Rnd 11.

Rnd 13: Sl st in next dc and in next ch-2 sp; ch 3, in same sp work beg shell, * ch 3, sc in next ch-3 lp, ch 3, in next ch-1 sp work (dc, ch 1, dc); ch 3, sc in next ch-3 lp, ch 3, shell in next shell; rep from * 14 times more, ending last rep without working last shell; join in 3rd ch of beg ch-3.

Rnd 14: Sl st in next dc and in next ch-2 sp; ch 3, in same sp work beg shell, * ch 5, sk next 2 lps, in next ch-1 sp work (dc, ch 1, dc), ch 5, sk next 2 lps, shell in next shell; rep from * 14 times more, ending last rep without working last shell; join in 3rd ch of beg ch-3.

Rnd 15: Ch 3, dc in next dc, * 2 dc in next ch-2 sp, dc in next 2 dc, 4 dc in next ch-5 lp, dc in next dc, dc in next ch-1 sp, dc in next dc, 4 dc in next ch-5 lp, dc in next 2 dc; rep from

* 14 times more, ending last rep without working last 2 dc; join in 3rd ch of beg ch-3: 255 dc.

Rnd 16: Ch 3, dc in next 82 dc, keeping last lp of each dc on hook, dc in next 2 dc, YO and draw through all 3 lps on hook: dec made; dc in next 83 dc, dec as before; dc in next 83 dc, dec as before; join in 3rd ch of beg ch-3: 252 dc.

Rnd 17: Ch 3, dc in each dc; join in 3rd ch of beg ch-3.

Rnd 18: Ch 3, dc in next 6 dc, * † ch 5, sk next 2 dc, sc in next 7 dc, ch 5, sk next 2 dc †, dc in next 7 dc; rep from * 12 times more, then rep from † to † once; join in 3rd ch of beg ch-3.

Rnd 19: Ch 4 (counts as a dc and ch-1 sp in this and following rnd), dc in next dc, (ch 1, dc in next dc) 5 times; * † ch 5, sk next sc, sc in each of next 6 sc, ch 5 †, (dc in next dc, ch 1) 6 times; dc in next dc; rep from * 12 times more, then rep from † to † once; join in 3rd ch of beg ch-4.

Rnd 20: Ch 4, dc in next dc, (ch 1, dc in next dc) 5 times; * † ch 5, sk next sc, sc in each of next 5 sc, ch 5 †, (dc in next dc, ch 1) 6 times; dc in next dc; rep from * 12 times more, then rep from † to † once; join in 3rd ch of beg ch-4.

Rnd 21: Ch 5 (counts as a dc and ch-2 sp in this and following rnd), dc in next dc, (ch 2, dc in next dc) 5 times; * † ch 5, sk next sc, sc in next 4 sc, ch 5 †, (dc in next dc, ch 2) 6 times; dc in next dc; rep from * 12 times more, then rep from † to † once; join in 3rd ch of beg ch-5.

Rnd 22: Ch 5, dc in next dc, (ch 2, dc in next dc) 5 times; * † ch 5, sk next sc, sc in next 3 sc, ch 5 †, (dc in next dc, ch 2) 6 times; dc in next dc; rep from * 12 times more, then rep from † to † once; join in 3rd ch of beg ch-5.

Rnd 23: Ch 6 (counts as a dc and ch-3 lp), dc in next dc, (ch 3, dc in next dc) 5 times; * † ch 5, sk next sc, sc in next 2 sc, ch 5 †, (dc in next dc, ch 3) 6 times; dc in next dc; rep from * 12 times more, then rep from † to † once; join in 3rd ch of beg ch-6.

Rnd 24: Ch 7 (counts as a dc and ch-4 lp), dc in next dc, (ch 4, dc in next dc) 5 times; * † ch 5, sk next sc, sc in next sc, ch 5 †, (dc in next dc, ch 4) 6 times; dc in next dc; rep from * 12 times more, then rep from † to † once; join in 3rd ch of beg ch-7.

Rnd 25: Ch 8 (counts as a dc and ch-5 lp), dc in next dc, (ch 5, dc in next dc) 5 times; * ch 2, sk next sc, (dc in next dc, ch 5) 6 times; dc in next dc; rep from * 12 times more; ch 2; join in 3rd ch of beg ch-8.

Rnd 26: Sl st in next lp; ch 1, sc in same lp, * (ch 6, sl st in 3rd ch from hook: picot made; ch 3, sc in next ch-5 lp) 5 times; ch 6, sl st in 3rd ch from hook: picot made; ch 3, sc in next ch-2 sp, ch 6, sl st in 3rd ch from hook: picot made; ch 3, sc in next ch-5 lp; rep from * 13 times more, ending last rep without working last sc; join in first sc. Finish off and weave in ends.

Counted Cross Stitch

Counted Cross Stitch

Many of us learned to embroider as young children, patiently making stumbling stitches over small Xs stamped on cheap towels and pillowcases purchased at the dime store.

Today there aren't many dime stores left, and beginning embroiderers of any age are learning to stitch beautiful designs, from charts, onto blank evenweave fabric.

In fact, this skill that we now call counted cross stitch -- to differentiate it from the old stamped cross stitch -- is the most popular of all needlework skills today.

There's a special thrill to seeing a colorful design appearing on the fabric. Counted cross stitch is easy to learn and do, is inexpensive, and the projects can be carried from place to place to take advantage of every spare moment. Cross stitchers become addicted to this skill.

To feed the cross stitch habit, literally hundreds of new design books are published each year, with projects of all types and sizes available .

Because cross stitch is quick to do and the materials are not costly, many projects are done as gifts. Even the smallest cross stitch design, nicely framed or finished, makes a very special gift.

On the following pages we've given you a selection of designs to appeal to a wide variety of tastes. We hope you'll find a favorite here.

Materials

The materials required for counted cross stitch are few and inexpensive: a piece of evenweave fabric, a tapestry needle, some 6-strand cotton floss, and a charted design. An embroidery hoop is optional. All of these are readily available at most needlework shops.

Evenweave Fabrics

These are designed especially for embroidery, and are woven with the same number of vertical and horizontal threads per inch. Cross stitches are made over the intersections of the horizontal and vertical threads, and because the number of threads in each direction is equal, each stitch will be the same size and perfectly square.

The evenweave fabrics most commonly used for cross stitch are:

Aida Cloth

A basketweave fabric in which horizontal and vertical threads are grouped, making the intersections for stitches very easy to see. Aida is woven with the intersections spaced in three different sizes: 11- count (11 stitches to the inch); 14-count (14 stitches to the inch) and 18-count (18 stitches to the inch).

The number of stitches per inch of any evenweave fabric determines the size of a design after it is worked. The photos in **Fig 1** show the same heart design worked on all three sizes of Aida. The more stitches to the inch, the smaller the design will be. Thus a design stitched on 18-count fabric will be considerably smaller than one stitched on 11-count fabric.

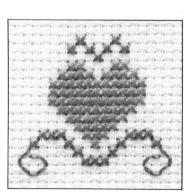

11-count Aida

14-count Aida

18-count Aida

Fig 1

76

Hardanger Cloth

Woven with pairs of vertical and horizontal threads, the intersections in Hardanger are visible but not as pronounced as in Aida. All Hardanger is 22-count fabric (22 stitches to the inch) which makes the stitches very small and delicate (**Fig 2**). Working on Hardanger becomes easier with practice.

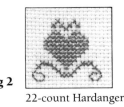

Fig 2

22-count Hardanger

Linen

To cross stitchers, linen is considered the ultimate fabric, the stuff of heirlooms. Evenweave linen is composed of single woven round threads. The intersections are not as clearly defined as in Aida or Hardanger; cross stitch on linen is always worked over two threads of linen both horizontally and vertically.

Most linen fabrics come with 18 to 36 threads to the inch (which is the equivalent of 9 to 18 stitches per inch) and in neutral colors such as white, ivory and natural. Stitching on linen is a bit different than working on the other fabrics, so on the following pages you will find special techniques for linen work.

Perforated Paper

It's not fabric, but you can cross stitch on it, and with exciting results. Heavy paper, evenly perforated with 14 holes to the inch, comes in a wide variety of colors and most any cross stitch design can be worked on it. Perforated paper is easy to finish: just cut it out, and there are no raveling edges.

Pre-made Projects

Do you want to make a cross-stitched fingertip towel, pillow or perhaps a baby bib, but you don't like to sew? Then you will love the many pre-made accessories available with the evenweave fabric made part of the construction. You'll find so many lovely pre-sewn items; in addition to those we've mentioned, there are place mats, kitchen accessories, afghans, bookmarks, and many baby accessories.

Hoops

Counted cross stitch can be done with or without a hoop. If you choose to stretch the fabric in a hoop, use one made of plastic or wood with a screw type tension adjuster. You may use a hoop large enough to accommodate the whole design or choose a small hoop, whichever you prefer. Placing the small hoop over existing stitches will slightly distort them

but a gentle raking with the needle will restore their square shape. Be sure to remove the fabric from the hoop when you have finished stitching for the day.

If you are going to use a hoop, center it on the fabric with the tension screw at 10 o'clock if you are right handed, or at 2 o'clock if you are left handed. Pull fabric taut and tighten screw.

Needles

Cross stitch is done with a blunt-pointed tapestry needle. The needle slips between the threads, not through them. **Fig 3** will tell you which size needle is appropriate for each kind of fabric.

Floss

Any six-strand cotton embroidery floss can be used for cross stitch. The six-strand floss can be divided to work with one, two or three strands as required by the fabric. **Fig 3** tells how many floss strands to use with the various fabrics.

For our charts the brands of embroidery floss colors are specified by number in the Color Keys. Each brand has its own color range, so these suggestions are not perfect color matches, but are appropriate substitutions. Cut floss into comfortable working lengths - we suggest about 18". Generic color names are given for each floss color in a design; for example, if there is only one green it will be so named, but if there are three greens, they will be labeled lt (light), med (medium), and dk (dark).

Fabric	Stitches Per Inch	Strands of Floss	Tapestry Needle Size
Aida	11	3	24
Aida	14	2	24 or 26
Aida	18	1 or 2	24 or 26
Hardanger	22	1	24 or 26

Fig 3

Scissors

A pair of small, sharp-pointed scissors is necessary, especially for snipping misplaced stitches. You may want to hang your scissors on a chain or ribbon around your neck—you'll need them often.

Charts

Counted cross stitch designs are worked from charts. Each square on a chart represents one cross stitch. The symbol in each square represents the floss color to be used. Straight lines over or between symbols indicate back stitches. Each chart is accompanied by a color key, which gives the number of the suggested colors. If a color name appears without a preceding symbol and equal sign, the color is only used for one of the decorative stitches. Backstitches are indicated by straight lines and should be worked the length and direction shown. French Knots are designated by a dot or starburst symbol. Each chart also gives you the number of stitches in width, then height of the design area.

Charts can be foolers: *the size of the charted design is not necessarily the size that your finished work will be.* The work size is determined by the number of threads per inch of the fabric you select. For example, if you work a motif that is 22 stitches wide and 11 stitches high on 11- count Aida, the worked design will be 2" wide and 1" high. Worked on 22-count Hardanger, the same design will be 1" wide and 1/2" high. **Fig 4** shows how much fabric is required for designs under 100 stitches in either direction.

Fig 4

Fabric	Number of Stitches in Design									
	10	20	30	40	50	60	70	80	90	100
11 Aida	1"	2"	2 3/4"	3 3/4"	4 1/2"	5 1/2"	6 1/2"	7 1/4"	8 1/4"	9"
14 Aida	3/4"	1 1/2"	2 1/4"	2 3/4"	3 1/2"	4 1/4"	5"	5 3/4"	6 1/2"	7 1/4"
18 Aida	1/2"	1 1/4"	1 1/2"	2 1/4"	2 3/4"	3 1/2"	4"	4 1/2"	5"	5 1/2"
Hardanger	1/2"	1"	1 1/2"	2"	2 1/4"	2 3/4"	3 1/4"	3 3/4"	4"	4 1/2"

Measurements given to next larger quarter inch.

Getting Started

Unless otherwise directed, work your design centered on the fabric. Follow arrows to find center of charted design; count threads or fold fabric to find its center. Count up and over to the left on chart and fabric to begin cross stitching.

To begin, bring threaded needle to front of fabric. Hold an inch of the end against back, then anchor it with your first few stitches. To end threads and begin new ones next to existing stitches, weave through the backs of several stitches.

The Stitches

Note: Unless otherwise noted in the Color Key, use two strands of floss for all cross stitching, French Knots, and lazy daisies, and one strand for backstitching and straight stitches.

Cross Stitch: A single cross stitch is formed in two motions. Following the numbering in **Fig 5**, bring threaded needle up at 1, down at 2, up at 3, down at 4, completing the stitch. When working on Aida cloth, as in **Fig 1** on page 76, your stitch will cover one "block" of fabric.

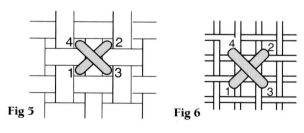

Fig 5   Fig 6

Hardanger has a simple weave and is described as having 22 threads per inch—it actually has 22 **pairs** of threads per inch. Work cross stitches over each intersection, **Fig 6**, to produce 22 stitches per inch. Be sure to use the "stab stitch" method (pull thread completely through fabric after each entry of the needle) rather than a "sewing" method to form cross stitches.

Work horizontal rows of stitches, **Fig 7**, whenever possible. Bring thread up at 1, holding tail end of thread beneath fabric and anchoring it with your first few stitches. Bring thread down at 2; repeat to end of row, forming first half of each stitch. Complete the stitches (3-4, 3-4) on the return journey right to left. Work second and subsequent rows below first row.

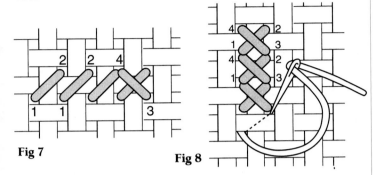

Fig 7

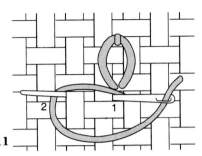

Fig 8

When a vertical row of stitches is appropriate, complete each stitch then proceed to the next, **Fig 8**. No matter how you work the stitches, make sure that all crosses slant in the same direction.

End thread by running the needle over and under several stitches on the wrong side of fabric; begin new threads in this manner if stitches are available. Trim thread ends close to fabric. Because knots in embroidery cause lumps that show under the fabric when it's framed or sewn into finished projects, never begin or end with a knot.

Backstitch

Backstitches are usually worked after cross stitches have been completed. They may slope in any direction and are occasionally worked over more than one fabric block or thread. **Fig 9** shows the progression of several stitches; bring thread up at odd numbers, down at even numbers.

French Knot

Bring thread up where indicated on chart. Wrap floss once around needle, **Fig 10,** and reinsert needle close to where thread first came up. Hold wrapping thread tightly, close to surface of fabric. Pull needle through, letting thread go just as knot is formed. For a larger knot, use more strands of floss, but wrap only once.

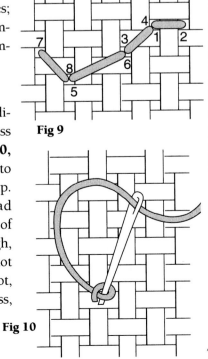

Fig 9

Fig 10

Lazy Daisy Stitch

This stitch creates pointed oval shapes that resemble flower petals. Bring thread up at center hold (1), **Fig 11**. Loop floss, insert needle in same hole, and bring it out two squares from center (2) or as indicated on chart, with loop beneath point of needle. Pull needle through, adjusting size and shape of loop. Stitch down over loop, one thread farther from center, to secure it. Repeat for each oval shape. Anchor ending thread especially well on the wrong side.

Fig 11

Planning a Project

The designs in this book are shown finished as suggested projects. You may wish to use some of these cross stitch designs for other projects. Whichever project you work, select your chart and type of fabric. Next determine the finished dimensions of a stitched area. Divide the number of stitches in width by the number of stitches per inch of fabric. This tells you how many inches wide the fabric must be. Repeat for the height of the design.

Add enough additional fabric for unworked area around the design plus an additional 2" all around for use in finishing and mounting. If your design is a small one, be sure to allow enough fabric to fit over your smallest hoop. The excess fabric can be cut off after stitching.

Cut your fabric exactly true, right along the holes of the fabric. Some ravelling will occur as you handle the fabric; however, an overcast basting stitch, machine zigzag stitch, or masking tape around the raw edges will minimize ravelling.

At bottom and sides of each chart are arrows which indicate the center (which may be a row of stitches, or between two rows of stitches). Find the center of the fabric by folding it in half horizontally and then vertically. Baste along both fold lines; the basting (which is removed when stitching is completed) will cross at the middle and aid in counting stitches.

It is best to start stitching at the top of the design (or the top of a color area) and work downward, whenever possible. This way your needle comes up in an empty hole and goes down in a used hole. This makes your work look neater and is easier than bringing the needle up through an already occupied hole.

To begin stitching, count up from the center hole of the fabric to the top stitches indicated on the chart.

Finishing

Cross stitch on any evenweave fabric is fully washable. When you have finished stitching, dampen embroidery (or wash in lukewarm mild soap suds if soiled and rinse well); roll it briefly in a clean towel to remove excess moisture. Place embroidery face down on a dry, clean terry towel and iron carefully until dry and smooth. Make sure all thread ends are well anchored and clipped closely. Then proceed with desired finishing.

Several of the projects shown can also be framed as pictures. For cross stitch to look its best in a frame it should be stretched taut over a piece of heavy cardboard with the following method of lacing. You will need white cardboard or mat board the size of your frame, 1 spool of white heavy duty sewing thread, pins and four strips of paper.

Step 1: Lay stitchery (washed and pressed) face up on table. Lay strips of paper about 1/2" out from each side of design. Adjust paper until a pleasing border surrounds stitched area. Mark inside edge of paper strips with pins; remove paper. Measure horizontally and vertically between pins and cut board that size. (If you have a frame, cut board same size as glass.)

Step 2: Cut fabric about 3" out from pins on all sizes.

Step 3: Place stitchery face down on table. Place cardboard within pins, aligning top edge of board with weave of fabric. Fold extra fabric toward you over cardboard; pin every 1/2" into edge of board (**Fig 12**). Follow weave while pinning to keep design straight. Pulling fabric taut, fold up bottom fabric and pin. Repeat on sides. Remove marking pins from fabric.

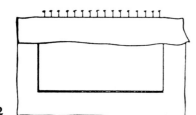

Fig 12

Step 4: Working off a spool of white sewing thread, thread a sharp needle. Beginning at right edge, make a small stitch on top hem, then a small stitch directly below in bottom hem. Now go back to top hem and make another small stitch about 1/2" from first; then back to bottom hem, pulling thread from spool through stitches as you go (**Fig 13**). Continue across, secure thread at top when you reach left

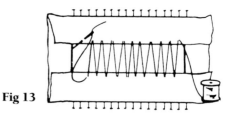

Fig 13

edge of board. Cut needle off. Now working backwards, pull every other lacing thread taut with right hand (hold stitch just tightened with left forefinger). When you reach right side, cut thread off spool, leaving 8" end. Re-thread needle and secure lacing thread. Remove pins. Repeat for sides.

Working On Linen

Location of Selvages

In doing counted cross stitch on linen, a slight difference can be noted in a design worked with the selvages on the right and left and a design where the selvages are held at the top and bottom. The correct way is to have the selvages on the left and right vertically.

Using a Thimble

While no pushing of the needle is required to poke through the linen holes, a sewing stitch rather than a stab stitch is used on linen. Those who normally sew with a thimble will feel more comfortable wearing one.

Needles

Use a blunt-pointed tapestry needle that slips easily through the fabric, and is not so large that it distorts the holes in the fabric. Sizes 24 and 26 are the size needles usually used for all counted cross stitch; size 24 is larger than size 26.

Threads

Embroidery Floss

Any six-strand cotton embroidery floss can be used. The floss can be divided to work with one, two or three strands as required by the linen fabric.

The chart below gives guidelines for the number of strands of floss to use on popular linen fabrics.

Thread Count of Linen	Strands of Floss
18-20	3
26-27-28-30	2
35-36	1 or 2

Charted Designs

For linen work, one square on the chart equals one cross stitch but the cross stitch is worked over two threads of the linen vertically (warp) and two threads horizontally (weft). See **Fig 14**. Often a darker line divides the grid into ten square sections to make counting easier.

Fig 14

Square on Chart = 4 Threads of Linen

Stitching on Linen

An embroidery hoop is not needed for linen cross stitching, so the stitches are made with a sewing stitch: the needle goes in and out in one motion. Place the fabric over your fingers keeping them relaxed, as shown in **Fig 15**. The thumb and index finger hold the fabric and the little finger anchors the fabric. On a tiny piece of fabric it may be necessary to anchor it with the ring finger.

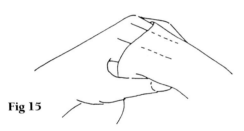

Fig 15

Basic Rules

• Do not sew with fabric wrapped around one finger only. Use the entire hand, three fingers or at the very least two fingers to avoid distorting the fabric or having incorrect tension.

• Do not sew with the work on a table or in your lap but rather sit up straight and hold the embroidery at about eye level.

• The important number for linen work is two. The stitch crosses diagonally over two threads of the linen each way, as shown in **Fig 16**, up two over two. Each square on the chart equals two threads of warp and two of weft, or to say it differently, count over two threads of the linen and up two

Fig 16

threads for each square on the chart. Count the threads of the linen, not the spaces. Think of a ladder and count rungs not holes. This will be tedious but only for about three stitches. After that the eye begins to see in twos. Should a mistake occur – too many or too few threads counted – it will be immediately obvious by the slant, as shown in **Fig 17**.

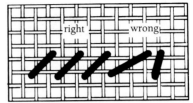

Fig 17

Starting to Stitch

Begin with a waste knot; see page 83. In placing the first stitch on linen, bring the needle up at "x" to the left of a vertical linen thread as shown in **Fig 18**. Make sure that this vertical thread is on top of the horizontal linen thread (rather than under it) as this will help keep the first half of your cross stitch "on top of" the linen weave, resulting in a prettier stitch. The space between linen threads at the left of a vertical thread is larger, so that starting your stitch at this location will also make it easier on your eyes. Work a row of stitches by doing the understitches across, then the overstitches back, never by completing each stitch individually. The only exception is isolated stitches which can be completed individually. If you prefer, when working a vertical row of stitches, only one stitch wide, you can cross each stitch individually.

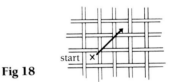

Fig 18

Never carry a thread over more than four threads of the open fabric (four threads equals two stitches). When the distance is greater than two stitches, end the thread and start again.

Work from the top, or center, of the chart down. In stitching, stitch each stitch from the bottom of the stitch to the top, but work the design from the top down. Why? When a needle comes up in an unoccupied (empty) space and down in a occupied (full) space, it will not ruffle the previous stitch. Therefore the results are the desired smoother stitches and the previously finished stitch is reinforced.

Stitching with Several Colors

If a design uses several colors in any area, it is useful to do the stitches of one color leaving the last stitch unfinished (work understitch only) and then bring the thread which is on the front side of the fabric up and to the side, out of the way of stitching, temporarily. Do the next color in the same way using another needle, and the next, etc. See **Fig 19**. When a previously used color is required run the thread of that color through the intervening stitches to the new area.

Use this technique discreetly, such as for areas of intricate shading. Remember the best work will have mostly vertical lines on the reverse.

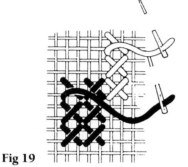

Fig 19

Planning a Project on Linen
Determining Size
To determine size of your finished project and the amount of fabric required:

1. Count the number of threads per inch in the linen.

2. Divide this number by two (remember you are crossing over two threads with each stitch).

3. Now count the number of stitches (or squares) in the design, first vertically, then horizontally.

4. Divide each number of design stitches by the number of stitches per inch.

Example: The linen to be used is 28 threads per inch. Divided by 2 this equals 14. The design is 42 stitches (or squares) vertically. Divided by 14 this equals 3. The design is 28 stitches (or squares) horizontally. Divided by 14 this is 2. The image size is 3 inches by 2 inches. Add 6 inches to each measurement for framing, turn over, or border. Cut the fabric 9 inches by 8 inches. If your arithmetic is doubtful at best, cut extra cloth. It will be easier to stitch on a small linen piece if there is enough fabric to wrap around your hand as in **Fig 15**. Even expensive linen is cheaper than your time. Waste a little fabric rather than waste your work.

Preparing the Fabric
A basting thread marking the center line can be an aid in counting. Start at a vertical thread (as shown in **Fig 18**), as you would for a cross stitch, and baste by two being sure not to deviate from the thread line. Repeat horizontally. It is then simple to count up 20 stitches or over 15, etc.

Initial and Date Your Work

It may not seem important to you now, but a piece of embroidery that has a signature and date will be much more valuable when it becomes an antique. Choose a thread color that has been used in the piece and position your initials and date unobtrusively at or near the bottom.

Below are the alphabet and numbers to use to personalize your projects.

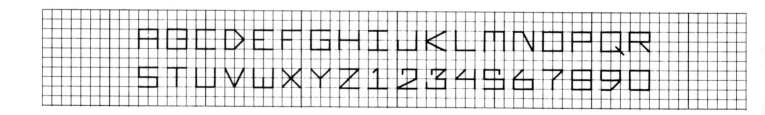

At-A-Glance Reference Guide

Waste Knot Method

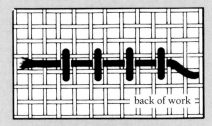

Working Over Method

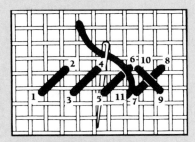

Cross Stitch

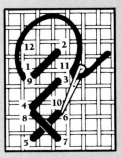

Single Vertical Row
Thread ends where you began

Single Vertical Row
Thread ends where you stop

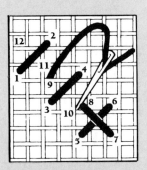

Single Diagonal Row
Thread ends where you began

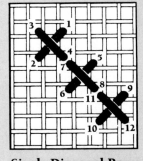

Single Diagonal Row
Thread ends where you stop

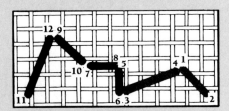

Backstitch

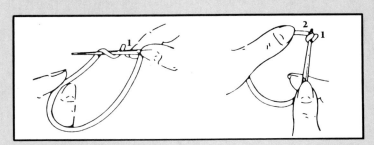

French Knot

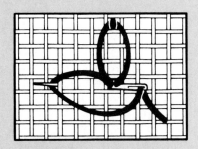

Lazy Daisy

Home Sweet Home

designed by Sam Hawkins

Perforated paper provides the background for this tribute to the warmth and joy of a home. Perforated paper can be used for just about any cross stitch design; it is wonderful for a design like this one.

Design

103 wide x 42 high
Stitched on a 12" x 9" piece of ecru 14-count perforated
  paper, shown in a 9" x 5" green & gold frame

Color Key

		Anchor	Coats	DMC
~	= cream	386	2386	746
○	= lt pink	48	3067	818
+	= med pink	76	3176	3731
★	= dk pink	65	3004	3350
⊗	= med yellow	306	2307	725
⊟	= dk yellow	308	5308	782
◇	= lt green	241	6238	704
×	= med green	244	6226	702
◆	= dk green	246	6246	986
▫	= lt blue	120	7031	800
▲	= dk blue	122	7022	792
✳	= dk green French Knots			
●	= dk blue French Knots			
I	= Backstitch: dk green			

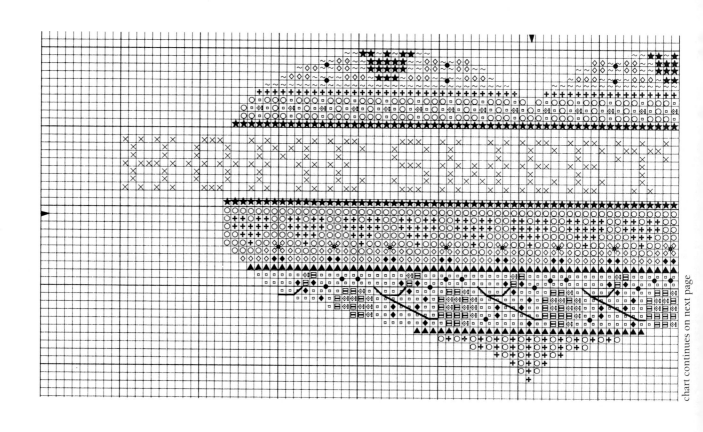

chart continues on next page

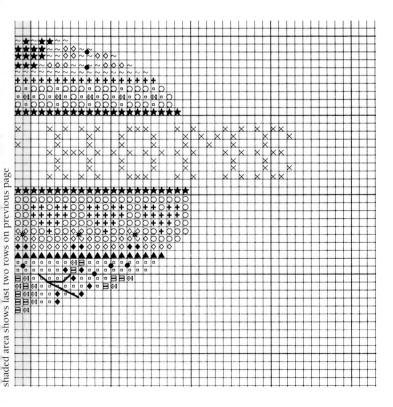

shaded area shows last two rows on previous page

Beribboned Roses Table Runner

designed by Sam Hawkins

These floral corner motifs can be used on a table runner or on a tablecloth. A graceful ribbon twines among the beautifully shaded roses.

Design

73 wide x 62 high
Stitched on pre-finished 13 1/2" x 27" ivory table runner
    made from 14-count Sal-Em cloth

Stitching notes

Work Lower Left and Lower Right designs in respective corners at one (or both) end(s) of table runner. Center your work about 1" from fringed end, leaving 9 fabric squares vacant between the two designs.

Color Key

		DMC	Anchor	Coats
▫	= very lt rose	3713	23	3068
○	= lt rose	3326	25	3152
◎	= med rose	899	27	3127
⊕	= dk rose	335	42	3153
●	= very dk rose	326	59	3019
⋇	= lt yellow	727	293	2289
▣	= med yellow	725	306	2307
◇	= very lt green	472	264	6253
▨	= lt green	471	266	6010
+	= med green	470	267	6268
▦	= dk green	469	268	6269
▲	= very dk green	937	269	6317
□	= lt purple	211	108	4303
⊞	= med purple	210	109	4302
★	= dk purple	208	111	4301
−	= lt tan	951	366	3335
△	= med tan	945	347	5345

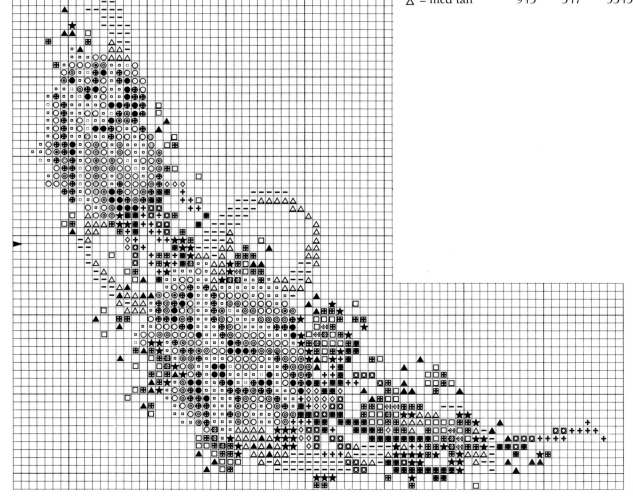

Lower Left

Lower Right

87

Little Red School House

designed by Polly Carbonari

The two students and their teacher are dramatically silhouetted against a bright quilt in the Little Red School House traditional pattern. This is a lovely gift for a teacher, student or quilter.

Design

139 wide x 97 high
Stitched on 14-count cream Aida
Frame is 10" x 12"

Color Key

		DMC	Anchor
◇	= lt rust	760	9
✦	= med rust	3328	11
+	= dk rust	347	13
●	= black	310	403
•	= French Knot: black		
|	= Backstitch: black		

chart continues on next page

Grandma's Lockets

designed by Sam Hawkins

There's an old-fashioned feel to this delightful picture of flowers entwined with ribbon.

Design

91 wide x 147 high

Stitched over two threads on a 17" x 22" piece of cream
    25-count Dublin linen, shown in a 9" x 14" gold frame

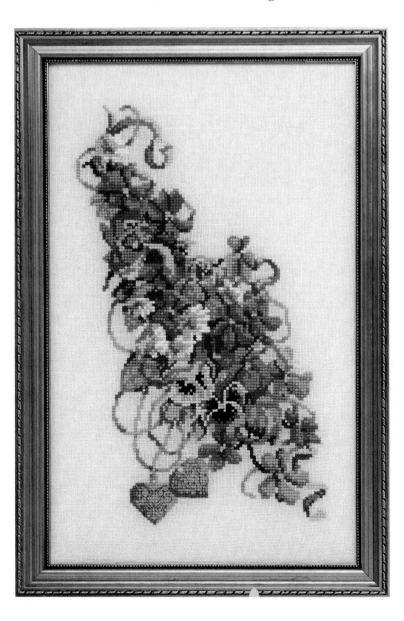

Stitching note

Use three strands for cross stitches, two strands for French
knots, and one strand for backstitches.

Color Key

		Anchor	Coats	DMC
–	= white	1	1001	blanc
O	= lt pink	24	3173	963
©	= med pink	27	3127	893
⊕	= dk pink	28	3152	892
∿	= lt rose	48	3067	818
=	= med rose	50	3151	605
⊠	= dk rose	54	3128	956
✖	= very dk rose	59	3065	815
×	= yellow	305	2298	743
▫	= lt gold	306	2307	725
+	= med gold	307	5307	783
✖	= dk gold	309	5309	781
◇	= lt green	240	6016	368
⊞	= med green	244	6226	702
◆	= dk green	246	6246	986
▣	= very dk green	683	6880	890
~	= lt gray-green	214	6875	504
✣	= med gray-green	216	6876	502
▨	= dk gray-green	218	6880	500
∧	= lt blue	128	7031	800
ω	= med blue	130	7021	809
⊖	= dk blue	132	7080	798
☆	= lt blue-violet	117	7005	341
>	= med blue-violet	118	7110	340
★	= dk blue-violet	119	7150	333
△	= lt purple	96	4104	554
⊟	= med purple	98	4097	553
▲	= dk purple	94	4089	917
	brown	310	5365	780
•	= lt gray	398	8398	415
◉	= dk gray	235	8399	414
●	= black	403	8403	310
●	= French Knots: brown			
	= Backstitch: brown			

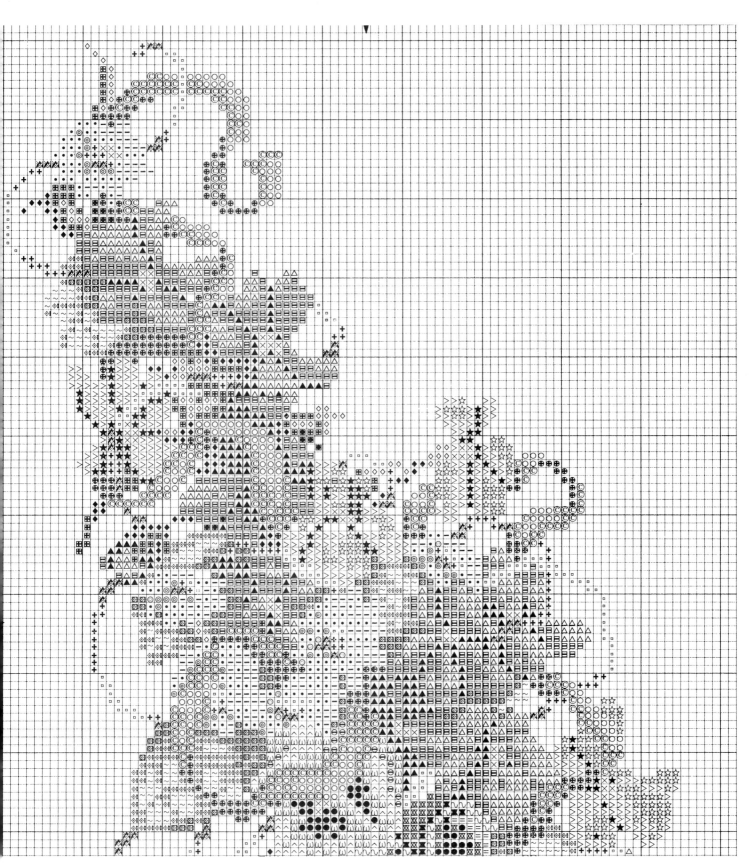

chart continues on next page

Shaded area shows last two rows on previous page

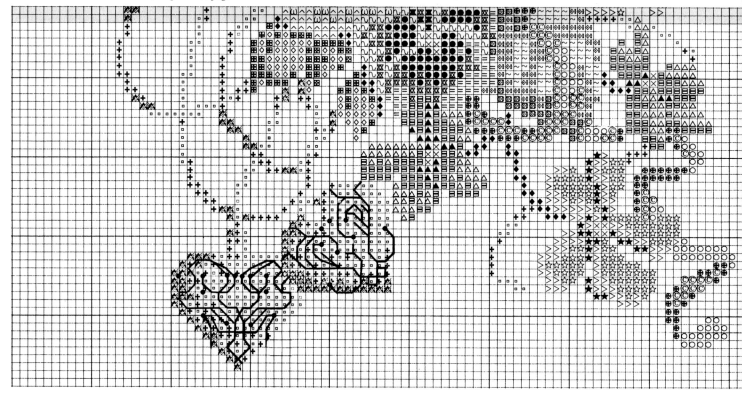

Color Key

	Anchor	Coats	DMC
− = white	1	1001	blanc
○ = lt pink	24	3173	963
◎ = med pink	27	3127	893
⊕ = dk pink	28	3152	892
∿ = lt rose	48	3067	818
= = med rose	50	3151	605
⬗ = dk rose	54	3128	956
⬛ = very dk rose	59	3065	815
× = yellow	305	2298	743
▫ = lt gold	306	2307	725
+ = med gold	307	5307	783
⬕ = dk gold	309	5309	781
◇ = lt green	240	6016	368
⊞ = med green	244	6226	702
◆ = dk green	246	6246	986
⬛ = very dk green	683	6880	890
~ = lt gray-green	214	6875	504

	Anchor	Coats	DMC
⊛ = med gray-green	216	6876	502
⊠ = dk gray-green	218	6880	500
∧ = lt blue	128	7031	800
ω = med blue	130	7021	809
⊖ = dk blue	132	7080	798
☆ = lt blue-violet	117	7005	341
> = med blue-violet	118	7110	340
★ = dk blue-violet	119	7150	333
△ = lt purple	96	4104	554
⊟ = med purple	98	4097	553
▲ = dk purple	94	4089	917
brown	310	5365	780
• = lt gray	398	8398	415
◎ = dk gray	235	8399	414
● = black	403	8403	310
● = French Knot: brown			
I = Backstitch: brown			

The Four Seasons Sampler

designed by Polly Carbonari

Each season in the country is charmingly depicted in this lovely picture.

Design

151 wide x 213 high
Stitched on 14-count ivory Aida
Frame is 14" x 18"

Summer	Fall
Winter	Spring

The charts for this design are on pages 94-97. Refer to placement diagram and photo when positioning each design section on your fabric.

Summer

Color Key

		DMC	Anchor
ı	= white	blanc	2
□	= lt rose	3326	25
☆	= lt red	891	35
✦	= red	349	13
❧	= lt brick	3328	11
●	= dk brick	347	13
⊙	= orange	721	324
◉	= dk cream	738	942
▪	= yellow	725	306
+	= dk gold	782	308

Continue stitching from chart on next pages 95-97.

94

Color Key

		DMC	Anchor
∘	= lt green	704	256
◇	= med green	911	205
◀	= dk green	986	246
▷	= lt turquoise	993	186
⊡	= dk turquoise	991	189
O	= lt blue	519	167
◆	= med blue	334	145
⊕	= dk blue	824	164
⊠	= lavender	209	105

		DMC	Anchor
ω	= brown	975	355
✖	= gray-beige	640	903
▣	= med gray	318	399
■	= black	310	403
	dk brown	801	357
✳	= French Knots: Angel's eye, deer's eye, sheep's eye, and strawberries - black		
❘	= Backstitch: All outlining - dk brown		
	Season names - match color of symbols		

Fall

shaded area shows last two rows on previous page

Continue stitching from chart on next pages 96-97.

Color Key

		DMC	Anchor			DMC	Anchor			DMC	Anchor
ı	= white	blanc	2	●	= dk brick	347	13	○	= lt green	704	256
□	= lt rose	3326	25	⊙	= orange	721	324	◇	= med green	911	205
☆	= lt red	891	35	◎	= dk cream	738	942	◀	= dk green	986	246
★	= red	349	13	·	= yellow	725	306	▷	= lt turquoise	993	186
❀	= lt brick	3328	11	+	= dk gold	782	308	▣	= dk turquoise	991	189

Winter

shaded area shows last two rows on previous page

chart continues on next page

Color Key

		DMC	Anchor
○	= lt blue	519	167
◆	= med blue	334	145
⊕	= dk blue	824	164
⊠	= lavender	209	105
ᴈ	= brown	975	355
✖	= gray-beige	640	903

		DMC	Anchor
⊡	= med gray	318	399
■	= black	310	403
	dk brown	801	357

✳ = French Knots: Angel's eye, deer's eye,
sheep's eye, and strawberries - black

| = Backstitch: All outlining - dk brown
Season names - match color of symbols

Spring

shaded area shows last two rows on previous page

97

Cross Stitch Afghans

Cuddle up under a soft, warm afghan featuring a beautiful cross stitch design. Cross stitch afghans are usually stitched on fabric especially designed for this purpose. We've specified the fabrics for which each design was created; if you change fabric, you must carefully count the stitches in each design to be sure it fits the new fabric. Both of the afghan designs are stitched over two fabric threads.

Our Neighborhood   **Romance**

Special Hints for Afghans

Our designs were developed so that each design section fits a fabric section of a particular afghan fabric. If you want to substitute one design for another or work with a different fabric, make sure you have the right number of threads to make it workable.

Note: All stitches are worked over two fabric threads.

Pay special attention to the threads on the back of these afghans. With only seven stitches per inch, you'll need to bury fairly long ends to secure the stitches, especially backstitches, from normal wear and tear. You may even want to run threads through in two directions by including a "U-turn." Occasionally, stitching will be visible on the back, so if it's tidy, it will just look like any other wrong side.

Each fabric has a woven layout for which these designs have been planned. Make sure the fabric cut is the size and layout required for the design. Mark the top of the fabric and keep it as the top while stitching the design, turning only the chart(s) so that all stitches cross the same direction. Baste the vertical and horizontal centers of any large sections before you begin, to ensure proper placement.

It is sometimes difficult to tell one side from the other on afghan fabric. One way is to check the selvages. If thread ends are visible where they turn back on themselves, that will be the wrong side. Also, look at the decorative section bars or bands—one side may appear more "finished" than the other and should be chosen as the right side. When weaving ribbons through a border, make sure there are properly spaced cross threads. Finally, if you absolutely cannot tell the difference, then it really doesn't matter!

Fringe makes an attractive and easy edging for an afghan. First, trim selvage ends. Along each side to be fringed, use matching thread to machine zigzag over two threads, right next to the woven pattern. Trim fabric to desired fringe width. Then carefully remove the cross threads, leaving the fringe intact. If desired, reinforce the fringe base by hand with a row of backstitches or even cross stitches. Use ravelled thread for a perfect match.

To hem the sides, use matching thread to machine zigzag along the raw edge; if desired, apply fray retarding solution and let dry. Turn edge under and topstitch with a straight or zigzag setting. Add a simple lining if you wish the wrong side to be covered. Cut a piece of prewashed lightweight fabric 1" wider and longer than the area to be lined. Press raw edges under 1/2". With wrong sides together, slipstitch to back of afghan. If desired, tack layers together at occasional points.

Romance

designed by Sam Hawkins

This colorful formal bouquet is accented with ribbon trim and fringe on the afghan. It will be a breath of spring to the lucky owner of this magnificent piece.

Design

110 wide x 167 high
Stitched on Gloria Cloth, 14-count, Antique White
    Cut size is about 48" x 56".
Fabric has an interior block of 285 x 399 threads and the design requires 220 threads x 336 threads; the surrounding border is approximately 12 1/2" deep on all sides.
Ribbon trimming requires 8 yds of 1/8" wide lt blue satin woven edge ribbon.

Instructions

Step 1: Place fabric on a flat surface. Refer to layout guide and make sure you have enough fabric for ribbon-trimmed border and desired length of fringe.

Step 2: Mark top of fabric. Refer to Special Hints for Afghans and color key to stitch design **centered** in large middle block.

Step 3: Trim selvages. To prepare a space for 1/8 inch ribbon to be woven into outer woven border, a fabric thread must be removed. Look closely at the fabric—there are three threads between and parallel to the pair of woven bars that form this outer border. Beginning at one raw edge, use tip of your needle to lift out middle thread only. Clip and discard each thread section until thread is completely withdrawn. Repeat on remaining three sides.

Step 4: Cut ribbon into four 2-yard pieces. Thread one piece into your needle. Beginning at a corner where prepared spaces intersect, weave ribbon over two threads, then under two threads to reach the next intersection. Center the ribbon along the channel. Repeat on the remaining three sides.

Step 5: On each side, use matching thread to reinforce base of fringe. Zigzag over two threads, 3 1/2" beyond woven ribbon border. Trim evenly on all sides, then remove cross threads beyond reinforcement to make fringe. Tie ribbon ends in bows, tack at corners, and trim ends.

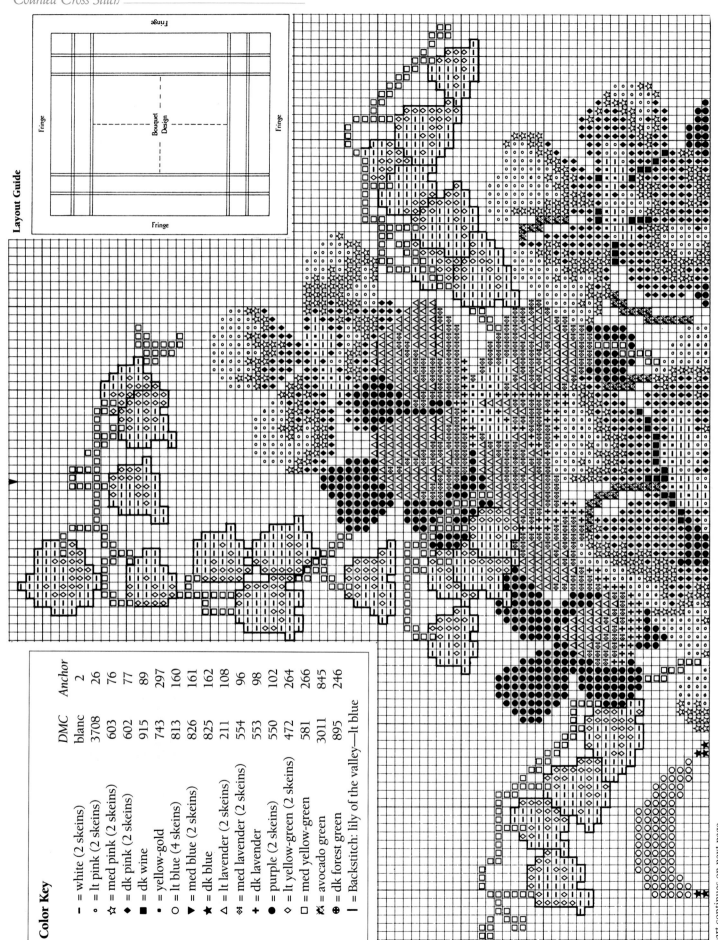

Layout Guide

(Layout diagram shows: Fringe around all four sides, with "Bouquet Design" in the center)

Color Key

		DMC	Anchor
=	= white (2 skeins)	blanc	2
○	= lt pink (2 skeins)	3708	26
☆	= med pink (2 skeins)	603	76
◆	= dk pink (2 skeins)	602	77
■	= dk wine	915	89
•	= yellow-gold	743	297
○	= lt blue (4 skeins)	813	160
▼	= med blue (2 skeins)	826	161
★	= dk blue	825	162
△	= lt lavender (2 skeins)	211	108
✷	= med lavender (2 skeins)	554	96
+	= dk lavender	553	98
●	= purple (2 skeins)	550	102
◇	= lt yellow-green (2 skeins)	472	264
□	= med yellow-green	581	266
✕	= avocado green	3011	845
⊕	= dk forest green	895	246
	= Backstitch: lily of the valley—lt blue		

chart continues on next page

Our Neighborhood

designed by Carol Wilson Mansfield

Homespun and Blue—what ideal teammates to create a feeling of nostalgia for the old hand-woven coverlets. Using a fabric woven in checkerboard fashion, four charming motifs are repeated around the edges and are combined with a series of heart designs. Using only one color of floss, the afghan is stitched on a 14-count blue fabric. An easy-to-make fringe surrounds the pattern.

Afghan Fabric

Liberty Square, 14-count, Colonial Blue

Cut size is about 48" x 64".

Layout has 5 squares x 7 squares plus partial squares for fringing. Each square has 100 x 100 threads and is approximately 6 3/4" x 6 3/4".

Instructions

Step 1: Place fabric on a flat surface. Refer to layout guide and make sure all sections needed for afghan design are complete.

Step 2: Mark top of fabric. Refer to Special Hints for Afghans and color key to stitch each design **centered** in appropriate square on the fabric. Use six strands of floss for all stitching. Turn each chart—not the fabric—as needed so top of each design is toward center of fabric.

Step 3: Trim selvages so fabric margins match on all sides. Finish with a narrow hem or fringe. For fringe, use matching thread to machine zigzag over two threads next to outside woven border and remove cross threads.

Layout Guide

Corner Heart	Tree	House A	Tree	Corner Heart
House B	Inner Heart Corner	Inner Heart Border	Inner Heart Corner	House B
Tree	Inner Heart Border		Inner Heart Border	Tree
House A	Inner Heart Border		Inner Heart Border	House A
Tree	Inner Heart Border		Inner Heart Border	Tree
House B	Inner Heart Corner	Inner Heart Border	Inner Heart Corner	House B
Corner Heart	Tree	House A	Tree	Corner Heart

Fringe (top, bottom, left, right sides)

Our Neighborhood design area: 48" x 64"

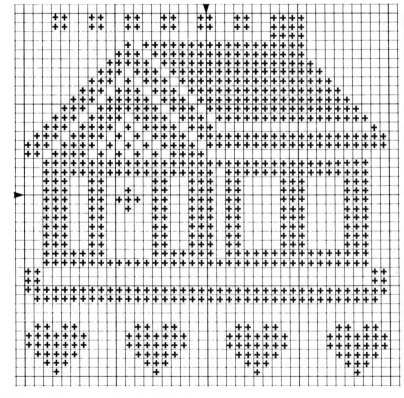

House A design area: 40 wide x 40 high

Color Key

	DMC	Anchor
+ = cream (50 skeins)	ecru	926

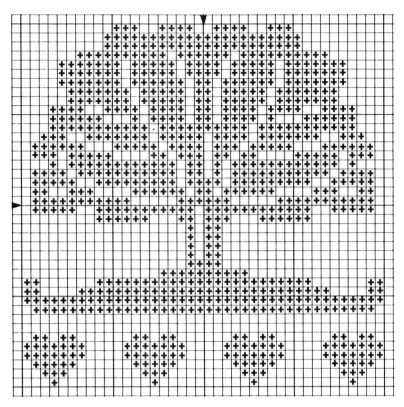

Color Key

	DMC	*Anchor*
+ = cream (50 skeins)	ecru	926

Tree design area: 40 wide x 40 high

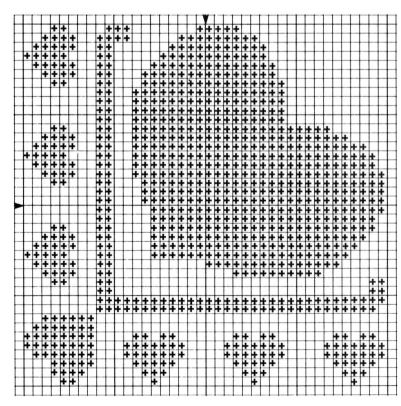

Corner Heart design area: 40 wide x 40 high

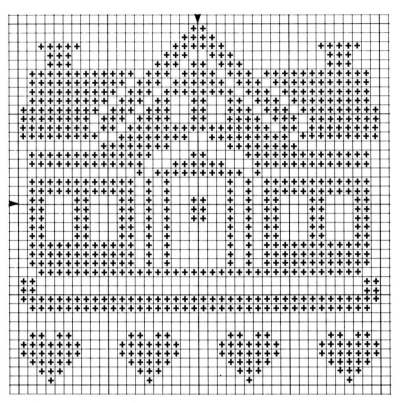

House B design area: 40 wide x 40 high

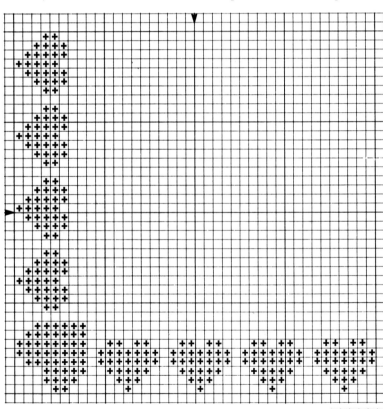

Inner Heart Corner design area: 40 wide x 40 high

Color Key

	DMC	Anchor
+ = cream (50 skeins)	ecru	926

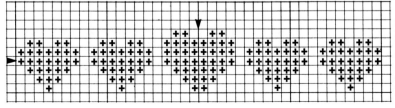

Inner Heart Border design area: 40 wide x 6 high

Delphiniums and Roses

designed by Sam Hawkins

Sam designed this especially for a friend who loves these two flowers. The blue and pink floral combination is as striking in this picture as in a vase — and the flowers never fade.

Design

93 wide x 151 high
Stitched over two threads on a 20" x 23" piece of cream
    25-count Dublin linen, shown with a marbleized blue
    11" x 14" oval mat in a 14" x 17" frame

Stitching note

Use three strands for cross stitches, two strands for backstitches.

105

Color Key

		DMC	Anchor	Coats
▫	= lt pink	818	48	3067
○	= med pink	776	24	3125
◉	= dk pink	899	27	3152
⊕	= very dk pink	309	42	3154
□	= yellow	3078	292	2292
ω	= lt yellow-green	3348	265	6266
✖	= med yellow-green	3346	257	6267
●	= dk yellow-green	895	268	6021
=	= lt green	989	242	6017
✖	= med green	988	243	6108
▨	= dk green	986	246	6246
∿	= lt blue	3753	282	7050
✦	= med blue	827	159	7159
▨	= dk blue	813	160	7161
■	= very dk blue	312	979	7979
◇	= lt purple	211	108	4303
+	= med purple	210	109	4302
★	= dk purple	208	111	4301
◆	= gray-black	317	400	8512
	= Backstitch: dk yellow-green			

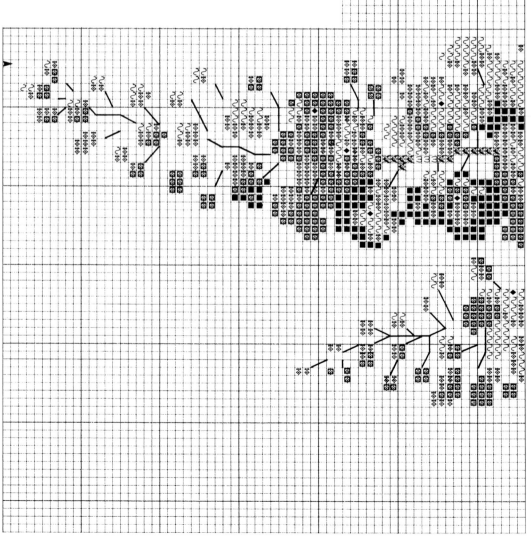

chart continues on next page

shaded area shows last two rows on previous page

Simple Pleasures Sampler

designed by Anne Ambler Murray

Life's simple pleasures—a letter from a friend, a cup of tea, a church service, a loving kitten—these and more are showcased on this sweet sampler, to be crafted by loving hands. This is an easy project, and would make a wonderful housewarming gift.

Design

101 wide x 112 high

Color Key

		DMC	Anchor
−	= white	blanc	2
○	= pink	893	27
+	= red	326	59
▪	= med blue	931	921
▲	= dk blue	311	149
◇	= lt green	470	267
★	= dk green	935	862
▽	= tan	436	363
✖	= med brown	434	309
◆	= dk brown	898	360
☆	= lt gray	3023	900
✪	= med gray	646	8581
■	= dk gray	844	401

✿ = French Knot: cat's eye - dk blue

| = Backstitch:
      border lines - med brown
      border hearts - match color of center stitches
      mailbox heart - red
      mailbox leaf - dk green
      yarn basket - dk blue around blue yarn
          dk green around green yarn
      knitting needles - med gray
      church roof, steeple - dk gray
      church windows, cross - dk blue
      church fence - med gray
      heart bow - dk blue
      "Home" - pink
      tiny house roof peak (left) - dk blue
      "Sweet" - lt blue
      tiny house roof peak (right) - red
      "Home" - lt green
      watering can grass - dk green
      apples - red
      apple stems - dk green
      cat hearts - red and dk green
      heart strings - med gray
      quilt "thread", edges - dk blue
          (add real needle)
      swing chain - med gray

Home is Where Your Heart Is

designed by Sam Hawkins

Home for this little mother is a cozy nest secure on a floral branch. Lucky are the tiny birds who will soon hatch.

Design

89 wide x 98 high

Stitched on a 14" x 14" piece of 14-count Fiddler's Lite, shown in a 8-1/2" x 8-1/2" wood frame

Color Key

		Anchor	Coats	DMC
▫	= white	2	1001	blanc
■	= yellow	305	2298	743
◇	= lt green	254	6266	3348
◆	= dk green	257	6018	988
~	= very lt blue	128	7031	800
○	= lt blue	130	7021	809
©	= med blue	132	7080	798
⊕	= dk blue	134	7100	820
△	= med rust	370	5349	975
▲	= dk rust	359	5475	801
□	= lt brown	376	2337	950
▤	= med brown	379	5379	840
⋈	= dk brown	936	5936	632
‐	= lt gray-brown	390	5387	3033

		Anchor	Coats	DMC
⬙	= med gray-brown	392	5388	3032
▨	= dk gray-brown	393	5393	640
×	= lt gray	234	8398	3072
+	= med gray	399	8511	318
★	= dk gray	400	8399	414
●	= black	403	8403	3310
		= Backstitch:		

green bud stems—dk green
green leaf stems—dk rust
nest—dk gray-brown
vines (thin lines)—med rust
vines (thick lines)—dk rust
wings—dk brown

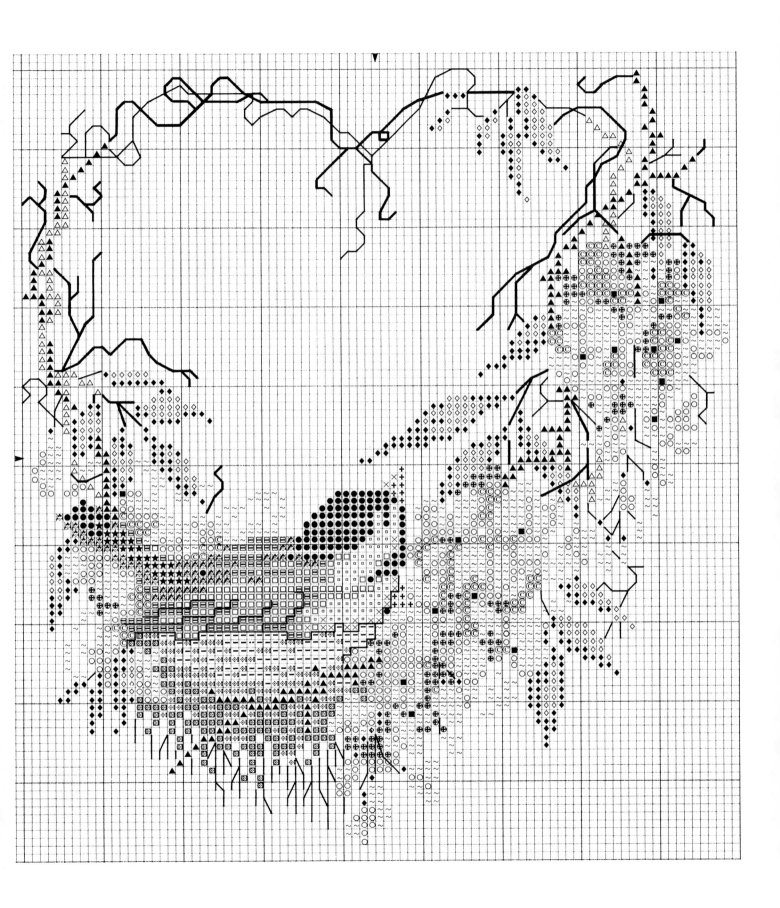

Delft Sampler

designed by Polly Carbonari

Two shades of blue thread on white fabric are used to create the authentic look of Dutch Delft on this lovely sampler. The individual motifs also could be used in other projects, perhaps a table runner or placemats.

Design

113 wide x 134 high
Stitched on 14-count white Aida
Frame is 10" x 12"

Color Key

		DMC	Anchor
+	= lt blue	799	130
●	= dk blue	797	132
❘	= Backstitch: Delft-dk blue		

Kitchen Towels

designs by Sam Hawkins

Pre-made kitchen towels, designed especially for cross stitch, are used to showcase this delightful collection of designs. They can easily be adapted for other uses, too. Sam has included a wide variety of colorful motifs. As a matter of fact, these designs cover such a range of decorative pattern and style, we could have called this section "not only for the kitchen."

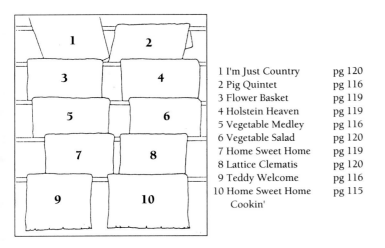

Home Sweet Home Cookin'

Color Key

		DMC	Anchor
+	= pink	893	27
o	= yellow	725	306
☆	= blue	518	168
✖	= lt green	703	238
▶	= dk green	910	228
I	= Backstitch:		

stems - lt green (2 strands)

Note: repeat background to meet selvages.

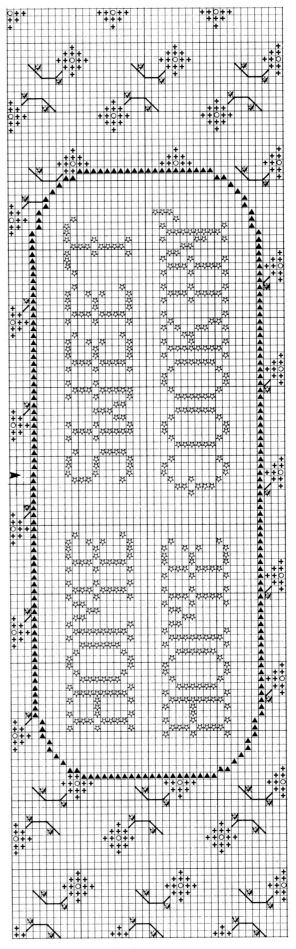

Home Sweet Home Cookin'

115

Vegetable Medley

Color Key

		DMC	Anchor
○	= white	blanc	2
◇	= lt red	892	28
✚	= med red	321	47
▶	= dk red	816	44
□	= lt orange	970	316
✩	= med orange	947	330
⊕	= dk orange	900	333
ı	= lt yellow	676	891
○	= med yellow	444	291
▣	= gold	783	307
◁	= lt yellow-green	472	264
❆	= lt leaf green	907	255
★	= med leaf green	906	256
●	= dk leaf green	904	258
■	= dk green	935	862
◆	= brown	780	310
◎	= gray	647	8581
ı	= Backstitch:		

     pea vine - dk leaf green
     carrots, corn - brown

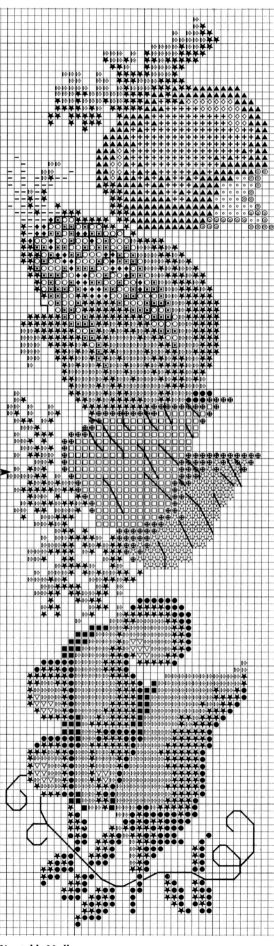

Vegetable Medley

Pig Quintet

Color Key

		DMC	Anchor
ı	= white	blanc	2
○	= pink	3708	26
▷	= dk rose	3328	11
✚	= blue	518	168
✖	= rose-brown	221	897
★	= dk brown	938	381
ı	= Backstitch:		

     all outlines - dk brown

Teddy Welcome

Color Key

		DMC	Anchor
○	= white	blanc	2
▫	= lt pink	957	50
✩	= med pink	956	40
●	= dk pink	600	59
□	= lt yellow	973	290
✚	= lt gold	725	306
❆	= dk gold	782	308
◁	= lt blue	519	167
✖	= med blue	518	168
◇	= lt green	704	256
▶	= med green	701	227
⊕	= dk green	895	246
ı	= lt tan	437	362
☺	= lt brown	435	369
▣	= med brown	433	371
★	= dk brown	898	360
•	= gray	452	399
■	= black	310	403
ı	= Backstitch: shelf, scalloped		

     edge - gray
     basket, teddy seams &
     mouth, HELLO - dk brown

| ı | = Backstitch: flower outlines | | |

     details, WELCOME - dk pi
     leaves - dk green
     hat, peg, strings - med brow
     ribbon - med blue
     lamb - black

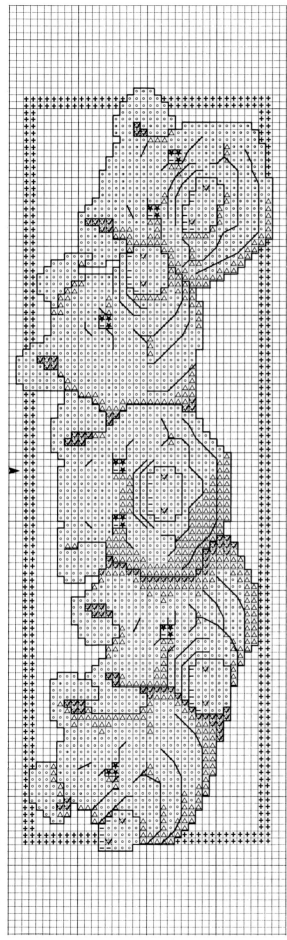

Pig Quintet

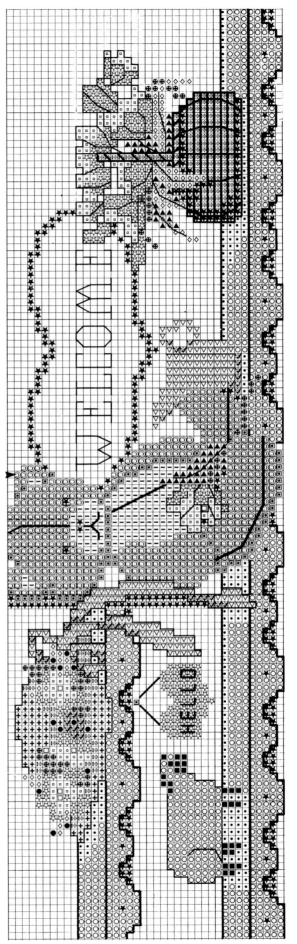

Teddy Welcome

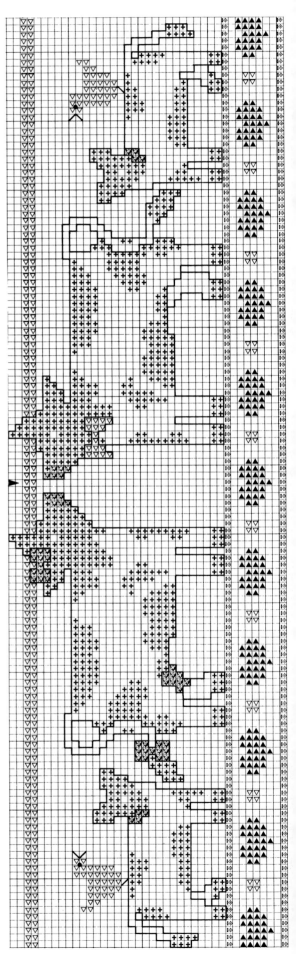

Flower Basket

Holstein Heaven

Holstein Heaven

Color Key

		DMC	Anchor
✖	= lt pink	894	26
▶	= dk pink	309	42
	gold	783	307
◁	= blue	517	169
✿	= green	702	239
+	= black	310	403
●	= French Knots: bird eyes - black		
		= Backstitch: birds - gold		
	cows - black (2 strands)		

Note: repeat borders to meet selvages

Flower Basket

Color Key

		DMC	Anchor
▪	= lt pink	894	26
✿	= med pink	956	40
◎	= lt orange	3341	328
+	= med orange	351	11
□	= yellow	726	295
○	= yellow-orange	742	303
		= lt gold	3046	887
●	= dk gold	783	307
○	= lt blue	3325	159
✖	= med blue	334	145
◁	= lt green	704	256
◆	= med green	905	258
★	= dk green	986	246
◇	= lt lavender	554	96
▶	= med lavender	553	98
☆	= med brown	434	309
▣	= dk brown	300	352
●	= French Knots: med lavender		
		= Backstitch: ribbon outline-		
	med brown		
	flower outlines - med green		
	stems - med green (2 strands)		
	basket - dk brown (2 strands)		

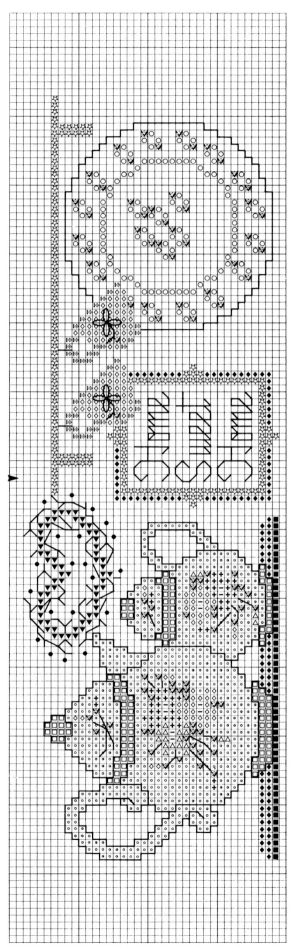

Home Sweet Home

Home Sweet Home

Color Key

		DMC	Anchor
°	= cream	739	885
□	= lt tan	422	373
◇	= pink	3326	25
	dk rose	309	42
▷	= peach	3341	328
✿	= gold	783	307
		= yellow	743	297
○	= lt blue	799	13
	med blue	798	131
✖	= green	913	209
+	= lavender	209	105
☆	= med brown	301	349
◆	= dk rust brown	918	341
■	= very dk brown	801	357
◀	= gray-brown	611	898
●	= French Knots: lavender		
0	= Lazy Daisy: dk rose		
		= Backstitch:		
	tea set - very dk brown		
	cup hooks - very dk brown		
	stems - green		
	heart wreath - gray-brown		
	flowered plate - med blue		
	Home Sweet Home - dk rose		

Lattice Clematis

Color Key

		DMC	Anchor
○	= gold	742	303
ı	= lt lavender	210	104
◇	= med lavender	553	98
✿	= blue-violet	333	119
▶	= purple	550	102
◁	= lt green	704	256
✖	= med green	702	239
■	= dk green	986	246
○	= lt brown	437	362
★	= med brown	433	371
ı	= Backstitch: stems - dk green		
	flowers - purple		

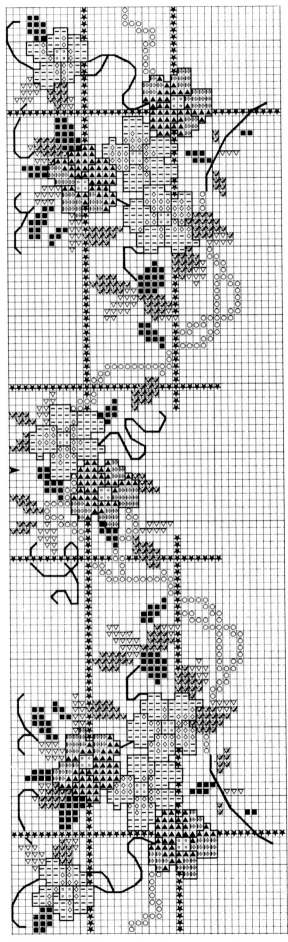

Lattice Clematis

I'm Just Country

Color Key

		DMC	Anchor
▷	= lt red	3705	35
◆	= dk red	347	13
○	= blue-gray	932	920
□	= lt green	704	256
✿	= med green	988	243
★	= dk green	319	246
✖	= lt brown	611	898
	dk brown	938	381
ı	= Backstitch: all outlines - dk brown		

Note: repeat background to meet selvages.

Vegetable Salad

Color Key

		DMC	Anch
○	= white	blanc	2
◇	= lt red	3705	35
+	= med red	321	47
▣	= dk red	816	44
ı	= lt yellow	744	301
▷	= med gold	783	307
✿	= dk gold	781	309
☆	= lt green	704	256
◆	= med green	988	243
■	= dk green	986	246
□	= yellow-green	472	264
✖	= brown	300	352
ı	= Backstitch: onion - brown		
	cucumber - dk green		

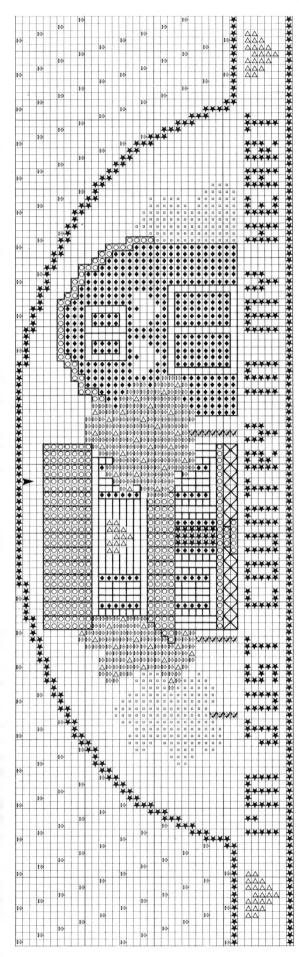

I'm Just Country

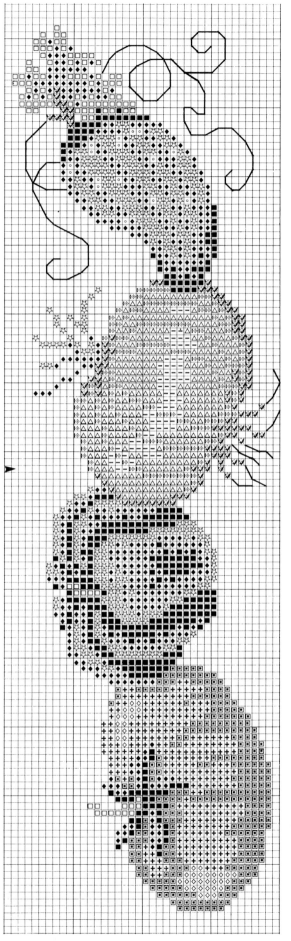

Vegetable Salad

Quilts Sampler

designed by Polly Carbonari

Blocks from favorite quilt patterns are combined to make a unique sampler for the quilter, or anyone who loves the look and feel of country.

Design

84 wide x 112 high
Stitched on 14-count
  rose Aida
Frame is 9" x 12"

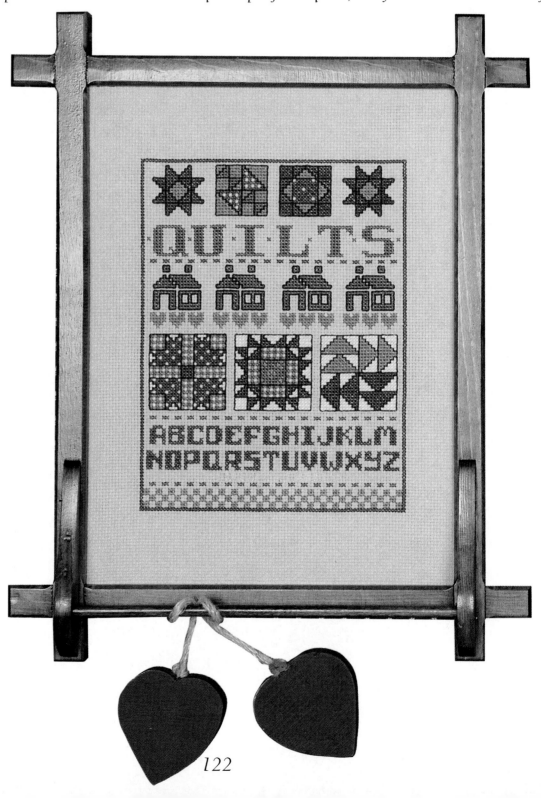

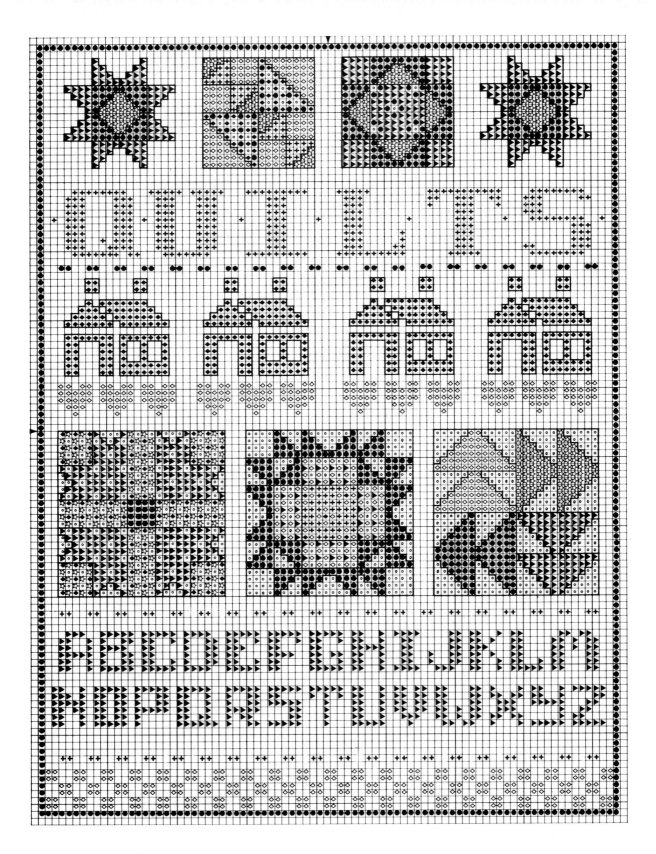

Color Key

		DMC	Anchor			DMC	Anchor
○	= white	blanc	2	◆	= med blue	517	169
◇	= lt pink	899	27	●	= lavender	327	101
▶	= dk pink	309	42	+	= green	988	243
	burgundy	3685	70	❘	= Backstitch: outlines - burgundy		
☆	= lt blue	518	168				

123

Cross Stitch with Waste Canvas

designs by Sam Hawkins

Waste canvas is a wonderful evenweave product that makes it possible to stitch cross stitch designs on non-evenweave fabrics such as sweatshirts, blouses, T-shirts, and children's clothes. Any cross stitch design can be worked over waste canvas; when the design is completely stitched, the canvas threads are dampened and then withdrawn — actually, wasted. The beautiful design remains.

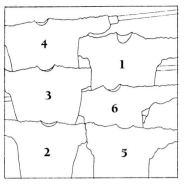

General Directions

What is waste canvas?

This unique canvas, also called waste fabric or blue-line canvas, is a disposable counted cross stitch surface. It is actually an inexpensive double-thread canvas that provides a temporary, countable surface on a non-evenweave fabric.

Waste canvas comes in several mesh sizes, ranging from 8 1/2 to 16 threads (actually pairs of threads) per inch. Every 5th pair of threads on the canvas has a dark blue thread as a counting aid and also to distinguish the piece from regular needlepoint canvas. Some sizes are available in pre-packaged smaller pieces; all sizes are available on the bolt, although some shops may not carry all of them.

We have worked most of our designs on 8 1/2-mesh waste canvas with just a few on 10-mesh (noted with the color key). A higher number mesh will produce slightly smaller finished designs.

The canvas is basted on the front of the garment or fabric. Then the design is stitched with embroidery floss, the surface dampened, and the canvas threads removed.

Supplies

Six-strand cotton embroidery floss was used for all of our models. The Anchor, Coats and DMC numbers are given in each color key. Unless otherwise noted, we used 6 strands for cross stitches and 3 strands for backstitches on the 8 1/2 mesh waste canvas; on 10-mesh, we used 4 strands for cross stitches and 2 strands for backstitches. Experiment with your chosen mesh size and decide the number of strands which give the look you like. Use 18" lengths for all stitching; for better coverage, you may want to separate the strands then put them back together to thread the needle.

Because the finished work will be dampened when canvas threads are removed, it is wise to test dark floss colors for color fastness - especially the reds. Just stitch an inch or two of floss through a piece of white fabric, dampen it, and let dry. If there is any hint of dye coming from the floss, do not use it unless you pre-wash the floss to remove the excess color.

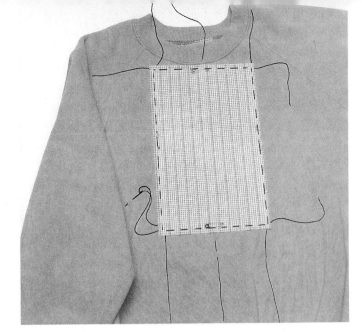

Waste canvas basted on fabric

Use a tapestry needle large enough to carry the number of strands with which you are stitching. A size 22 or even the smaller 24 can be used for six strands or less of floss. If you prefer to use a sharp needle, be careful not to pierce the canvas threads. A hoop will not be necessary as the waste canvas stabilizes the fabric.

You will need some extra supplies in addition to the usual embroidery scissors and thimble if you use one. Have on hand some shears (not good ones) for cutting the canvas, a sewing needle, thread, and pins. You will also need a spray bottle with water and tweezers after the design is stitched.

Preparation of Canvas and Fabric

To cross stitch on waste canvas, determine the finished size of the design on the chosen mesh (number of stitches divided by the mesh size equals the number of inches in width or height), then cut canvas two or more inches larger all around. If the canvas piece is large or the canvas feels coarse, tape the sides so threads and fabric do not snag on the rough edges.

Align the blue threads (horizontally or vertically) with the weave of the fabric and/or the seams of the garment. Pin the canvas over the center of the area where the design is to be stitched. You may even want to baste center lines on a large garment as a placement guide. Baste the waste canvas in place and remove pins. Usually a basting line around the edges is enough, but on a large design you may baste across the centers so the canvas does not shift. If canvas curls, turn it so the edges curve downward.

Note: A piece of cardboard or foam core board placed between the front and back of a garment keeps a good separation between the layers and provides a convenient work surface as you baste.

Waste canvas basted on fabric

Getting Started

Count the canvas threads, treating each pair as a single thread and stitch the design as you would on any evenweave fabric. Specific stitch instructions follow. Make sure to work the design centered (or in the desired position) on the garment. Start stitching at the top of the design and work downward. This way the needle comes up in an empty fabric hole and goes down in a fabric hole already occupied by a stitch.

There are several ways to secure the end of the floss when you begin. You can bring the threaded needle to the front and hold an inch or two of the tail end against the back and anchor it with your first few stitches, **Fig 1**.

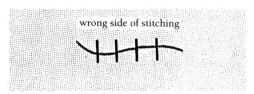

Fig 1

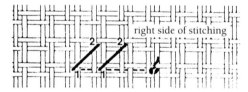

Fig 2

Or, you can make a knot on the front of the fabric about an inch away from where you intend to start and along the intended route, **Fig 2**; anchor the thread with your first few stitches and clip off the knot when you reach it. End threads and begin new ones by weaving through some stitches on the back.

Because garments are laundered frequently, you may wish to begin and end threads with a small knot for added security. Here's a neat way to make knots and keep the back tidy so thread ends do not catch when the item is worn. When beginning a thread, weave through some stitches on the back, then make a knot on the back and proceed to stitch. When ending threads, make your last stitch and end with a knot on the back, but do not cut the thread. Weave the thread end after the knot under some stitches on the back then clip the end. All the little tails will be secured.

The stab stitch method of pulling the thread completely through the fabric each time the needle goes in or out is the best way to work on waste canvas. The sewing method (in and out in one motion) can be used, but the canvas tends to shift out of position and the stitches are difficult to keep aligned.

Charted Designs

Each square on the chart represents one cross stitch. The symbol in each square represents the color to be used for that stitch. Backstitches are indicated with a straight line. The color key will specify the symbol and color used plus additional information.

The Stitches

The construction of cross stitches and backstitches on waste canvas is the same as for regular counted cross stitch. However, there are two ways to place the stitches and the choice is up to you. Practice to determine which one you like - just be consistent throughout the design. When canvas is removed, the method used should not be detectable.

Cross Stitch

Method A treats the larger waste canvas holes as if they were squares on evenweave fabric. The needle goes into and out of the small hole at the center of each intersection. To make a single cross stitch bring needle up at 1, down at 2, up at 3, and down at 4 (**Fig 3**). Follow this sequence for single stitches and all vertical rows of one color. For horizontal rows, work half of each stitch (1-2) from left to right across the row and complete each stitch on the return journey (3-4). Because the numbered spaces are exactly defined by the canvas intersections, your stitches will be right next to each other and share the same holes.

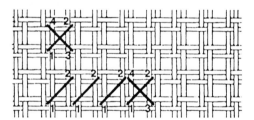

Fig 3—Method A

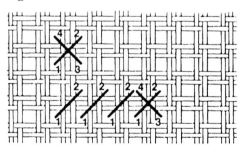

Fig 4—Method B

In Method B, make your stitches over the intersections with the thread traveling through the center of the larger canvas holes (**Fig 4**). This placement involves a bit of guesswork, but you'll get the feel of it shortly. The drawback is locating the center of that space so adjacent stitches share the same holes and keep their shape.

Backstitch

Work backstitches after cross stitches have been completed. Make sure to use the same method as you did for cross stitches. Backstitches can slope in any direction and are occasionally worked over more than one square.

Follow the numerical sequence in **Figs 5 and 6** to backstitch by Method A or B.

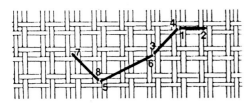

Fig 5—Method A

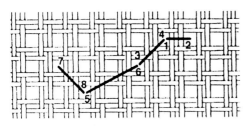

Fig 6—Method B

Removing waste canvas

Now comes a special fun part! Make sure your stitching is completed. Cut away the extra canvas, leaving about 1/2" all around the design.

Moisture Method

Dampen the right side with a spray or two of water and let it rest for a few minutes until the sizing softens. Use your tweezers to pull each of the canvas threads out. Pull them one at a time—resist the temptation to do more. Add moisture if needed and remove all canvas. Like magic...the finished design!

Place embroidery wrong side up over a dry towel. Steam lightly if desired, but be careful not to flatten the stitches by letting the iron rest on them.

Dry Method

For fabrics which are dry cleanable only, soften the canvas threads by rubbing (or scrunching) them together. It is then possible to remove the threads one by one without using water.

Glorious Gander

Design

42 wide x 53 high
Model worked with 8 1/2-mesh canvas on turquoise
    sweatshirt

Color Key

		DMC	Anchor
·	= white	blanc	2
×	= lt red	892	28
♥	= dk red	304	47
o	= med orange	722	323
☆	= dk orange	720	326
▫	= med blue	996	433
◉	= dk blue	824	164
◇	= lt gray	318	399
●	= dk gray	413	401
l	= Backstitch: dk gray		

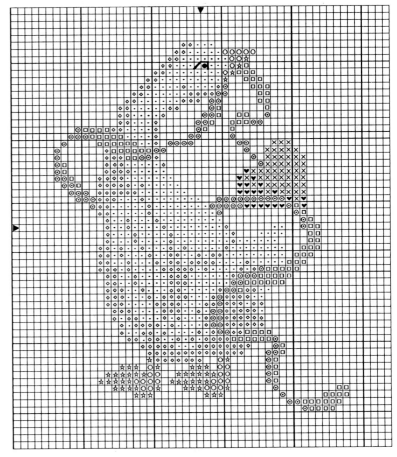

Tweetie Birds

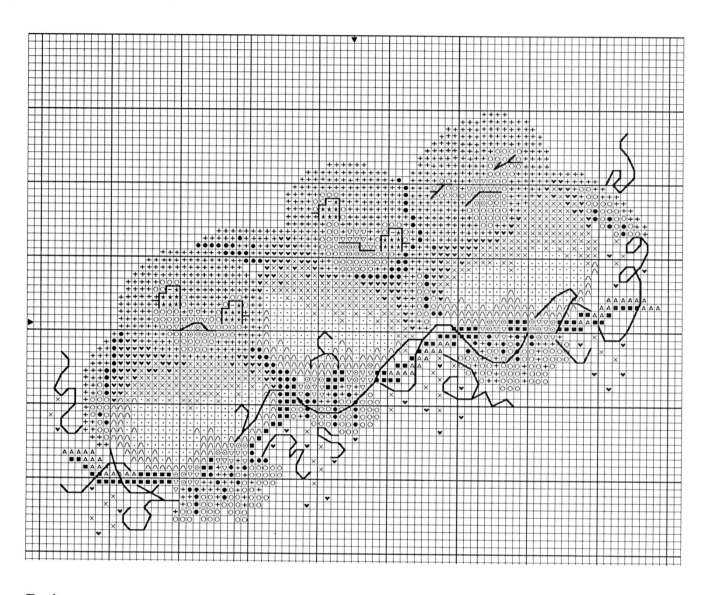

Design

88 wide x 58 high

Model worked with 8 1/2-mesh canvas on peach
sweatshirt

Color Key

		DMC	Anchor
-	= white	blanc	2
·	= lt cream	739	885
∧	= dk cream	437	362
×	= lt coral	352	10
♥	= dk coral	3705	35
▽	= lt gold	783	307
⊙	= dk gold	781	309
○	= lt blue	3325	159
+	= med blue	322	978
●	= dk blue	824	164
	green	703	238
▲	= lt brown	975	355
■	= dk brown	898	360
★	= black	310	403
I	= Backstitch: vines - green		
	beaks - dk brown		
	eyes - black		

Teddy with Chapeau

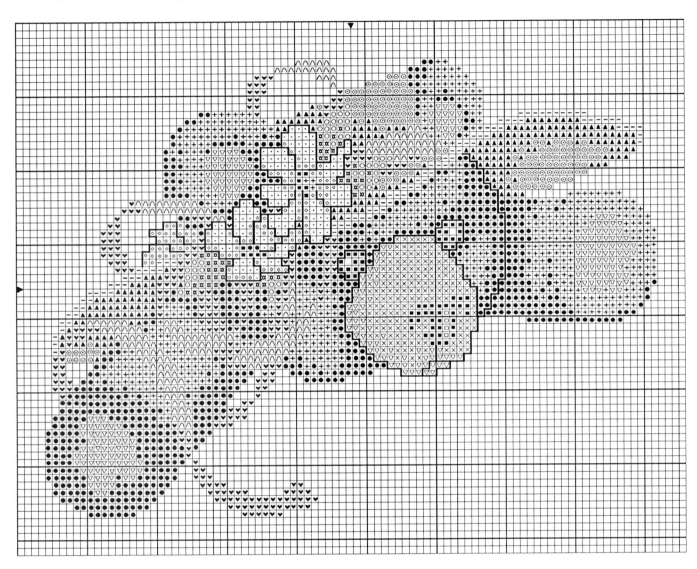

Design

88 wide x 62 high

Model worked with 10-mesh canvas on lt aqua
sweatshirt

Color Key

		DMC	Anchor
∧	= lt pink	894	26
♥	= dk pink	335	42
·	= lt yellow	444	291
○	= dk yellow	972	298
−	= lt gold	676	891
⊙	= med gold	680	901
▲	= dk gold	781	309
○	= lt green	562	210
✖	= dk green	986	246
×	= lt tan	758	868
∨	= dk tan	407	882
+	= med brown	920	339
●	= dk brown	300	352
▫	= gray	414	400
■	= black	310	403
❘	= Backstitch: face and muzzle - black		
	flowers - dk gold		

$\mathcal{ABC}$

Design

89 wide x 53 high
Model worked with 10-mesh
canvas on white sweatshirt

Color Key

		DMC	Anchor
·	= peach	353	8
⊙	= med pink	894	26
❤	= dk pink	961	76
o	= yellow	725	306
×	= blue	807	168
▫	= lt green	704	256
+	= dk green	988	243
▽	= lt brown	436	363
●	= dk brown	400	351
❙	= Backstitch: shirt - blue		
	blouse - dk green		
	mouths, faces, hair &		
	hat - dk brown		

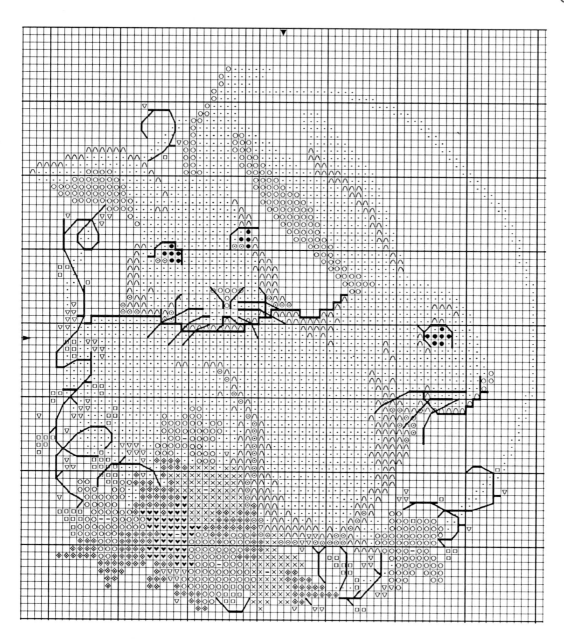

Wonderful Bunnies

Design

73 wide x 74 high
Model worked with 8 1/2-mesh canvas on lavender
sweatshirt

Color Key

		DMC	Anchor
·	= white	blanc	2
o	= lt pink	894	26
×	= med pink	892	28
❤	= dk pink	326	59
–	= yellow	742	303

		DMC	Anchor
▽	= blue	996	433
▫	= lt green	906	256
◆	= dk green	904	258
∧	= lt gray	318	399
⊙	= dk gray	317	400
●	= black	310	403
❙	= Backstitch: vines - lt green; eyelashes - black;
	body edges & whiskers - dk gray

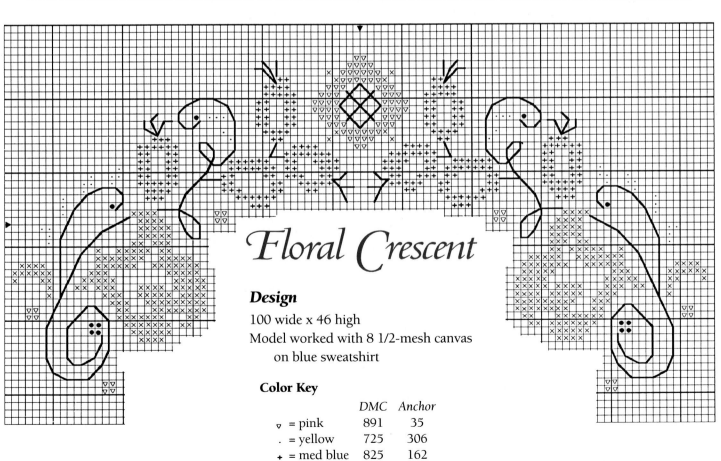

Floral Crescent

Design

100 wide x 46 high
Model worked with 8 1/2-mesh canvas
on blue sweatshirt

Color Key

		DMC	Anchor
▽	= pink	891	35
.	= yellow	725	306
+	= med blue	825	162
×	= green	3346	257
●	= brown	301	349
I	= Backstitch: brown		

Country Welcome

designed by Sam Hawkins

And a grrreat big country welcome to you! On hand to provide greetings is a gaggle of geese, cavorting among the delightful calico letters.

Design

158 wide x 51 high
Stitched on 14 ct Aida
Shown in a 15 1/4" x 7 1/4" wood frame

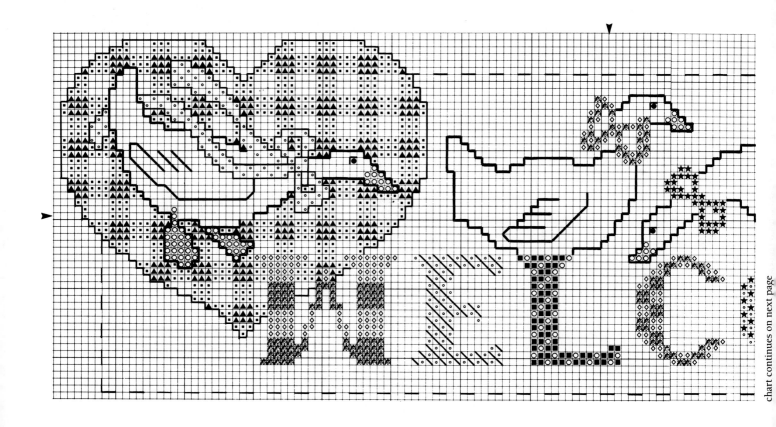

chart continues on next page

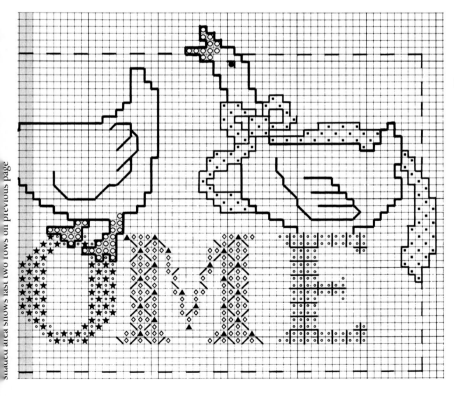

Color Key

		DMC	Anchor
∘	= pink	957	40
★	= dk red	326	59
○	= orange	3341	328
•	= lt blue	813	160
▲	= dk blue	517	169
◇	= lt green	913	209
✖	= dk green	988	243
■	= brown	301	349
●	= dk gray	844	401

| = Backstitch. outline of geese, eyes - dk gray
| = Backstitch: first "E", second "E", pink
        ribbon outline - dk red
        "M", heart outline, blue ribbon outline -
        dk blue
        running stitch border (each stitch 2
        squares long)- dk blue (3 strands)

Bread Cloths

designed by Sam Hawkins

What better way to dress up a dining table than with a pretty basket or bowl lined with a cross stitch cloth? The cloths keep bread, rolls and biscuits warm, and are a homey touch. We've given you several designs to suit any occasion. You can make your own cloth from an 18" square of 14-count evenweave fabric, or use the pre-made breadcovers you'll find at your local needlework shop.

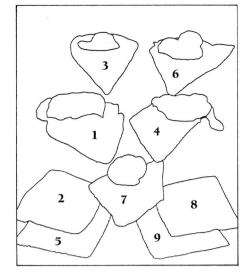

Summersweet Lilies

Design

67 wide x 64 high
Fabric is pink

Color Key

		DMC	Anchor	Coats
▫	= cream	746	386	1002
❖	= lt pink	604	75	3001
▨	= med pink	602	77	3063
	dk pink	600	59	3065
∿	= yellow	972	298	2298
◇	= lt green	472	264	6253
▣	= med green	3347	266	6256
▦	= dk green	701	227	6227
	brown	838	380	5360
	= Backstitch:			
	lilies—dk pink			
	stamens—brown			

Fringe

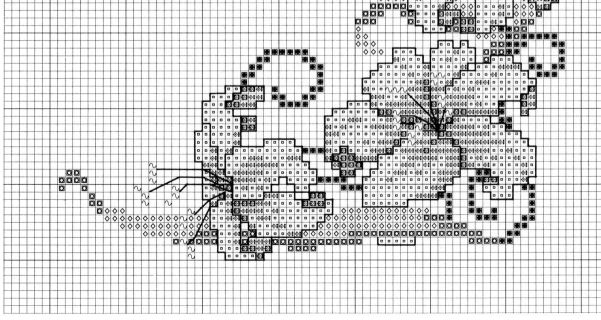

Fringe

135

Fringe

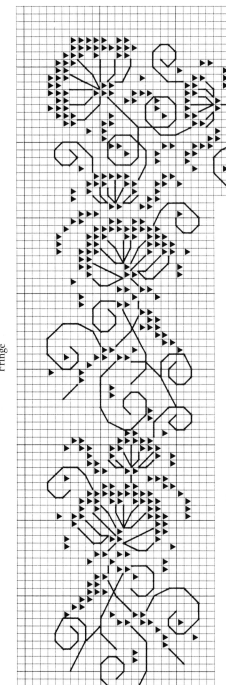

Fringe

Fantasy in Blue

Design

87 wide x 87 high

Fabric is white

Color Key

		DMC	Anchor	Coats
▶	= blue	798	137	7080
Ɩ	= Backstitch:			
	blue (2 strands)			

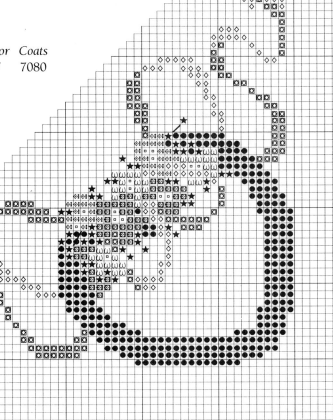

Fringe

Fringe

Heartstrings

Design

50 wide x 50 high

Fabric is lt blue

Color Key

		DMC	Anchor	Coats
●	= pink	957	50	3152
▫	= yellow	744	301	2296
★	= green	702	239	6226
◇	= lt blue	826	161	7180
⊡	= dk blue	824	164	7182
ω	= lt purple	210	104	4104
◈	= med purple	208	110	4101
⊠	= dk purple	550	102	4107
Ɩ	= Backstitch: green (2 strands)			

Butterflies in Flight

Design
63 wide x 63 high
Fabric is yellow

Color Key

		DMC	Anchor	Coats
▫	= lt orange	3341	328	2329
◻	= dk orange	350	11	2335
✷	= green	367	216	6018
◙	= rust	355	5968	3340
	purple	340	118	7110
◼	= brown	938	381	5477
●	= French Knots:			
	antennae—brown (2 strands)			
	flower buds—purple			
❘	= Backstitch:			
	tendrils—green			
	antennae—brown (2 strands)			
	bodies—brown			

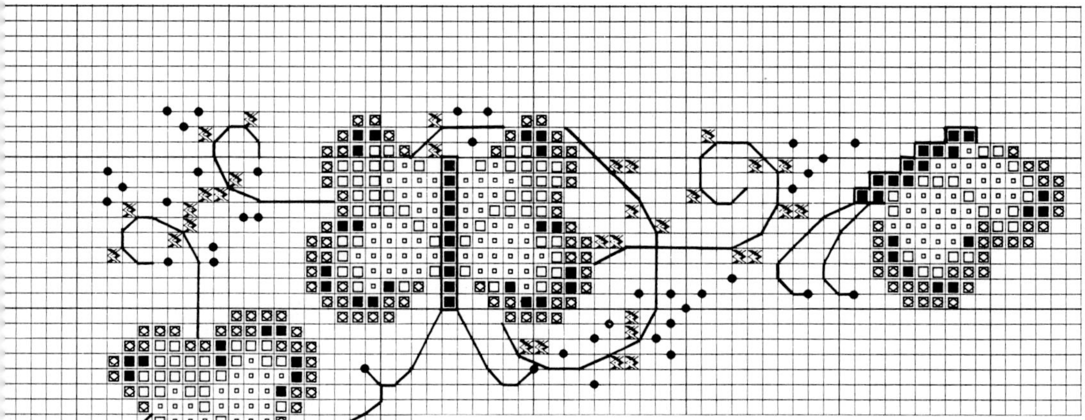

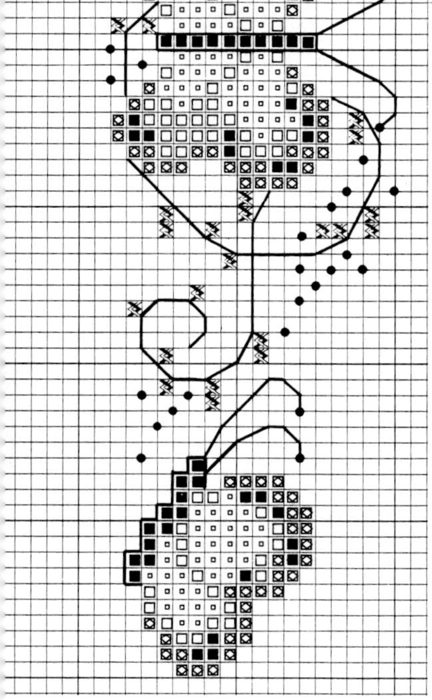

Strawberry Sunshine

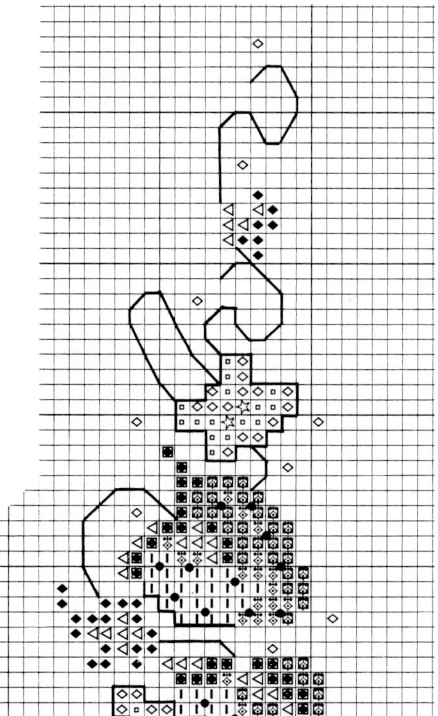

Color Key

		DMC	Anchor	Coats
▫	= white	blanc	2	1001
◇	= pink	3689	49	3086
❘	= lt red	894	26	3126
✸	= med red	891	35	3012
▣	= dk red	498	20	3072
☆	= yellow	743	297	2296
◁	= lt green	704	256	6238
◆	= med green	702	239	6226
◼	= dk green	910	228	6031
●	= French Knot: yellow			
❘	= Backstitch:			
	blossoms—pink			
	berries—med red			
	tendrils—dk green			

Design
65 wide x 65 high
Fabric is white

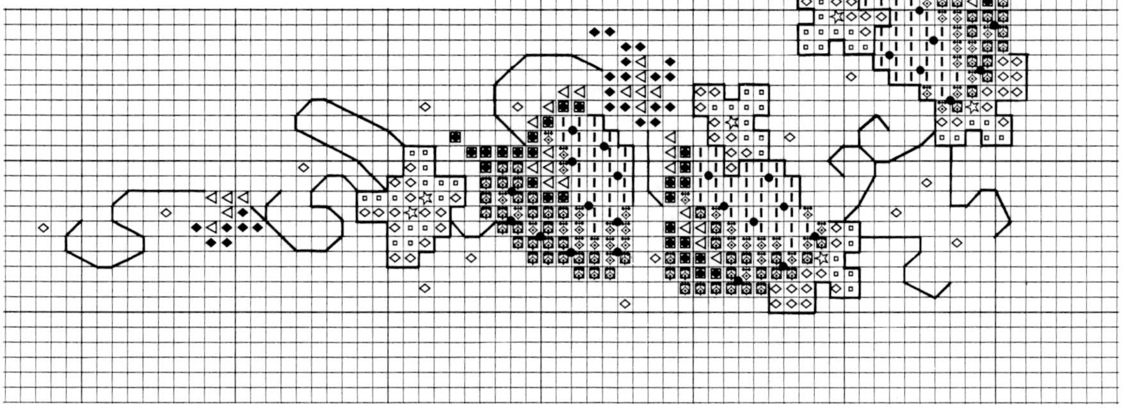

Fringe

Country Geese

Design

75 wide x 75 high
Fabric is med blue

Color Key

		DMC	Anchor	Coats
▫	= white	blanc	2	1001
❀	= lt pink	605	50	3151
	dk pink	603	76	3063
◇	= orange	3341	328	2329
○	= yellow	726	295	2294
◀	= green	3348	265	6266
+	= lt blue	827	159	7159
	med blue	826	161	7180
	dk blue	930	922	7052
■	= gray	431	401	5382

| = Backstitch:
     eye, bill, wing & feet—gray
     body—dk blue
     blue flowers—med blue
     pink flowers—dk pink

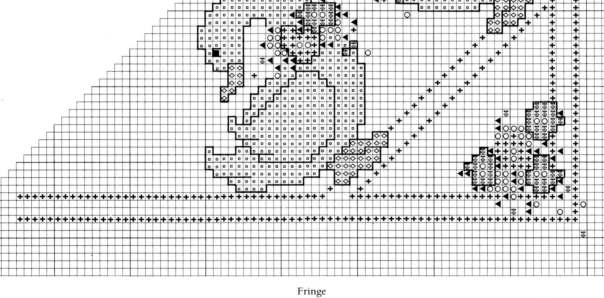

Fringe

Fringe

Elegant Floral

Design

91 wide x 91 high

Fabric is tan

Color Key

	DMC	Anchor	Coats
○ = med rose	3354	74	3003
⊕ = dk rose	3350	42	3004
− = lt orange	3341	328	2329
⊗ = med orange	351	11	3011
▫ = yellow	726	295	2294
☆ = gold	783	307	2308
⋈ = green	367	216	6018
△ = lt blue	3325	159	7976
★ = dk blue	322	978	7978
© = lt purple	210	104	4104
● = dk purple	208	110	4101
+ = med rust (initial)	356	5975	2326
◆ = dk rust	355	5968	3340
❘ = Backstitch: green			

Note: Choose desired initial from the alphabet on pages 140-141. Match placement symbols (•) on the letter and the circle to work the initial. This alphabet is not symmetrical so the symbols place the initial to be visually centered; alter the arrangement as desired.

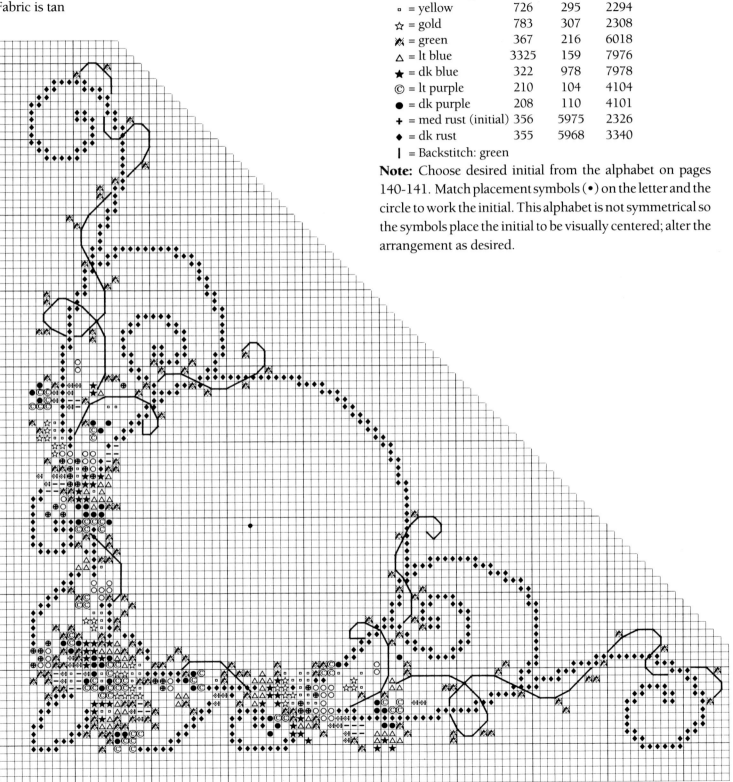

Fringe

139

Alphabet

Choose desired initial for the Elegant Floral design on page 139.

chart continues on next page

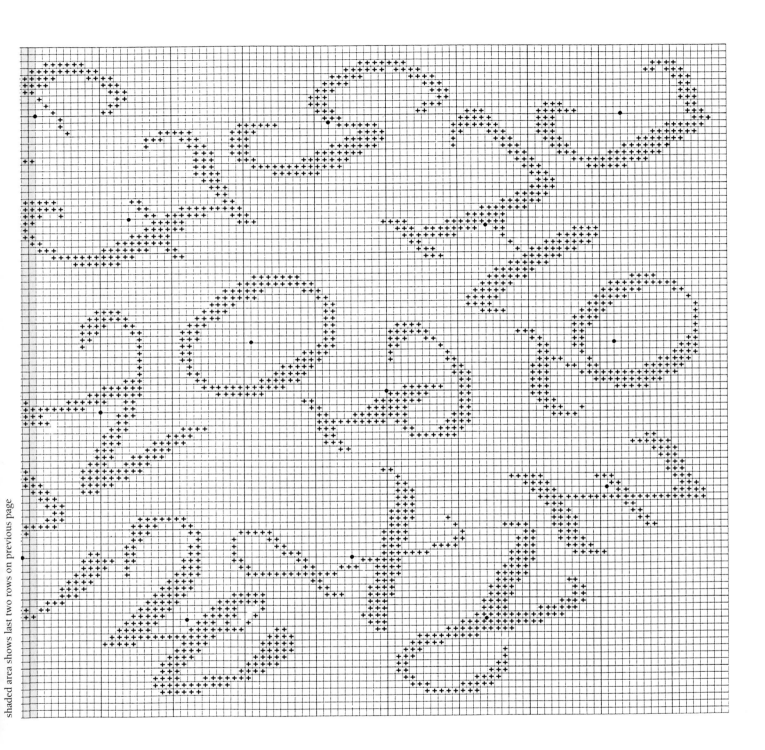

Fringe

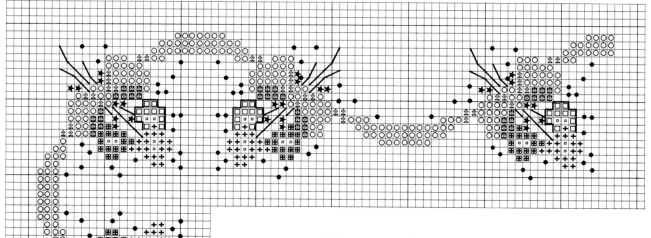

Fringe

Beribboned Bouquets

Design

76 wide x 78 high

Fabric is cream

Color Key

		DMC	Anchor	Coats
O	= lt pink	957	50	3152
❈	= med pink	956	40	3153
⊞	= dk pink	600	59	3065
▫	= yellow	726	295	2294
★	= green	910	228	6031
□	= lt blue	813	160	7161
+	= med blue	825	162	7181
⊞	= dk blue	791	941	7045
●	= French Knot: dk blue (2 strands)			
I	= Backstitch:			
	stems—green (2 strands)			
	blue flowers—med blue			

May Our Home Be Warm

Design

89 wide x 89 high

Fabric is pink

Color Key

		DMC	Anchor	Coats
●	= mauve	3687	69	3088
◁	= med green	989	242	6020
★	= dk green	987	244	6258
×	= lt blue	519	167	7167
+	= dk blue	517	169	7162
│	= Backstitch: dk green			

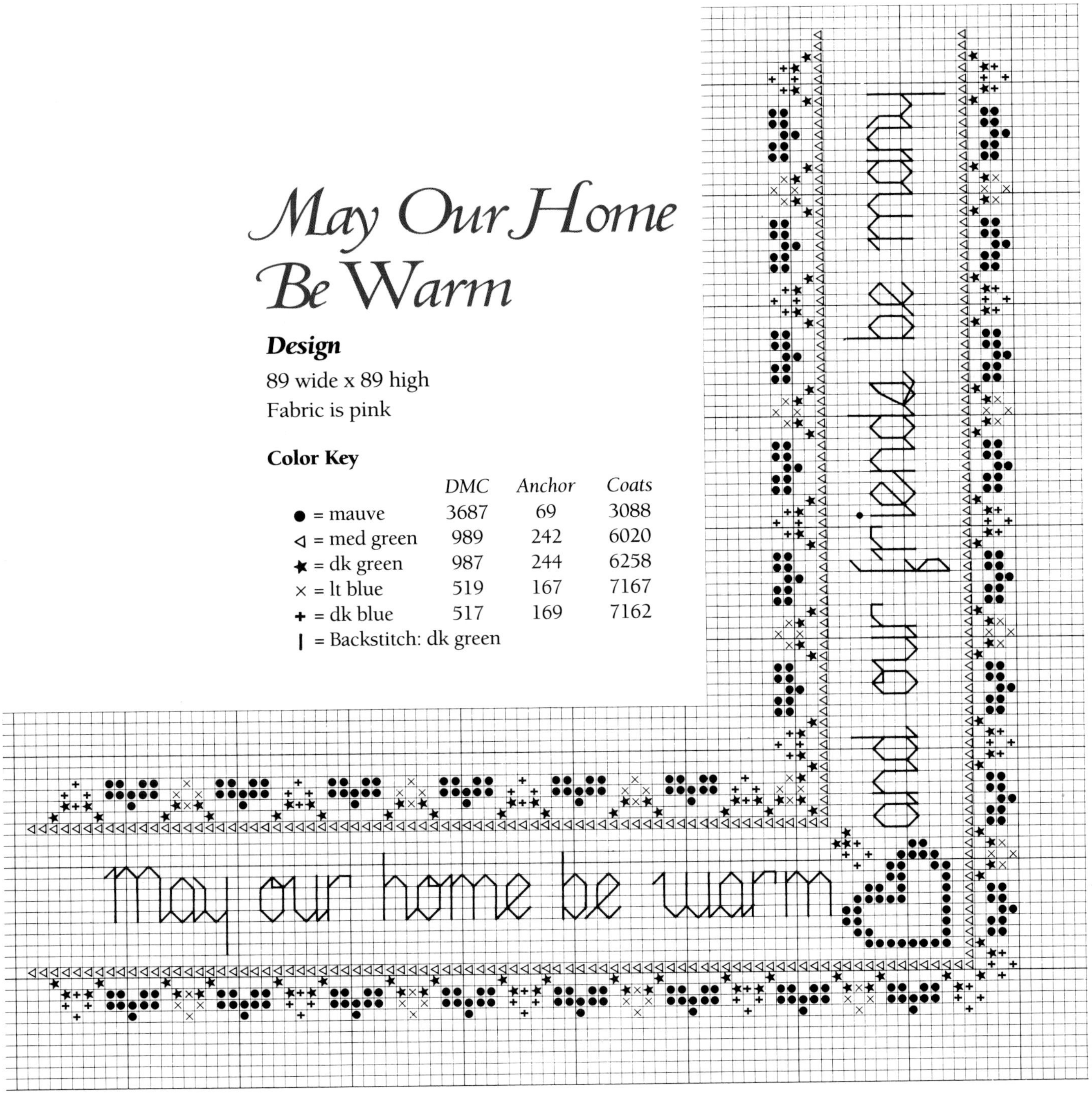

Fringe

Fringe

143

Country Trains Sampler

designed by Polly Carbonari

A train of old-fashioned cars winds through the countryside of a house, barn, cow, pig, fences and trees.

Design area

98 wide x 112 high
Stitched on 14-count lt blue Aida
Frame is 9" x 10"

Color Key

		DMC	Anchor
•	= white	blanc	2
ı	= pink	3708	26
✢	= dk pink	892	28
+	= red	349	13
✶	= dk red	347	19
○	= yellow	744	301
◁	= med blue	826	161
◆	= dk blue	311	149
♣	= green	989	242
✖	= brown	301	349
◇	= med gray	3022	8581
●	= dk gray	3021	382
■	= black	310	403

✳ = French Knots: train wheels and
    pig's eye - dk blue

ı = Backstitch: trains, trees, houses,
    fences, pig and cow - dk blue

Traffic Jam Session

designed by Anis Duncan

You can almost hear the wonderful zoom-zoom engine sounds a child will make while wrapping up in this fun-filled afghan. The bright colors and clever designs make it an imaginative playtime companion. The charming design motifs could be used as pictures, to decorate clothing, or other purposes. For hints on working on afghan fabric, see page 99.

Afghan Fabric

Hearthside, 14-count, Beige with Blue cross threads.
Layout has 6 squares in width x 5 squares in length plus
partial squares for fringing. Each square has 97 x 97
threads and measures approximately 7" x 7".

Instructions

Step 1: Place fabric on a flat surface. Refer to Layout Guide and make sure all sections needed for afghan design are complete.

Step 2: Mark top of fabric. Read the Special Hints for Afghans, page 99, for specific stitching information and floss recommendations. Each chart has 48 x 48 squares representing 96 x 96 fabric threads. Work each motif as positioned on the chart according to the Layout Guide and following the Color Key. Turn the chart (not the fabric) as needed so the base of each one is toward the center of the afghan.

Step 3: Trim selvages so fabric margins match on all sides. Use matching thread to zigzag over two threads just outside the outer woven border. Remove cross threads for fringe.

Layout Guide

			Fringe			
Traffic Signal	Tractor	Sailboat	Tow Truck	Dump Truck	Traffic Signal	
School Bus					Fire Engine	
Fringe / Tugboat					Tugboat	Fringe
Fire Engine					School Bus	
Traffic Signal	Dump Truck	Tow Truck	Sailboat	Tractor	Traffic Signal	
			Fringe			

48"

60"

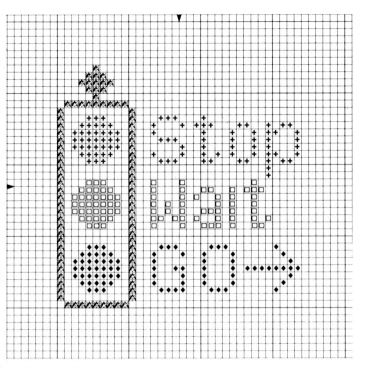

Traffic Signal design area: 34 wide x 34 high

Fire Engine design area: 32 wide x 22 high

Color Key

		DMC	Anchor
+	= red (6 skeins)	666	46
▲	= dk red	498	20
✣	= orange	608	333
□	= yellow (6 skeins)	741	304
◆	= green (2 skeins)	700	229
★	= blue (3 skeins)	798	131
✖	= gray (3 skeins)	414	400
■	= black (3 skeins)	310	403

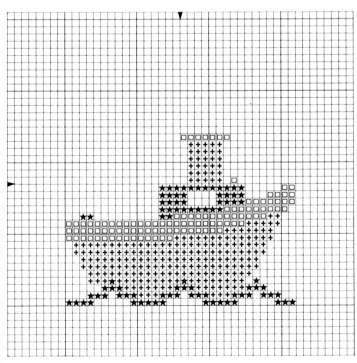

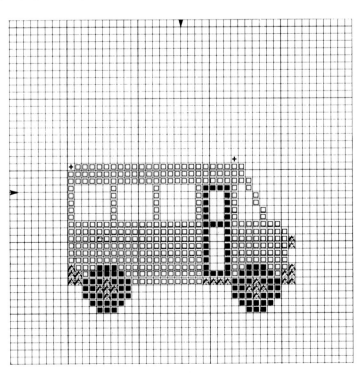

Tugboat design area: 32 wide x 24 high

School Bus design area: 32 wide x 22 high

147

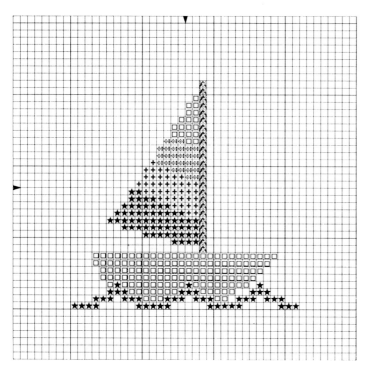

Sailboat design area: 32 wide x 32 high

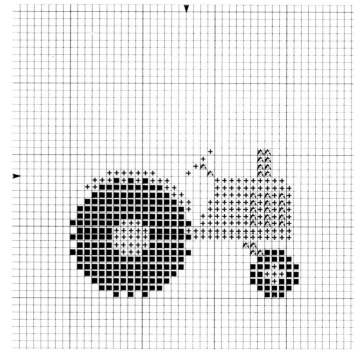

Tractor design area: 32 wide x 21 high

Color Key

	DMC	Anchor
+ = red (6 skeins)	666	46
▲ = dk red	498	20
⬧ = orange	608	333
□ = yellow (6 skeins)	741	304
◆ = green (2 skeins)	700	229
★ = blue (3 skeins)	798	131
✄ = gray (3 skeins)	414	400
■ = black (3 skeins)	310	403

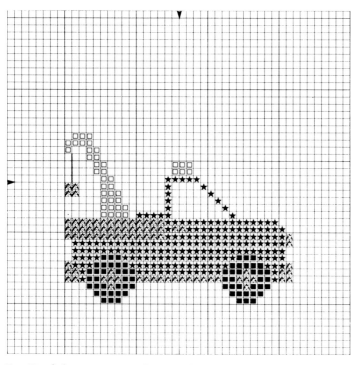

Tow Truck design area: 32 wide x 24 high

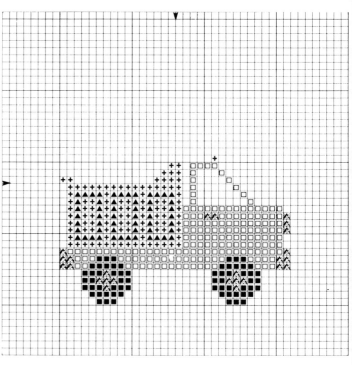

Dump Truck design area: 32 wide x 21 high

Plastic Canvas

Plastic Canvas

Needlepoint, traditionally worked on evenweave canvas fabric to create projects such as chair seats, pillows, and wall hangings, has been popular for centuries. But though the stitching is fun, the finishing of a needlework project requires blocking and extensive finishing, often best done by a professional.

When sheets of plastic grid, molded with evenly spaced holes, was introduced in the 1960s, it brought a new kind of magic to needlepoint stitching.

Plastic canvas is supple and easy to stitch, but strong enough to require no blocking and no difficult finishing. It is rigid enough to hold its shape, so it can be used for a wide variety of dimensional projects such as tissue box covers, door stops, baskets and even clocks.

Plastic canvas can be cut to shape easily with scissors, and the cut edges don't ravel. The most popular canvas, which works to seven stitches to the inch, has holes that are large enough to see easily, making it especially nice for senior citizens and children.

Plastic canvas projects are usually colorful and fun to stitch. They are wonderful gifts and sell well at craft fairs and bazaars.

The limits of what can be done with plastic canvas are set only by the imagination.

Types of Plastic Canvas

The canvas is available in several forms. Most commonly used are flat canvas sheets that come in several sizes; in clear or a variety of colors; and in four mesh sizes. Mesh simply means the number of stitches per inch.

The canvas consists of holes into which the threaded needle is inserted, and bars over which the stitches are made. Canvas called 7-mesh has 7 stitches, or bars, to the inch.

Most projects are made from clear canvas sold in sheets of about 10-1/2" x 1 3-1/2", and with 7 bars to the inch.

The canvas is also available in sheets of 11" x 14" with 10 bars to the inch. A project worked on 10-mesh canvas will be considerably smaller than the same project worked on on the larger 7-mesh canvas. **Fig 1** shows the same project worked on the two mesh sizes of canvas. 14-mesh canvas is also available.

7-mesh   10-mesh

Fig 1

Hint: Always be sure to use the mesh size canvas specified in your project instructions if the finished project must be a certain size (such as to fit over a tissue box).

Plastic canvas is manufactured by several different companies. Not all canvas is exactly the same, so be sure to use just one brand of canvas in a project, or the pieces may not fit together exactly.

The clear 7-mesh canvas comes in three weights: regular, extra stiff, and extra soft. The stiff canvas is ideal for projects needing added strength, while the soft canvas is best for pieces that must be curved or shaped.

Types and Sizes of Canvas

regular weight sheets: 10-1/2" x 13-1/2",
   12" x 18" and 13-1/2" x 21-1/2"
extra stiff sheets: 12" x 18"
extra soft sheets: 12" x 18"
specialty shapes: 12" x 18" oval (for placemats)
3" and 4" squares
3-1/2" x 4 1/2" diamonds
various sized circles
Other specialty shapes include butterflies, dimensional pieces, purse forms and precut alphabet and numbers. **Fig 2** shows some of the available forms of plastic canvas.

Fig 2

Colored canvas is bright and fun, and is often used in projects that leave some areas of canvas unstitched for a special effect. For instance, red and green canvas is frequently used for Christmas projects.

About the Yarn

Any yarn that covers the canvas well can be used. Experiment with different types of yarn to achieve the coverage and effect you desire.

Worsted Weight Yarn, available in many colors in both synthetic and wool fibers, is easy to work with and widely available. This yarn has a tendency to "pill," so it is not good for an item such as a tote bag that will get a lot of wear. One strand of worsted weight will cover 7-mesh canvas well. It is too heavy for use on 10-mesh.

Sport Weight Yarn is thinner than worsted weight, and not available in as many colors. One strand covers nicely on 10-mesh canvas, but you will need two strands for coverage on 7-mesh.

Rug Yarn works well on 7-mesh with one strand, but is much too heavy for 10-mesh canvas.

Craft Yarns come in a variety of types and finishes, and most work well on 7-mesh canvas.

Persian Type Yarn is a twisted wool 3-ply yarn used frequently in regular needlepoint. Its greatest advantage is the many lovely colors available, with many shadings within one color family. The plies can be divided so that you can use one or two plies on 10-mesh canvas; for 7-mesh, use three-ply strands. Experiment to see what gives the coverage you like.

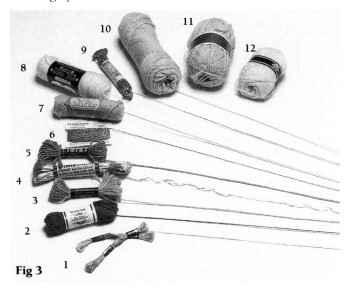

Fig 3

Sample of yarns suitable for plastic canvas:
1 cotton embroidery floss, **2** tapestry yarn, **3** acrylic Persian yarn, **4** rayon raffia, **5** nylon needlecraft yarn, **6** metallic needlepoint thread, **7** acrylic plastic canvas yarn, **8** acrylic sport weight yarn, **9** metallic plastic canvas cord, **10** and **11** worsted weight yarn, and **12** acrylic/wool blend sport weight yarn

Tapestry Yarn is another wool yarn used for regular needlepoint. One strand of tapestry yarn usually covers 10 mesh well; use two or three strands to give good coverage on 7-mesh.

Cotton Embroidery Floss comes in many colors, and is often used for detail work or overstitching. It is too thin to use in large areas on 7-mesh canvas, but on 10-mesh you can use it as desired, with three 6-strand pieces in the needle.

Specialty Yarns can give a unique look to a project. You can get wonderful effects using yarns such as angora, metallics, synthetic raffia, or narrow ribbon to accent certain projects. Experiment to get the look you like. There are also nylon yarns made especially for plastic canvas work.

Getting Started

Once you have chosen your project, read the instructions for making it.

Materials

First you'll find a list of materials, which tells you what size mesh plastic canvas you need and how many sheets; colors and yardage of yarn you will use; and any specialty trims such as beads, ribbon, etc. Materials lists usually do not include a tapestry needle or scissors–we assume you already know about those.

Pattern Charts

There usually is a pattern chart for each piece. The chart shows you the size and shape of the piece, how to stitch it, and with what color yarn.

Note that the chart is printed on a grid which looks like plastic canvas. This grid is not the exact size of your canvas. **Fig 3** shows a typical pattern chart.

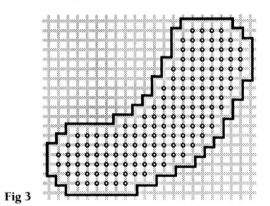

Fig 3

Front Leg 22 bars wide x 20 high

First, note that the size of the piece is given: bars wide by bars high. These are the outer dimensions of the piece. The actual piece is not an exact rectangle; the heavy outlines placed just outside the bars show the exact finished shape of the piece.

Now look for the Color Key (**Fig 4**). You will see a number of symbols on the left, followed by yarn color names and suggested stitch. The same symbols are on the chart, placed at the intersection of canvas bars where you will make a given stitch. If there are areas with no symbols on the chart, the color key will indicate what color is to be filled in, usually with a tent stitch (Continental or Half Cross).

Color Key

∘ = brown Continental

fill in white Continental

Fig 4

Cutting the Canvas

Cutting the canvas must be done very carefully; if you miscut, the piece is ruined and you'll have to cut another piece.

Cutting will be easier if you use a china marking pencil to draw the cutting outline on the canvas. This pencil will wipe off easily after cutting. For long straight edges, a ruler helps you draw more quickly.

Cut all the pieces for a project at one time before you start stitching.

Our charts show the shape of the pieces when they are cut out, making it easier to follow the cutting line. To cut, count bars, not holes. You may wish to cut the piece into a square or rectangle of the maximum width and length indicated on the chart, then stitch the piece; after stitching, do the final cutting. This method is especially good when the piece has a number of stairsteps or irregular edges, as it is easy to make a mistake when cutting these before stitching.

Cut the space between bars (**Fig 5**), rather than a bar. After cutting, you will need to trim off all of the plastic nubs that remain, using the smaller sharp scissors, or, in small hard to-reach areas, the craft knife.

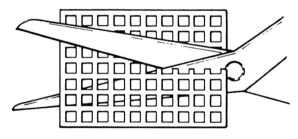

Fig 5

Trimming these nubs cleanly will make your work look much more finished. To make joining and overcasting of open edges neater, cut all corners carefully at a diagonal (**Fig 6**), being careful not to cut so closely that the corner is weakened. Clean the outline marks from the cut shape before stitching.

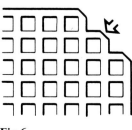

Fig 6

After you have cut out the pattern pieces, select the first piece you want to stitch. Look at the pattern chart for this piece. Generally you will start stitching at the top of a piece, and work across from right to left, or left to right; the next rows are worked consecutively below. Sometimes when there are isolated stitches of a color, there will be a bit of jumping around. Choose where to start, and from the color key, determine what color to use. Then thread the needle.

Threading the Needle

This may take practice, but will become an easy way to thread the tapestry needle (**Fig 7**). Fold yarn over needle (**A**). Pinch yarn fold tightly with thumb and first finger (**B**). Carefully slide needle out of fold and push pinched yarn into needle eye (**C**). When working with most synthetic yarn, use a 36" length for stitching. With some wool yarn it will be necessary to use 18" lengths to keep the yarn from fraying.

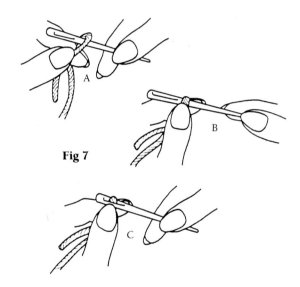

Fig 7

Beginning and Ending the Yarn

Hold cut piece in same position as the pattern is printed in the book. When beginning to stitch with a new strand of yarn, do not tie a knot (unless you are joining two pieces). Instead, bring needle up from underneath canvas, leaving an inch of yarn on the back. Hold end in place while making the first few stitches, working over the yarn end (**Fig 8**). If adjacent area is already stitched, you may run yarn through

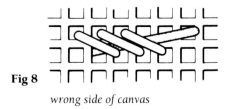

Fig 8

wrong side of canvas

back of stitched area to hold it. It is best to run yarn only through an area of the same color. When yarn strand is finished or color area is complete, turn canvas over and run yarn through back of a stitched area of the same color for about 1". Trim yarn close to work.

Stitching Hints:

When possible, work light-colored areas of a design first, leaving dark stitches for later. This keeps the lighter areas more free of "fuzz" from the dark colors.

Keep your stitch tension as even as possible, establishing a rhythm as you work. If you pull stitches too tightly, the yarn won't cover well; if stitches are too loose, they will not lie flat on the canvas, and will look unattractive.

As you stitch, the yarn in your needle will start to twist. To untwist, drop the needle and let the yarn untwist itself. Do this whenever needed.

The Stitches

Tent Stitch

Unless otherwise noted in special instructions for each project, the design area is worked in the tent stitch. This forms a flat, diagonal stitch on the front of the canvas (**Fig 9**). The tent stitch can be worked in one of two ways, each of which has an advantage.

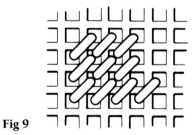

Fig 9

Method A– Continental Stitch

To work horizontal rows, bring needle up through canvas at odd numbers, down at even, as shown in **Fig 10**. First row is worked from right to left, next row from left to right.

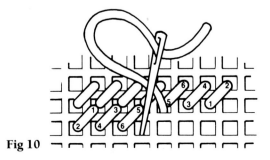

Fig 10

This method is slightly different than used in regular needlepoint, because our method is easier to understand and does not require turning the canvas upside down for alternate rows (this can make following a chart confusing). Vertical rows are used only when there is a long area of just one stitch in width. Vertical rows can be worked from bottom to top or top to bottom, depending on the design (**Fig 11**). Note the difference in the numbering depending on the direction.

Fig 11

Occasionally a design requires a Reverse Continental Stitch where the stitches slope in the opposite direction. To work horizontal rows (**Fig 12**), bring needle up through canvas at odd numbers, down at even numbers.

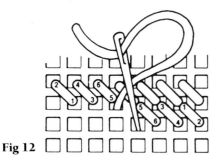

Fig 12

Advantage: Continental Stitch gives a padded back which is desirable for items such as placemats. It also makes the stitching appear a little fuller giving better coverage. Many of the projects that follow use the Continental Stitch.

Method B–Half Cross Stitch

To work horizontal rows, bring needle up at odd numbers, down at even, as in **Fig 13**. First row is worked from left to right, second row from right to

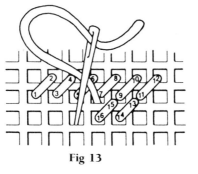

Fig 13

left. Again we have adapted the stitch so that work does not have to be turned upside down at the end of each row.

To work vertical rows, work as in **Fig 14**.

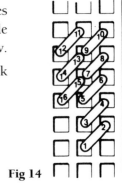

Fig 14

Occasionally a design requires a Reverse Half Cross Stitch where the stitches slope in the opposite direction. To work horizontal rows (**Fig 15**), bring needle up through canvas at odd numbers, down at even numbers.

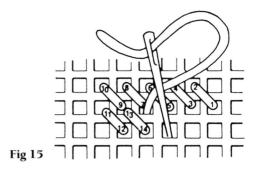

Fig 15

Advantage: Half Cross Stitch uses two-thirds as much yarn as Continental does to cover the same area. If you are making a large number of items, such as for a bazaar, this could be a significant cost saving factor. Yarn yardage listed allows for using the Continental Stitch.

Joining Pieces

When pieces are all stitched, it is time to join them. The most common way to join is with the Overcast Stitch.

Overcast Stitch

To join two straight edges, place pieces with wrong sides together (unless otherwise specified in individual project instructions). Anchor yarn firmly on the wrong side (it's okay to use a knot here). Start by taking two holding stitches through the first hole of the two pieces, then continue overcasting (**Fig 16**), going through holes of both pieces with each stitch. You can work

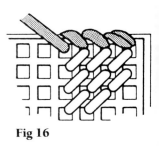

Fig 16

the stitch from left to right, right to left; top to bottom, or bottom to top, whichever works best for you.

For some projects you may need to join a diagonal edge to a straight edge; or a straight edge to a circle. The holes in the two pieces may not line up perfectly. In this case, just try to keep the pieces as even as possible and take extra stitches as needed to cover the edges.

> **Hint:** Take care not to pull yarn too tightly. There should be some "give" to the stitches or the canvas bars on the edge may break. To cover canvas well, you may need to put more than one stitch in each hole on the corners.

Finishing Unstitched Edges

When edges are not joined, they need to be finished, again using the Overcast Stitch. In this case, work through only one layer of canvas. This is easy on a straight edge. On a diagonal or uneven edge, take one stitch into an inside corner hole, and three stitches in an outside corner hole (**Fig 17**). You can take more stitches if needed for good coverage.

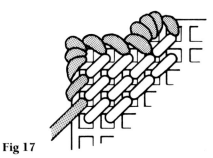
Fig 17

Backstitch

This is a straight stitch used for details and decoration, worked on top of an area of completed stitching (**Fig 18**). It is worked over one stitch in any direction. For some Backstitches we have used embroidery floss, specified in the materials list and color key. The placement of the Backstitches will be indicated on the charts.

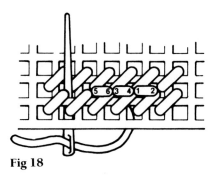
Fig 18

Braid Stitch

The Braid Stitch is a beautiful stitch that can be used instead of Overcasting for joining or finishing edges.

This stitch is more difficult to learn than Overcasting, but the beautiful, braided effect is well worth the effort. It can be worked easily along a straight edge and around a corner, but is more difficult for use on curved or uneven edges.

The stitch is always worked from left to right, with the right side of the stitched canvas facing you. Work as follows:

Step 1: Secure yarn in previous stitching (the stitch is shown on unstitched canvas for clarity), then bring needle up at **2**, over and around edge bar, then up at **1** (**Fig 19**).

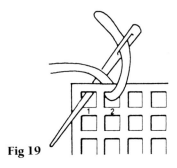
Fig 19

Step 2: Bring needle over and around edge bar, then up at 3 (**Fig 20**).

Step 3: Bring needle over and around edge bar, then up at 2 again (**Fig 21**).

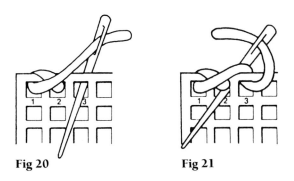
Fig 20   **Fig 21**

Step 4: Bring needle up in same manner two holes to the right (this will be an empty hole).

Step 5: Bring needle up in same manner one hole to the left (this will be a hole previously worked into).

Repeat Steps 4 and 5, advancing two holes, then going back one hole, for braided pattern.

To work corners, work to corner, then take two extra overcast stitches in corner. Turn corner and continue braid pattern. To use Braid Stitch for joining, work through both pieces with right sides facing out. Use a long piece of yarn so that you will not have to start a new piece often.

Door Stops

The rigidity of plastic canvas makes it ideal for constructing doorstops, those essential home decorating accents. Just when you think there isn't a single place left to put another needlework project, you can discover doorstops. Look at all those doors that need propping. Actually, these projects make terrific bookends, table decorations, or shelf sitters.

Grandfather Clock

Contented Cat

Clarabell Cow

Victorian Cottage

Victorian Cottage

designed by Cheryl Hofe

Complete with a front veranda, and lace curtains at the windows, you can make this charming period accent in any color to match your decor.

Material

three sheets 7-mesh plastic canvas
one 6mm gold bead
lace:
    three 1 1/2" x 2 1/2" pieces;
    one 1 1/2" x 1 1/2" piece
It blue ribbon or fabric:
    1 1/2" x 9"
worsted weight yarn:
    white   25 yds
    brown   25 yds
    blue   100 yds
    gray   40 yds
standard size brick or desired weight
tacky craft glue

Instructions

Step 1: Draw outlines and cut out four House and four House Roof pieces; six Porch and three Porch Roof pieces; four Railing pieces; and one Door, one Octagon Window, and one Base.

Step 2: Follow charts to stitch House Front (leaving shaded area unstitched), Sides, and Back; and Octagon Window. Match cutout section of Octagon Window to House Front; use white to overcast all Window edges to Front. Glue smallest lace piece behind Octagon Window opening and a matching piece of ribbon behind lace. Overcast windows and crossbars with white.

Step 3: Stitch all Porch pieces following charts. Using brown, join the following pieces: Porch Step Sides to Porch Step Front; then join Porch Step Top along unstitched row, overhanging Front and Sides by one Bar. See **Construction Diagram** at right. Attach step to Porch Front where indicated and overcast remaining edges of step. Join Porch Front to House Sides with brown.

Step 4: Using white, stitch all Railing pieces, then join each Front Railing to a Side Railing. See **Construction Diagram**. Set aside.

Step 5: Use matching yarn to overcast House Front to House Sides and Porch Floor to Front/Side unit along the unstitched

row. Stitch Door following chart and overcast inner edges of opening with blue. Clue lace with matching piece of ribbon behind it behind door opening. Join Door to House Front with white. Glue a piece of lace with a matching piece of ribbon behind each remaining window.

Step 6: Glue railings to Porch Floor over joining row.

Step 7: Use matching yarn to attach Base and House Back.

Step 8: Stitch all roof pieces following charts. Follow Construction Diagram to join Porch Roof pieces with gray; overcast edges with gray. Glue in place. Join House Roof pieces, using gray. Overcast with matching yarn. Place brick or desired weight into house, then glue roof in place. Glue on bead for door handle.

> **House Back 56 bars wide x 50 high**
> **(fill with blue Slanting Gobelin over 4 bars)**
> **Base 56 bars wide x 26 high (unstitched)**

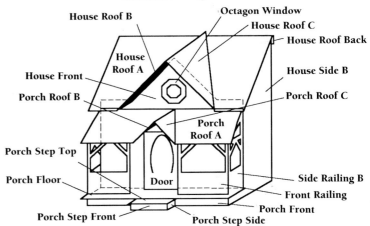

Construction Diagram

House Roof B — Octagon Window — House Roof C — House Roof Back — House Side B — Porch Roof C — House Front — House Roof A — Porch Roof B — Porch Roof A — Porch Step Top — Porch Floor — Door — Side Railing B — Front Railing — Porch Front — Porch Step Front — Porch Step Side

Color Key

☆ = white Continental
★ = white Reverse Continental
— = white Backstitch
    fill in blue Continental
♥ = brown Continental
🪶 = brown Slanting Gobelin
◇ = gray Continental
I = gray Brick Stitch
✕ = attach bead

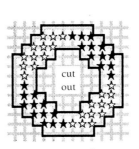

Octagon Window
12 bars wide x 12 high

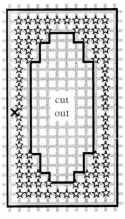

Door 12 bars wide x 21 high

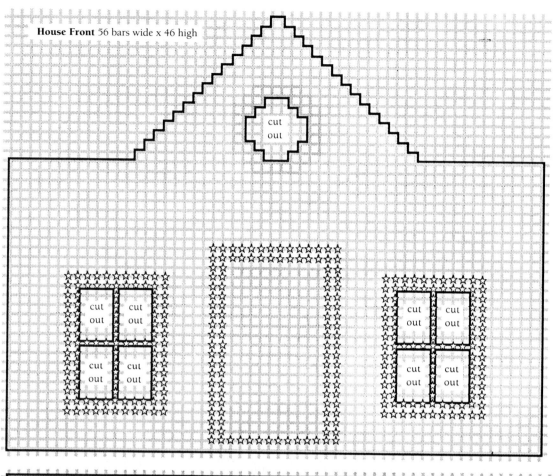

House Front 56 bars wide x 46 high

cut out

cut out

cut out

cut out

cut out

cut out

cut out

cut out

cut out

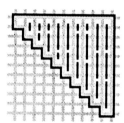

Porch Roof B
11 bars wide x 11 high

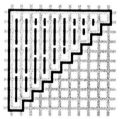

Porch Roof C 11 bars wide x 11 high

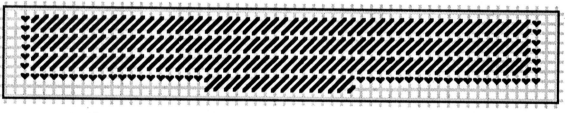

Porch Floor
58 bars wide x 10 high

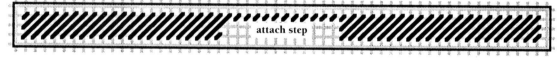

attach step

Porch Front 56 bars wide x 5 high

top peak

top peak

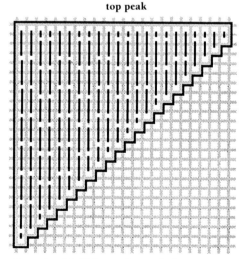

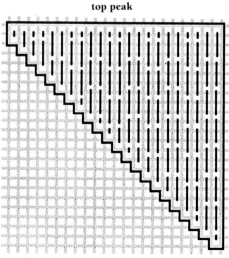

House Roof C 23 bars wide x 24 high

House Roof B 23 bars wide x 24 high

Color Key
☆ = white Continental
★ = white Reverse Continental
— = white Backstitch
fill in blue Continental
♥ = brown Continental
❚ = brown Slanting Gobelin
◇ = gray Continental
❘ = gray Brick Stitch
✕ = attach bead

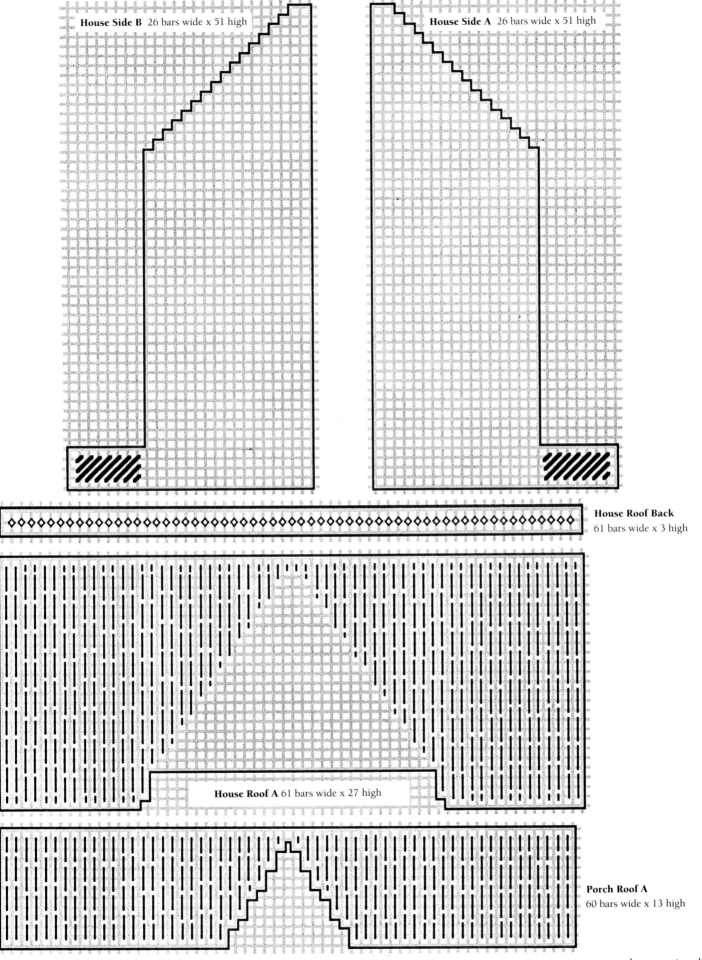

House Side B 26 bars wide x 51 high

House Side A 26 bars wide x 51 high

House Roof Back
61 bars wide x 3 high

House Roof A 61 bars wide x 27 high

Porch Roof A
60 bars wide x 13 high

charts continued

159

Color Key

- ☆ = white Continental
- ★ = white Reverse Continental
- — = white Backstitch
  fill in blue Continental
- ♥ = brown Continental
- ◢ = brown Slanting Gobelin
- ◇ = gray Continental
- | = gray Brick Stitch
- ✗ = attach bead

unstitched row

Porch Step Top
14 bars wide x 4 high

Porch Step Front
12 bars wide x 3 high

Porch Step Side
3 bars wide x 3 high
(make two)

**Cut Out
All
Small
Outlined
Areas**

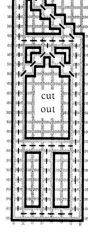

Side Railing A
8 bars wide x 26 high

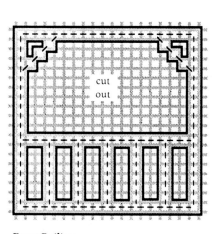

Front Railing
20 bars wide x 20 high (make two)

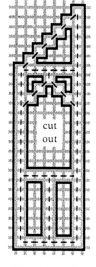

Side Railing B
8 bars wide x 26 high

Clarabell Cow

designed by Darla Fanton

Clarabell sports a real brass bell and an appealing face. She can double as a decoration for the breakfast table.

Materials

two sheets 7-mesh plastic canvas
1 yd 1/4"-wide leather thong
3/4" cowbell
standard size brick or desired weight
worsted weight yarn:

lt gray	2 yds	brown	1 yd
white	77 yds	black	65 yds
pink	1 yd	dk gray	2 yds
peach	5 yds		

Instructions

Step 1: Draw outlines and cut out one Front, one Back, one Head Front, one Head Back, one Side A, one Side B, and one Base.

Step 2: Stitch following charts, working Cross Stitches for the eyes, Continental Stitch for the remainder. Backstitch leg lines with lt gray. Backstitch tops of eyes with brown and eye highlights with white.

Step 3: To make tail, cut six 6" strands of white and six 20" strands of black. Center the group of white strands over midpoint of black strands. Bring ends of white strands together around black yarn and tie with a separate strand of white to form tassel. Bring the 12 black strands together and braid three groups of 4 strands for a length of 4". Tie ends in a knot. Working from the right side, insert 4 of the braid-end strands into each of the holes marked on Side B. Knot the ends on the wrong side to secure, and trim tassel to desired length.

Step 4: Join Side A to Front and Back with corresponding colors (see **Construction Diagram** on page 161). Join Side B to Front and Back with corresponding colors. **Note:** The top edge of the neck extensions on Front and Back should just meet.

Step 5: With right side of Head Back touching right side of Front neck extension, join along holes indicated using black yarn and stitching through Back neck extension, Front neck extension, and Head Back (three layers of canvas). With wrong sides together, join Head Front to Head Back with corresponding colors.

Step 6: Insert brick into body. Attach Base with white, being careful not to catch tail.

Step 7: Use leather thong to tie bell around neck.

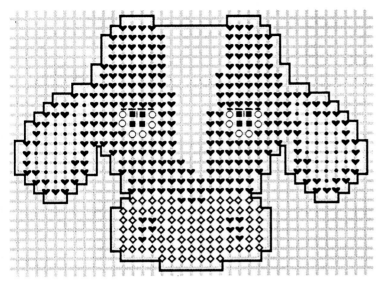

Head Front 37 bars wide x 27 high

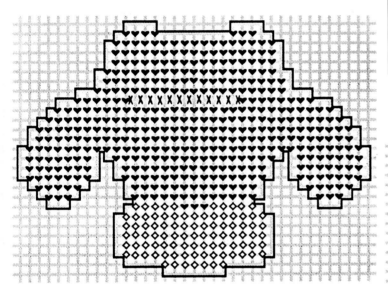

Head Back 37 bars wide x 27 high

Color Key

fill in white Continental
- − = white Backstitch
- • = pink Continental
- ◇ = peach Continental
- ▽ = lt gray Continental
- − = lt gray Backstitch
- ▲ = dk gray Continental
- ♥ = black Continental
- − = brown Backstitch
- ○ = brown Cross Stitch
- ■ = black Cross Stitch
- ⊙ = attach tail braid
- x = attach to peak

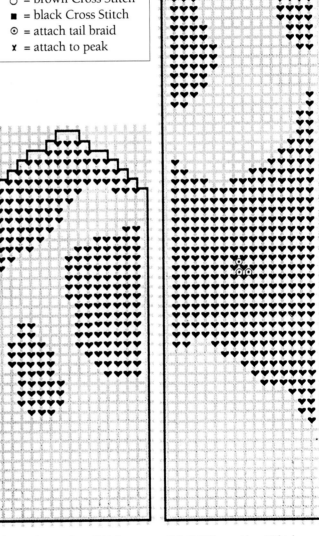

Side A 17 bars wide x 41 high   **Side B** 17 bars wide x 79 high

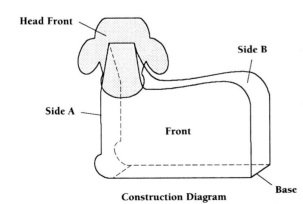

Construction Diagram

(labels: Head Front, Side B, Side A, Front, Base)

Base 57 bars wide x 17 high (fill in with white)

charts continued

161

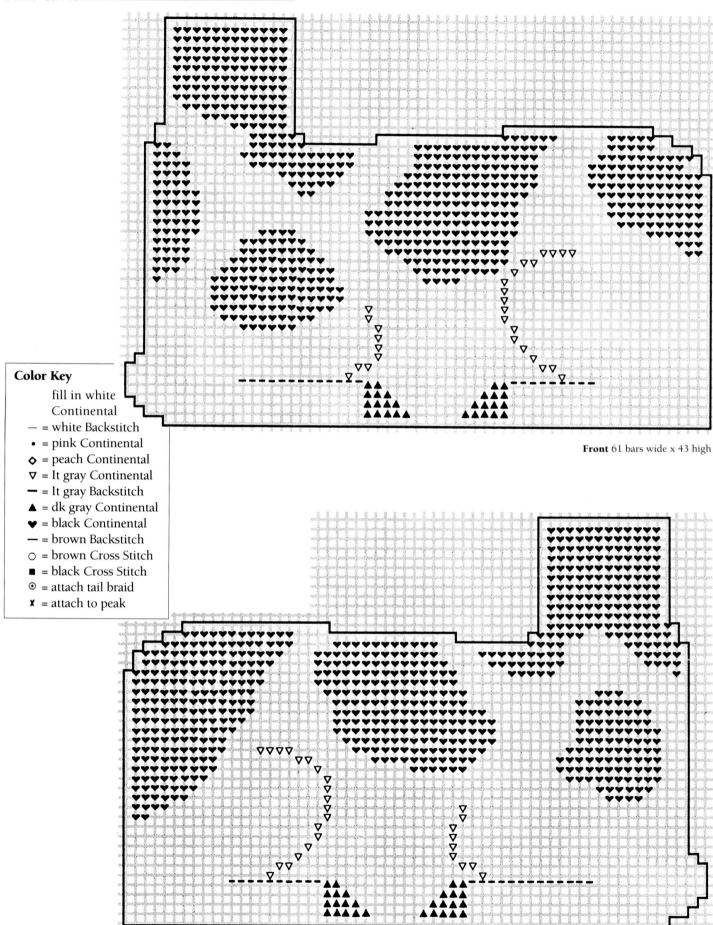

Color Key

fill in white
Continental
— = white Backstitch
• = pink Continental
◇ = peach Continental
▽ = lt gray Continental
— = lt gray Backstitch
▲ = dk gray Continental
♥ = black Continental
— = brown Backstitch
○ = brown Cross Stitch
■ = black Cross Stitch
⊙ = attach tail braid
✗ = attach to peak

Front 61 bars wide x 43 high

Back 61 bars wide x 43 high

Contented Cat

designed by Darla Fanton

Kitty is so cute you'll want to make her even if you don't have a door to stop! Use her as a shelf sitter or to hold down papers on a desk.

Materials

two sheets 7-mesh plastic canvas
one yard gray thread or monofilament
standard size brick or desired weight
worsted weight yarn:

white	5 yds	green	1 yd
pink	1 yd	lt gray	80 yds
dk pink	1 yd	dk gray	25 yds
red	4 yds	black	2 yds
dk red	1 yd		

Instructions

Step 1: Draw outlines and cut out one Front, one Back, one Tail, one Side A, one Side B, one Side C, one Side D, and one Base.

Step 2: Stitch following charts, working Cross Stitches for the nose and Continental Stitches for remainder. Backstitch mouth with dk pink. Backstitch eyes (**Fig 1**) with green, then black, and white for highlights.

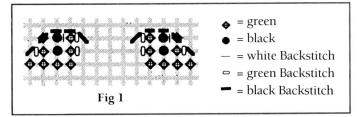

✦	= green
●	= black
—	= white Backstitch
◦	= green Backstitch
▬	= black Backstitch

Fig 1

Step 3: Overcast all edges of Tail with corresponding colors and set aside.

Step 4: Refer to **Construction Diagram** for assembly. Join the following pieces end-to-end to make the Side Strip: Side B to Side A with lt gray, Side C to Side B with lt gray, and Side D to Side C with red.

Step 5: Join Front to joined Side Strip using corresponding colors. Repeat to join Back and remaining edge of Side Strip.

Step 6: Attach Tail to Side D where indicated with dk gray.

Step 7: Bend tail around to front. Tack with monofilament to secure end to front; leave some slack so tail is not too close to body.

Step 8: Insert brick into body. Attach Base with lt gray, being careful not to catch tail in overcasting.

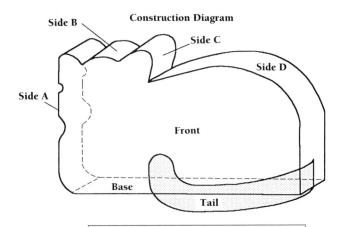

Construction Diagram

Side B · Side C · Side D · Side A · Front · Base · Tail

Base 56 bars wide x 17 high (fill in with lt gray)

Side D 17 bars wide x 61 high

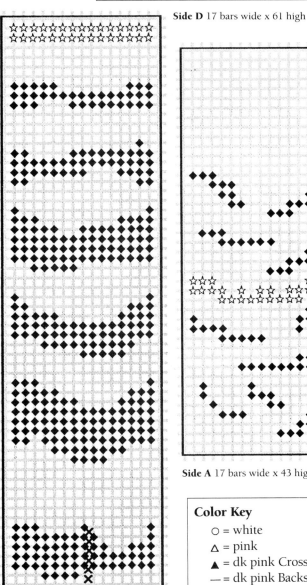

Side A 17 bars wide x 43 high

Color Key

○	= white
△	= pink
▲	= dk pink Cross Stitch
—	= dk pink Backstitch
☆	= red
★	= dk red
✦	= green
	fill in lt gray
◆	= dk gray
●	= black
—	= black Backstitch
✕	= attach tail

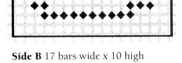

Side B 17 bars wide x 10 high

charts continued

163

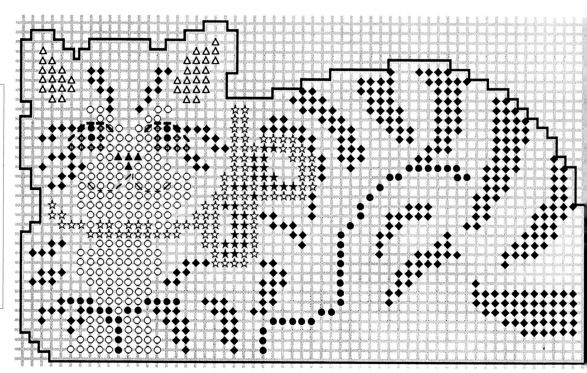

Color Key
- ○ = white
- △ = pink
- ▲ = dk pink Cross Stitch
- — = dk pink Backstitch
- ☆ = red
- ★ = dk red
- ◈ = green
    fill in lt gray
- ◆ = dk gray
- ● = black
- — = black Backstitch
- ✕ = attach tail

Front 59 bars wide x 36 high

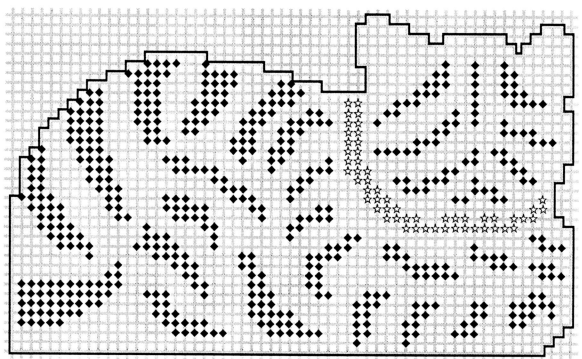

Back 59 bars wide x 36 high

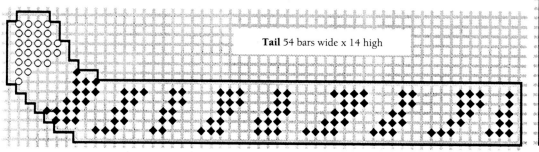

Tail 54 bars wide x 14 high

Side C 17 bars wide x 16 high

Grandfather Clock

designed by Wayne Fox

You really expect this doorstop to chime the hours, it looks so real! And like the song, may it stand 90 years on your floor.

Materials

two sheets 7-mesh plastic canvas
gold beads: two 5mm round, two 3mm round, two 3/4"
    spaghetti
gold chain, 1/8" or 1/4", one-quarter yard
invisible thread
tacky craft glue
worsted weight yarn:
    cream   5 yds
    med brown   80 yds
    dk brown   25 yds
embroidery floss, 6-strand: black
standard size brick or desired weight

Instructions

Step 1: Draw outlines and cut out one each Front, Front Trim, Back, and Base, and two each Sides, Side Trims, and Tops.

Step 2: Stitch following charts. Use 2 strands of yarn for all Upright Gobelin Stitches. On the Front, work the corners around the clock face as shown in **Fig 1**; backstitch the numerals and hands then work French Knots for remaining number positions. On the Front and Sides, leave the indicated areas unstitched.

Fig 1

Step 3: Use matching yarn to join top edge of Front Trim to the sixth bar from lower edge of Front. Repeat with Side Trims and Sides. See **Construction Diagram**. Attach each Side to the Front, joining Trim pieces at the same time.

Step 4: Cut a 3" and a 2" piece of chain. Insert invisible thread through one spaghetti bead, through smallest round bead, back through spaghetti bead, then tie ends onto end link of one chain. Repeat with matching beads and other chain. Tack opposite ends of chains to clock front. **Note:** If desired, chain ends can be glued in place after assembly is complete.

Step 5: Using med brown, join Back to Sides and Base to lower edge of entire unit. Overcast top edge of unit with dk brown.

Step 6: Glue round beads to front where indicated.

Step 7: With wrong sides together, join edges of Top A and Top B with dk brown. Insert brick and glue Top in place.

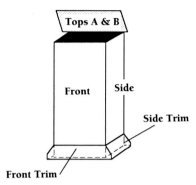

Construction Diagram

Top B 34 bars wide x 18 high
(work one outside row of dk brown Continental)
Base 19 bars wide x 34 high (unstitched)

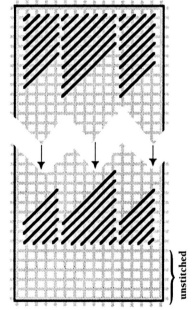

Side 16 bars wide x 67 high (make two)
(fill with med brown Slanting Gobelin Stitches)

Color Key

✓ = cream Continental Stitch
☆ = med brown Continental Stitch
✔ = med brown Upright or Slanting Gobelin Stitch
★ = dk brown Continental Stitch
● = dk brown Upright or Slanting Gobelin Stitch
— = black Backstitch
⊙ = black French Knot
✘ = attach bead

charts continued

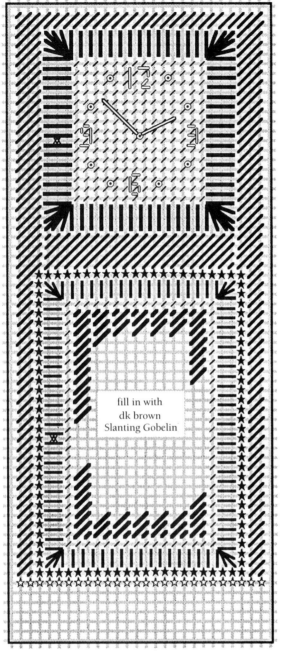

Front 28 bars wide x 67 high

fill in with
dk brown
Slanting Gobelin

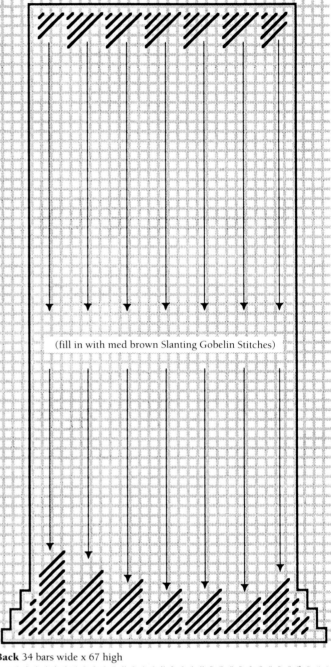

(fill in with med brown Slanting Gobelin Stitches)

Back 34 bars wide x 67 high

Left Trim 19 bars wide x 7 high

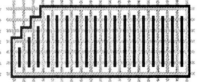

Right Trim 19 bars wide x 7 high

Front Trim 34 bars wide x 7 high

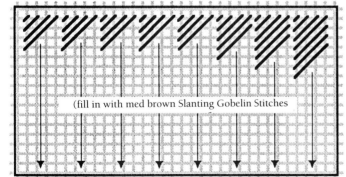

(fill in with med brown Slanting Gobelin Stitches)

Top A 34 bars wide x 18 high

Color Key

∕ = cream Continental Stitch

☆ = med brown Continental Stitch

● = med brown Upright or Slanting Gobelin Stitch

★ = dk brown Continental Stitch

● = dk brown Upright or Slanting Gobelin Stitch

━ = black Backstitch

⊙ = black French Knot

✖ = attach bead

166

Christmas Angels

designed by Carol Wilson Mansfield

Decorate your holiday home with choirs of angels from this selection of colorful designs. Each angel has a distinct personality. Some of them stand up, others are perfect for tree or package decorations, and six of them create a garland. You'll love our two skaters, with paper clips for their skate blades. These are great for gifts and Christmas bazaars.

Angel Garland

Materials

1 sheet 7-mesh plastic canvas

12 dark blue seed beads

navy sewing thread and needle

24" piece of 1/4" wide green ribbon

20 gold beads, 5mm

15 green beads, 8mm

worsted weight yarn:

cream	22 yds	lt green	6 yds
pink	11 yds	dk green	6 yds
red	3 yds	lt purple	10 yds
dk red	8 yds	dk purple	10 yds
peach	10 yds	brown	7 yds
rose	3 yds		

metallic yarn: gold, 11 yds

Optional: Small gold plastic musical instruments and tacky craft glue or hot glue.

Instructions

Step 1: Outline and cut out two Purple Angel, two Red Angel, and two Green Angel.

Step 2: Stitch following charts. Use two strands gold metallic. Hymnbook on Purple Angel is regular Straight Stitch, whereas halo and wing details with gold metallic on all Angels are worked over previous stitching after Step 3.

Step 3: For Purple Angel, overcast hair with brown, wing with cream, foot with peach, sleeve with pink, and robe with dk purple. For Red Angel, overcast hair with brown, wing with cream, foot with peach, and robe with red. For Green Angel, overcast hair with brown, wing with cream, foot with peach, sleeve with rose, and robe with lt green.

Step 4: Using two strands gold metallic, work Straight Stitches on wings and heads. For eyes, use navy thread and sew on seed beads.

Step 5: To construct Garland, alternate four gold beads and three green beads on a 6" piece of cream yarn. Tie to edge of hair of one Angel and top hem of robe on another Angel; trim yarn. Repeat four more times to connect all six Angels. Attach a 12" piece green ribbon to each end Angel for hanging. If desired, glue small decorations or bows on Angels.

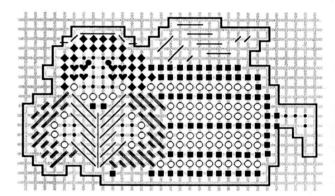

Purple Angel 31 bars wide x 18 high (make 2)

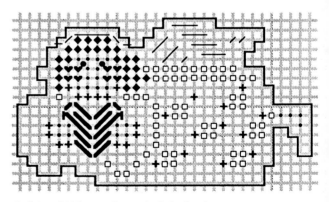

Red Angel 31 bars wide x 18 high (make 2)

168

Materials

1 sheet 7-mesh plastic canvas
2 blue seed beads
navy thread and sewing needle
12" piece of 1/2" pregathered cream lace
mini Christmas balls, 1/2" diameter
1 small white flower
mini natural basket, about 1" wide
tacky craft glue or hot glue
worsted weight yarn:

cream	17 yds
pink	8 yds
peach	3 yds
magenta	14 yds
purple	3 yds
dk purple	4 yds
dk brown	4 yds

metallic yarn: gold, 6 yds
Optional: 2 yds pink metallic thread

Home and Hearth

Instructions

Step 1: Outline and cut out Angel, Arms and Wing/Halo. Stitch following charts, except dk brown French knots. Use two strands pink on apron hearts. If desired, use one strand pink metallic to work over previous stitching of apron hearts and hem.

Step 2: Using navy thread, sew two blue seed beads for eyes.

Step 3: Overcast head with dk brown; stitch French Knots. Overcast right edge of Angel with magenta; Wing/Halo with two strands gold metallic; bottom edge of Angel and Arms with cream.

Step 4: Curve Angel skirt so center back overcast edge overlaps stitched area. Attach magenta yarn securely at top edge and stitch through both layers down to bottom, using small stitches over the overcasting. Using cream, tie Arms in place at shoulders. Tie top front corners of sleeves loosely together, leaving a 1/2" gap, and adding basket with balls and flower. To assemble Angel, see Step 5 of Angel Belle on page 172.

Color Key

fill in cream Continental
♥ = pink
✦ = pink Slanting Gobelin
◢ = red Slanting Gobelin
□ = dk red
• = peach
◣ = rose Continental and Reverse Continental
◇ = lt green
+ = dk green
○ = lt purple
■ = dk purple
◆ = brown
╱ = gold metallic Straight Stitch
● = seed bead

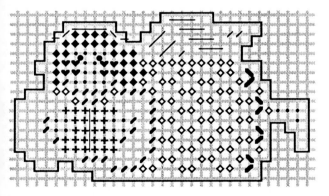

Green Angel 31 bars wide x 18 high (make 2)

charts continued

Color Key

fill in cream Continental
/ = cream Slanting Gobelin
♡ = pink
✎ = pink Slanting Gobelin
• = peach
▲ = magenta
⬗ = lt purple Slanting Gobelin
⧅ = dk purple Cross Stitch
◇ = dk brown
ж = dk brown French Knot
☆ = gold metallic
● = seed bead

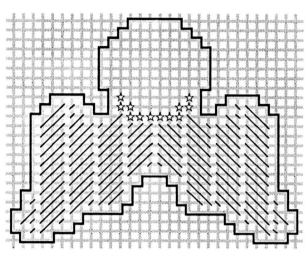

Wing/Halo 30 bars wide x 24 high

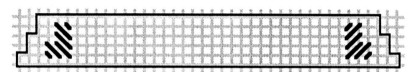

Arms 40 bars wide x 6 high

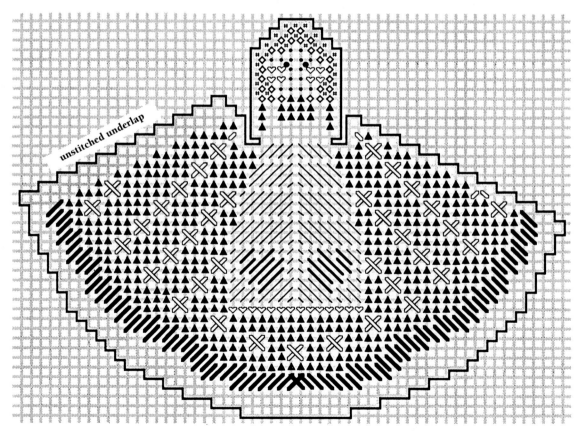

unstitched underlap

Angel 57 bars wide x 42 high

Rosebud

Materials

1 sheet 7-mesh plastic canvas
2 teal seed beads
navy thread and sewing needle
12" piece of 1/2" pregathered cream lace
sprig of holly
mini natural basket, about 1" wide
tacky craft glue or hot glue
worsted weight yarn:

cream	23 yds	gold	5 yds
pink	2 yds	dk green	3 yds
dk pink	3 yds	blue-green	11 yds
peach	2 yds	reddish-brown	2 yds

metallic yarn: gold, 6 yds

Color Key

    fill in cream Continental
/ = cream Straight Stitch and Slanting Gobelin
♡ = pink
✿ = dk pink French Knot
• = peach
╱ = gold Slanting Gobelin
◇ = blue-green
◢ = dk green Continental and Reverse Continental
■ = reddish-brown
● = seed bead

Instructions

Step 1: Outline and cut out Angel, Arms, and Wing/Halo. Stitch following charts. Work blue-green Continental first, then cream Straight Stitches. Make dk pink French Knots last.

Step 2: Using navy thread, sew two teal seed beads on face for eyes.

Step 3: Overcast head with reddish brown, Wing/Halo with two strands gold metallic, and Arms and Angel with cream, leaving underlap edge unstitched.

Step 4: Curve Angel skirt so center back overcast edge overlaps unstitched area. Attach cream yarn securely at top edge and stitch through both layers down to bottom, using small stitches over the overcasting. Using cream, tie Arms in place at shoulders. Tie top front corners of sleeves loosely together, leaving a 1/2" gap, adding basket with holly. To assemble Angel, see Step 5 of Angel Belle on page 172.

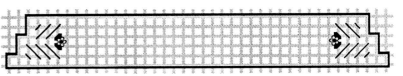

Arms 40 bars wide x 6 high

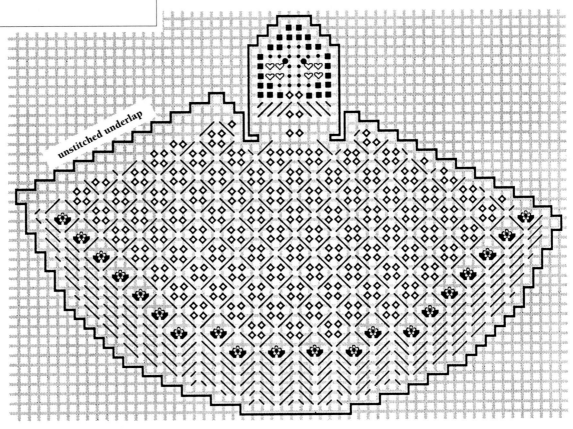

Angel 57 bars wide x 42 high

charts continued

Color Key

fill in cream Continental
/ = cream Straight Stitch and Slanting Gobelin
♡ = pink
🏵 = dk pink French Knot
• = peach
╱ = gold Slanting Gobelin
◇ = blue-green
🖌 = dk green Continental and Reverse Continental
■ = reddish-brown
● = seed bead

Wing/Halo 30 bars wide x 24 high

Angel Belle

Materials

1 sheet 7-mesh plastic canvas
2 blue seed beads; 34 red seed beads
10 gold beads, 3mm
34 gold star sequins; 5mm
navy and red thread and sewing needle
12" piece of 1/2" pregathered cream lace
tacky craft glue or hot glue
18" piece of l/4" green ribbon
l" gold-tone bell
worsted weight yarn:

cream	16 yds
pink	2 yds
red	10 yds

metallic yarn: gold, 6 yds

Instructions

Step 1: Outline and cut out Angel, Arms, and Wing/Halo. Stitch following charts, except gold metallic.

Step 2: Using navy thread, sew two blue seed beads on face for eyes. Using red thread, sew each gold bead as indicated on chart and sew a star sequin with a red seed bead in middle of each green circle on Angel and Arms. **Note:** If you prefer to glue beads and sequins, do so after Angel is assembled.

Step 3: Overcast head with gold, Arms with red, and Angel with cream, leaving underlap edge unstitched. Stitch Wing/Halo with two strands gold metallic and continue to overcast edges.

Step 4: Curve Angel skirt so overcast edge overlaps unstitched area. Attach cream yarn securely at top edge and stitch through both layers down to bottom, using small stitches over the overcasting. Using red, tie Arms in place at shoulders (see **Construction Diagram**). Tie top front corners of sleeves loosely together, leaving a 1/2" gap and adding bell. Tie a double bow with ribbon and glue at top of bell.

Step 5: Glue Wing/Halo to back of Angel over Arms, keeping center lower edge of Wing/Halo even with lower edge of Arms. Hold in place with pins or spring clothespin until dry. Glue lace inside bottom edge of Angel.

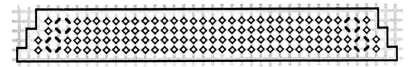

Arms 40 bars wide x 6 high

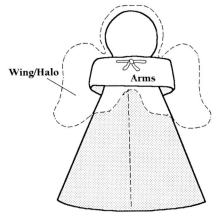

Construction Diagram

Wing/Halo 30 bars wide x 24 high

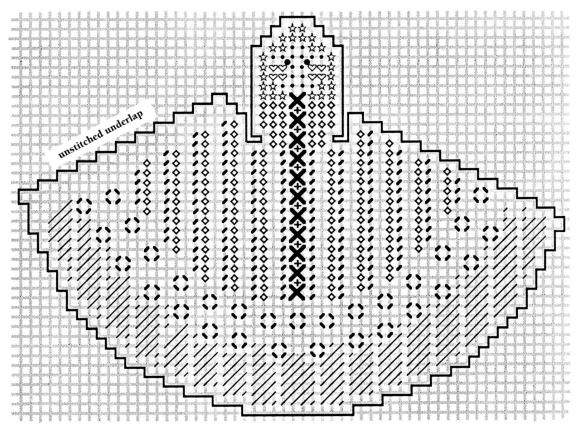

Angel 57 bars wide x 42 high

Heavenly Chimes

Materials

1/4 sheet 7-mesh plastic canvas
20mm wooden head
20mm wooden bead
1 jingle bell, 8mm
12" piece of 1/8" wide white ribbon
6" piece of 1/8" wide red ribbon
5" white curly chenille stem
4" gold metallic chenille stem
12" of 1/4" wide pregathered cream lace
2 spoked sequins, 5/8" diameter
tacky craft glue or hot glue
worsted weight yarn:

cream	12 yds
red	2 yds
gold	2 yds
green	2 yds
blue	3 yds

Optional: Heavenly Chimes can be changed by substituting a different color for the blue yarn. We used pink and lavender for our models.

Instructions

Step 1: Outline and cut out Front, Back, and Wing. Stitch following charts.

Step 2: Overcast Wing with cream. With wrong sides together, join Front and Back from A to B using cream; overcast all remaining edges. Join arms at ends.

Color Key
fill in cream Continental
♥ = red
◇ = gold
✎ = green Straight Stitch
○ = blue

Step 3: For hanger, knot ends of white ribbon together and glue in hole at top of head. For hair, curve curly chenille in a spiral around ribbon and glue to head. For halo, twist ends of gold metallic chenille together and glue on top of hair. Set head aside. Using cream yarn, go up through middle of skirt, out and around neck stem, and back down (**Fig 1**). String wooden bead onto yarn, then knot to secure bead as close to neck as possible. Tie jingle bell so half peeks out below skirt hem. Trim ends of yarn.

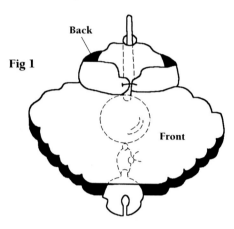

Fig 1

Step 4: Glue head to neck stem, Wing to back of angel, and sequins to hands. Glue lace along inside edge of skirt hem, starting at back. Tie red ribbon in a bow around neck; trim ends to desired length. Glue sequins to hands.

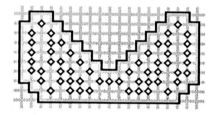

Wing 19 bars wide x 10 high

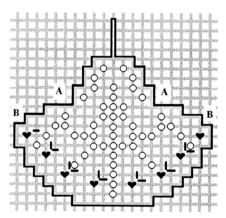

Front 21 bars wide x 20 high

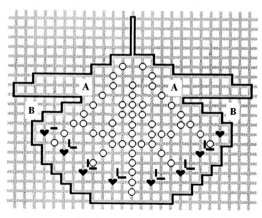

Back 25 bars wide x 20 high

Sonja and Dorothy– Skaters

Materials

1 sheet 7-mesh plastic canvas
4 indigo blue seed beads
navy thread and sewing needle
4 paper clips, 1 1/4" long
12" piece of 1/8" wide green ribbon
12" piece of 1/8" wide red ribbon
invisible thread for hangers
1 gold metallic chenille stem
tacky craft glue or hot glue
worsted weight yarn:

cream	10 yds	gold	8 yds
pink	4 yds	green	10 yds
red	2 yds	blue	8 yds
peach	4 yds	brown or tan	8 yds

Instructions

Step 1: Outline and cut out Sonja Front, Sonja Back, Dorothy Front, and Dorothy Back. Stitch following charts. With navy thread, sew on seed beads for eyes.

Step 2: With wrong sides together, join Fronts and Backs as follows:

Sonja: Join head with brown, wings with gold, hands with peach, and robe with blue.

Dorothy: Join hair with brown, face and hands with peach, cuff with red, wings with gold, and robe with green.

For both, join shoes with white, stitching in paper clips for skates at the same time (**Fig 1**).

Fig 1

Step 3: Cut 3 1/2" of chenille and twist ends together. Glue on head. For hanger, run a 12" length of invisible thread through top of head and knot ends together.

Sonja: Run green ribbon through a stitch under chin and make a bow. Trim to desired length.

Dorothy: Run red ribbon through edge at neck and make a bow. Trim to desired length.

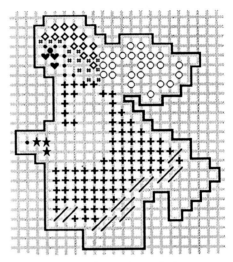

Dorothy Front 22 bars wide x 25 high

Color Key

fill in cream Continental

♥ = pink
★ = red
• = peach
○ = gold
+ = green
╱ = green Slanting Gobelin
▽ = blue
╱ = blue Slanting Gobelin
◇ = brown or tan
╫ = brown or tan French Knot
● = seed bead

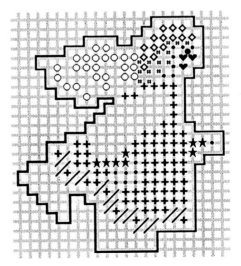

Dorothy Back 22 bars wide x 25 high

charts continued

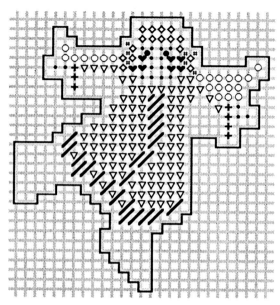

Sonja Front 27 bars wide x 29 high

Color Key
　　　fill in cream Continental
♥ = pink
★ = red
• = peach
○ = gold
+ = green
╱ = green Slanting Gobelin
▽ = blue
╱ = blue Slanting Gobelin
◇ = brown or tan
ⁿ = brown or tan French Knot
● = seed bead

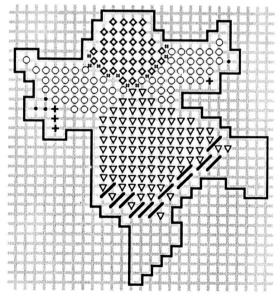

Sonja Back 27 bars wide x 29 high

Shooting Star

Materials

1 sheet 7-mesh plastic canvas
2 dk blue seed beads
navy thread and sewing needle
12" piece of 1/2" pregathered cream lace
1 yd piece of 1/4" wide green ribbon
8 gold star sequins, 1/2" diameter
tacky craft glue or hot glue
worsted weight yarn:

cream	27 yds	
pink	2 yds	
red	11 yds	
peach	2 yds	
brown	4 yds	

metallic yarn: gold, 9 yds

Instructions

Step 1: Outline and cut out Angel, Arms, and Wing/Halo. Stitch following charts. Stitch gold metallic in Wing/Halo last, using two strands.

Step 2: Using navy thread, sew two dk blue seed beads on face for eyes.

Step 3: Overcast halo only with two strands gold metallic; the rest of Wing/Halo with cream. Overcast head with dk brown and Arms and Angel with cream, leaving underlap edge unstitched.

Step 4: Curve Angel skirt so center back overcast edge overlaps unstitched area. Attach cream yarn at top edge and stitch through both layers down to bottom, using small stitches over the overcasting. Using cream, tie Arms in place at shoulders. Tie top front corners of sleeves loosely together, leaving a 1/2" gap. Make desired bow with ribbon and glue sequins to ends of streamers. To assemble Angel, see Step 5 of Angel Belle, on page 172.

Color Key

fill in cream Continental
- ♡ = pink
- ⁄ = red Continental and Mosiac
- • = peach
- ◊ = brown
- ⁄ = gold metallic Continental and Slanting Gobelin
- ● = seed bead

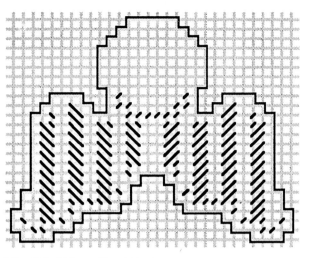

Wing/Halo 30 bars wide x 24 high

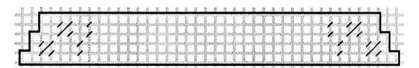

Arms 40 bars wide x 6 high

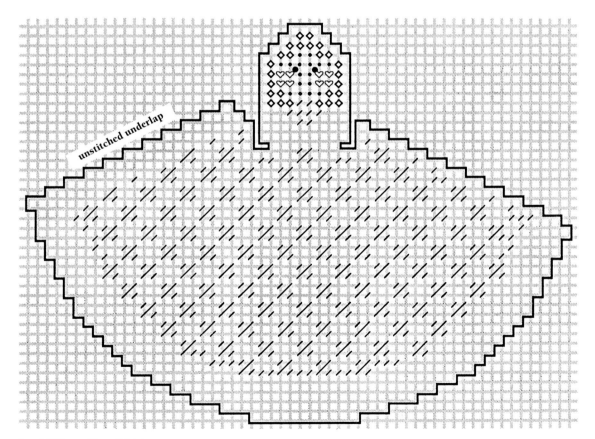

Angel 57 bars wide x 42 high

Country Quilt Basket

designed by Carol Wilson Mansfield

This is an easy-to-make basket designed to hold dried flowers. A pair would be nice on a dining table; change the color to fit your own decor.

Materials

one sheet 7-mesh plastic canvas
worsted weight yarn:

cream	24 yds
color (pink, blue or lavender)	20 yds

Instructions

Step 1: Draw outline and cut out one Handle and Upper Side, two Lower Sides, two Front/Backs and one Base piece. Stitch following charts, using Continental Stitch and Pattern Stitch (**Fig 1**). When stitching Handle, continue by turning piece over and working second side same as first side.

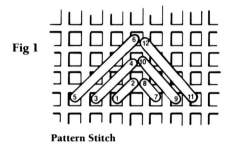

Fig 1

Pattern Stitch

Step 2: Join with cream overcasting; first add Lower Side pieces to Handle and Upper Side piece. Then join Front, Back and Sides as in **Construction Diagram**. The Base piece (unstitched) can be added last.

Step 3: Overcast top edge of finished basket and handle edges with cream.

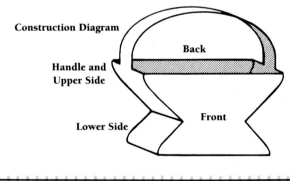

Construction Diagram

Back

Handle and Upper Side

Lower Side

Front

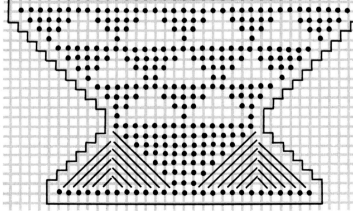

Front/Back 37 bars wide x 22 high (make two)

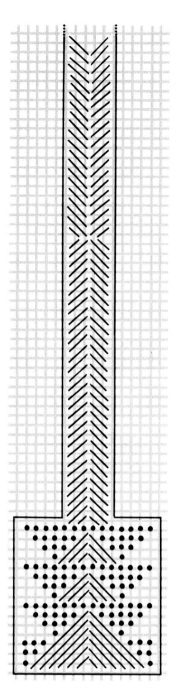

Handle & Upper Side 16 bars wide x 91 high

Color Key

fill in cream
/ = cream Pattern Stitch
• = color

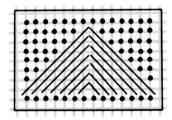

Lower Side
16 bars wide x 11 high (make two)

Base 16 bars wide x 29 high (unstitched)

179

Boutique Tissue Box Cover

designed by Carly Poggemeyer

Here's a pretty dress-up for that plain old box of tissues. The decorative stitch is easy to do, and the color shadings are subtle. For a bolder look, stitch it in just two strongly contrasting colors.

Materials

1 1/2 sheets 7-mesh plastic canvas
worsted weight yarn:

rose	13 yds
green	12 yds
blue	13 yds
beige	47 yds

Instructions

Step 1: Draw outlines and cut out Top and four Sides.

Step 2: Stitch following charts. Using beige, overcast cut out area of Top.

Step 3: Use beige and refer to **Construction Diagram** to assemble Tissue Box Cover. Join top edge of each Side to top. Join side edges of Sides; then overcast bottom edges.

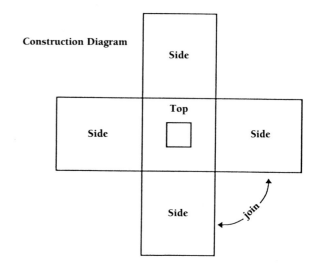

Construction Diagram

Color Key

- ╱ = rose Slanting Gobelin
- ╱ = green Slanting Gobelin
- ╱╱ = blue Slanting Gobelin
- ╱ = beige Slanting Gobelin

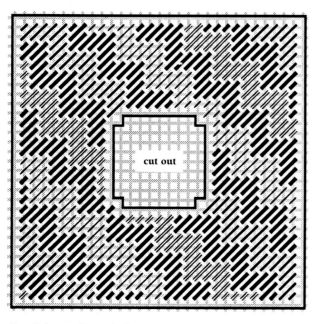

cut out

Top 31 bars wide x 31 high

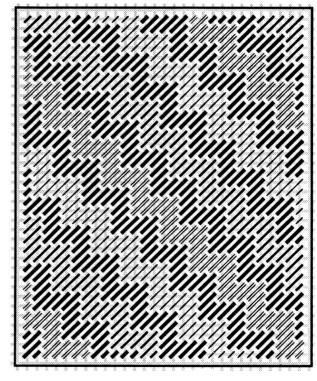

Side 31 bars wide x 38 high (make 4)

Mug Mats

These quick to stitch coasters are fun to make and to give. They are the perfect little gift that is both cute and practical, and are great projects for craft fairs and bazaars.

Coming of Age
designed by Carol Wilson Mansfield

Materials

1/4 sheet 7-mesh plastic canvas
red embroidery floss
worsted weight yarn:

white	23 yds
orange	5 yds
blue-green	6 yds
purple	4 yds

Instructions

Draw outline and cut out Mat. Stitch following chart, selecting desired inset. Work Backstitches and French Knots last over previous stitching. Overcast Mat with white.

Mat 32 bars wide x 32 high

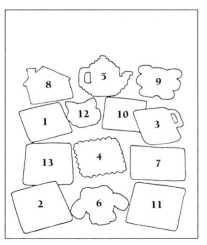

Inset

Color Key

       fill in white Continental
/ = red Backstitch (six strands floss)
★ = orange
♯ = orange French Knot
♥ = blue-green
/ = blue-green Backstitch
☆ = purple

Inset

Wake Up

designed by Carol Wilson Mansfield

Materials

1/4 sheet 7-mesh plastic canvas
black embroidery floss
worsted weight yarn:

white	6 yds	lt blue	10 yds
red	3 yds	dk blue	2 yds
orange	2 yds	black	3 yds
gold	2 yds		

Color Key

fill in white Continental
- ♥ = red
- ╱ = red Backstitch
- ♡ = orange
- ☆ = gold
- ∘ = lt blue
- • = dk blue
- ● = black
- ╱ = black Backstitch (six strands floss)

Instructions

Draw outline and cut out Mat. Stitch following chart. Work Backstitches last, over previous stitching. Overcast Mat with lt blue.

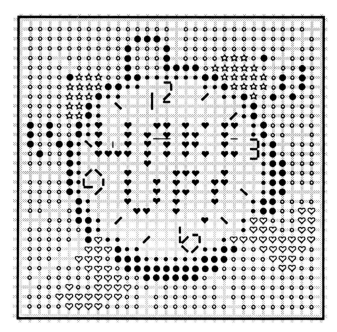

Mat 32 bars wide x 32 high

Coffee Break

designed by Meredith Montross

Materials

1/4 sheet 7-mesh plastic canvas
worsted weight yarn:

white	15 yds
red	4 yds
blue	4 yds
beige	2 yds

Instructions

Draw outline and cut out Coffee Cup. Stitch following chart. Work Backstitches last, over previous stitching. Overcast Coffee Cup with red.

Color Key

fill in white Continental
- ╱ = red Mosaic
- ╱ = blue Backstitch
- ♡ = beige

cut out outlined area

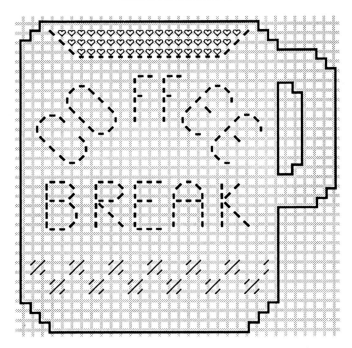

Coffee Cup 33 bars wide x 33 high

184

Sip n' Stitch

designed by Bobbie Matela

Materials

1/4 sheet 7-mesh plastic canvas
worsted weight yarn:

white	12 yds
peach	4 yds
yellow	2 yds
blue-green	8 yds

Instructions

Draw outline and cut out Mat. Stitch
following chart. Work Backstitches and
French Knots last, over previous stitching. Overcast Mat with blue-green.

Color Key

fill in white Continental
☆ = peach
o = yellow
✐ = blue-green Backstitch
= blue-green French Knot

Mat 32 bars wide x 32 high

Tea 4 Me

designed by Ann Harnden

Materials

1/4 sheet 7-mesh plastic canvas
worsted weight yarn:

white	17 yds
red	2 yds
blue	3 yds

Instructions

Draw outline and cut out Teapot. Stitch
following chart. Work Backstitches last,
over previous stitching. Overcast Teapot
with white.

Color Key

fill in white Continental
✐ = red Backstitch
♥ = blue

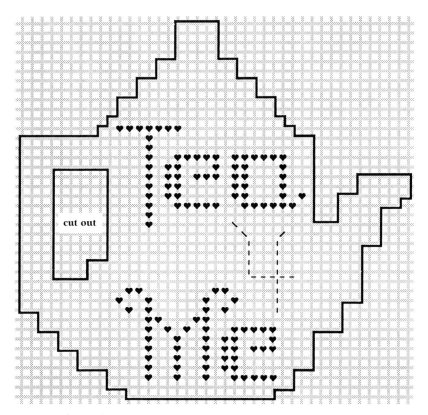

Teapot 41 bars wide x 40 high

185

Good Moo-ning

designed by Darla J. Fanton

Materials

1/4 sheet 7-mesh plastic canvas
worsted weight yarn:

white	2 yds
pink	2 yds
peach	3 yds
brown	2 yds
black	9 yds

Color Key	
	fill in with white Continental
⁄ =	white Backstitch
☆ =	pink
♡ =	peach
✖ =	brown Cross Stitch
⁄ =	brown Backstitch
• =	black
✕ =	black Cross Stitch

Instructions

Draw outline and cut out Cow. Stitch following chart. Work Backstitches last, over previous stitching. Overcast Cow with white, peach, and black to match previous stitching.

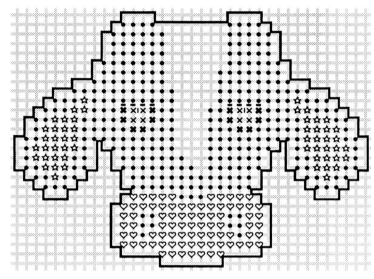

Cow 37 bars wide x 27 high

Antique Car

designed by Sam Hawkins

Materials

1/4 sheet 7-mesh plastic canvas
black embroidery floss
worsted weight yarn:

lt pink	4 yds
med pink	3 yds
dk pink	2 yds
lt gold	2 yds
dk gold	2 yds
lt blue	12 yds
black	3 yds

Color Key	
	fill in with lt blue Continental
○ =	lt pink
♡ =	med pink
♥ =	dk pink
◆ =	lt gold
◇ =	dk gold
★ =	black
⁄ =	black Backstitch (six strands floss)

Instructions

Draw outline and cut out Car. Stitch following chart. Work Backstitches last, over previous stitching. Overcast Car with lt blue.

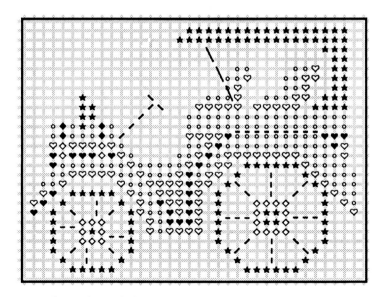

Car 36 bars wide x 28 high

Home Sweet Home

designed by Carol Wilson Mansfield

Materials

1/4 sheet 7-mesh plastic canvas

worsted weight yarn:

white	6 yds	med blue	3 yds
red	3 yds	dk blue	3 yds
green	3 yds	very dk blue	3 yds
lt blue	10 yds	tan	2 yds

Instructions

Draw outline and cut out House. Stitch following chart. Work Backstitches last, over previous stitching. Overcast House with red for chimney, tan for chimney top and steps, very dk blue for roof, and lt blue for remaining edges.

Color Key

fill in dk blue Continental	/ =	lt blue Slanting Gobelin
☆ = white		
✐ = white Backstitch	♥ =	med blue
♡ = red	◆ =	med blue Backstitch
// = green Upright Gobelin (two strands yarn)	▲ =	very dk blue
	★ =	tan

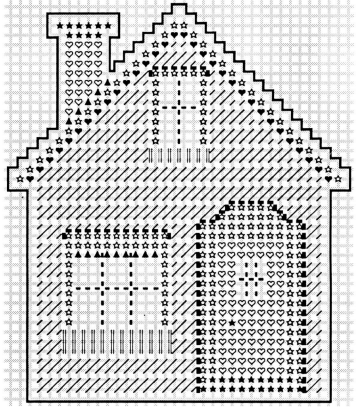

Home 36 bars wide x 42 high

Bear with Me

designed by Carly Poggemeyer

Materials

1/4 sheet 7-mesh plastic canvas

worsted weight yarn:

white	2 yds	blue	2 yds
pink	3 yds	lt brown	10 yds
lt red	4 yds	dk brown	4 yds
med red	3 yds	black	2 yds

Instructions

Draw outline and cut out Bear. Stitch following chart. Work Backstitches last, over previous stitching. Overcast ribbon with lt red, ribbon knot with med red, and remaining edges with dk brown.

Color Key

fill in lt brown Continental	★ =	med red
◇ = white	• =	blue
ı = white Backstitch	◆ =	dk brown
♡ = pink	♥ =	black
☆ = lt red		

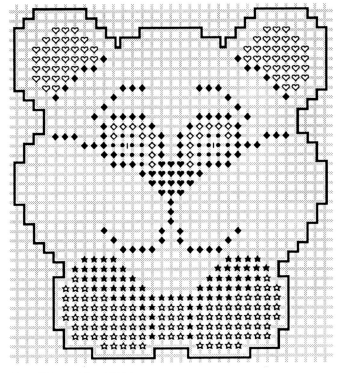

Bear 33 bars wide x 37 high

187

Bingo Card

designed by Meredith Montross

Materials

1/4 sheet 7-mesh plastic canvas
worsted weight yarn:

white	20 yds
red	7 yds
blue	5 yds

Instructions

Draw outline and cut out Bingo Card. Stitch following chart. Work Backstitches last, over previous stitching. Overcast Bingo Card with white.

Color Key
fill in white Continental
✔ = red Backstitch
╱ = blue Backstitch

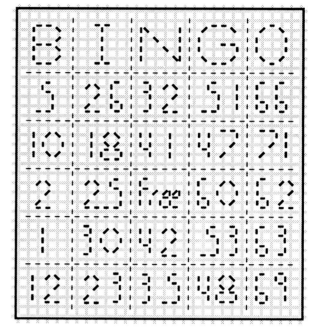

Bingo Card 30 bars wide x 33 high

Whose Deal?

designed by Meredith Montross

Materials

1/4 sheet 7-mesh plastic canvas
worsted weight yarn:

white	14 yds
red	4 yds
black	5 yds

Instructions

Draw outline and cut out Cards. Stitch following chart. Work Backstitches and French Knot last, over previous stitching. Overcast Cards with red.

Color Key
fill in white Continental
♡ = red
◆ = black
╱ = black Backstitch
♯ = black French Knot

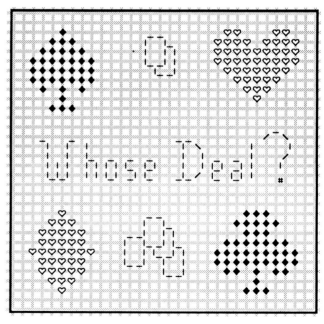

Cards 32 bars wide x 32 high

Coffee Cat
designed by Darla J. Fanton

Materials

1/4 sheet 7-mesh plastic canvas
worsted weight yarn:

white	1 yd	lt tan	4 yds
lt pink	2 yds	med tan	5 yds
med pink	2 yds	brown	3 yds
green	2 yds	black	2 yds

Instructions

Draw outline and cut out Cat. Stitch following chart. Work Backstitches last, over previous stitching. Overcast Cat with med tan.

Color Key

fill in med tan Continental	⟋ = green Backstitch
□ = white Backstitch	☆ = lt tan
♥ = lt pink	● = brown
♡ = med pink	• = black
✔ = med pink Backstitch	⟋ = black Backstitch
o = green	

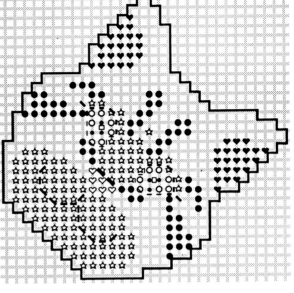

Cat 30 bars wide x 30 high

Amish Heart Quilt Design
designed by Carol Wilson Mansfield

Materials

1/4 sheet 7-mesh plastic canvas
worsted weight yarn:

off-white	4 yds	blue	4 yds
dk pink	6 yds	purple	3 yds
yellow	2 yds	grey	2 yds
green	2 yds	black	10 yds

Instructions

Draw outline and cut out Heart. Stitch following chart. Overcast Heart with black.

Color Key

fill in off-white Continental
- o = dk pink
- ★ = yellow
- ◇ = green
- ☆ = blue
- ♡ = purple
- ♥ = grey
- ● = black
- ⟋ = black Slanting Gobelin

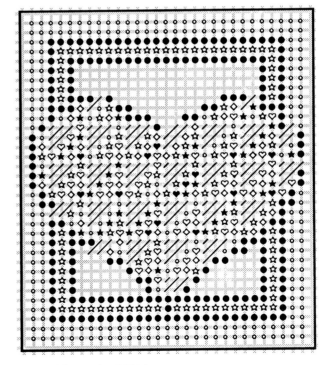

Heart 31 bars wide x 36 high

Prairie Doll Checkerboard

designed by Carol Wilson Mansfield

Our prairie girls with their calico dresses and white aprons add a whimsical touch to this checkerboard.

Materials

3 sheets 7-mesh plastic canvas (see Step 4)
worsted weight yarn:

white	8 yds
lt tan	55 yds
lt pink	6 yds
dk pink	2 yds
rust red	6 yds
gold	6 yds
lt blue	4 yds
dk blue	4 yds
green	9 yds
brown	4 yds
black	30 yds

Instructions

Step 1: Larger section of board is one full sheet of plastic canvas with one bar cut off the long side (70 bars x 91 bars). If you prefer, the one extra bar can be cut off after the stitching is completed. Follow the chart and stitch with Continental Stitch and Pattern Stitch (**Fig 1**).

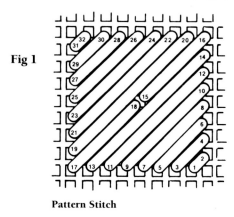

Fig 1

Pattern Stitch

Step 2: Smaller section of board should be cut 70 bars by 26 bars. Follow the top section of the chart to stitch the smaller section.

Step 3: Join the two sections of board with green and gold overcasting; match the green stitches of the design and continue with gold (see color photo at left).

Step 4: If you want the board to be firmer than a single sheet of plastic canvas, add a backing of plastic canvas; two pieces the same size as the front pieces. Seam the two pieces and join to front piece with black overcasting. Be sure the seam of the backing is at the opposite end from the seam of the front so the board will lie flat.

Step 5: For hanging, stitch yarn loops to the top back of the board.

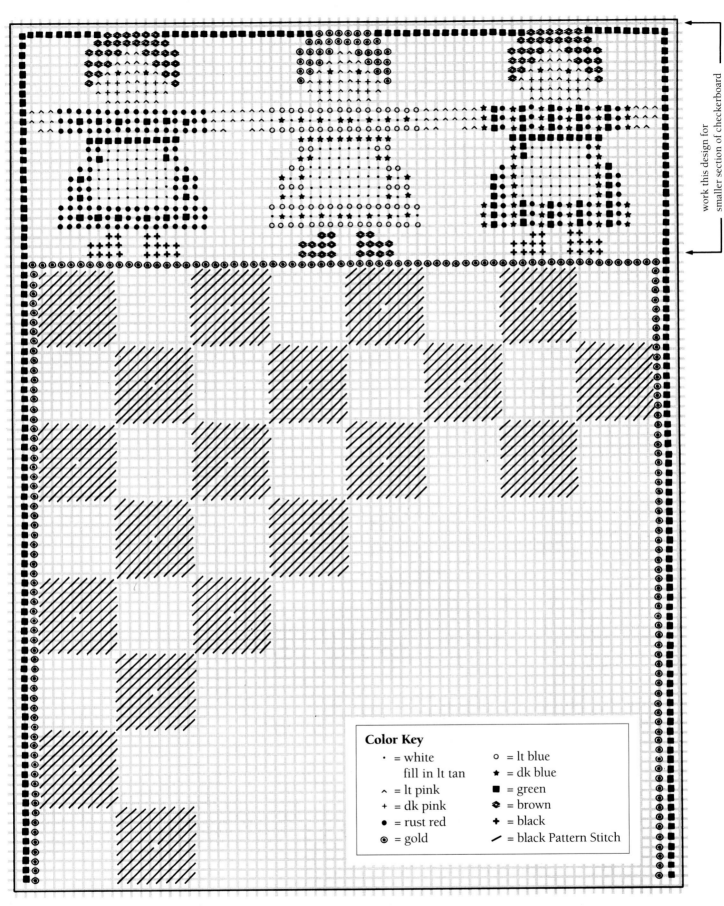

Color Key

·	= white fill in lt tan	○	= lt blue
∧	= lt pink	★	= dk blue
+	= dk pink	■	= green
●	= rust red	❧	= brown
◉	= gold	✛	= black
		╱	= black Pattern Stitch

Checkerboard - Larger Section 70 bars wide x 91 high

191

Coming Up Roses

designed by Carol Wilson Mansfield

Fill your home with the natural beauty of roses! Any plant in a pot 6" or less will fit in this rosy cover. It makes a lovely accent for a dresser, bedside table, or bathroom counter. This clock really works! The decorative hands and clock movement are available at craft stores. The boudoir clock is accented with roses and a cheerful sun face.

Flower Pot Cover

Boudoir Clock

Flower Pot Cover

Materials:

1 1/2 sheets 7-mesh plastic canvas
worsted weight yarn:

white	35 yds	lt blue	30 yds
lt pink	10 yds	dk blue	15 yds
med pink	10 yds	lt green	15 yds
dk pink	10 yds	lt green	10 yds

Instructions

Step 1: Cut out two Side 1 pieces, two Side 2 pieces, four Side 3 pieces and one Base. Stitch following charts; leave Base unstitched.

Step 2: Work all overcasting and joining with white. Overcast top edges of all Side pieces. Join Sides as in **Fig 1**.

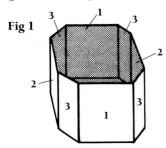

Fig 1

Step 3: Attach Base by matching holes in Sides 1 and 2 to the straight sides of the Base, and overcasting the holes in all Side 3 pieces to the diagonal sections of the Base. Overcast more than one stitch in a hole where necessary to cover on the diagonal sections.

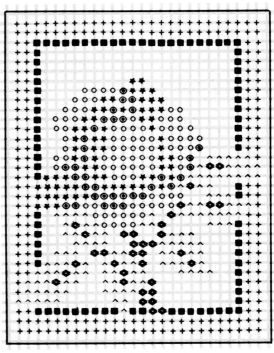

Side 1 28 bars wide x 35 high (make two)

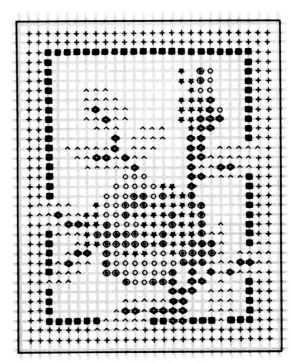

Side 2 28 bars wide x 35 high (make two)

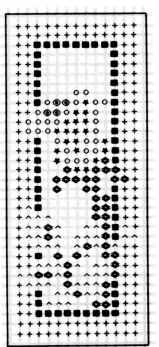

Side 3 15 bars wide x 35 high (make four)

Color Key
fill in white
o = lt pink
★ = med pink
◉ = dk pink
+ = lt blue
■ = dk blue
∧ = lt green
◈ = dk green

Base 48 bars x 48 bars
Note: Cut out Base; then cut off all four corners to match section of chart shown.

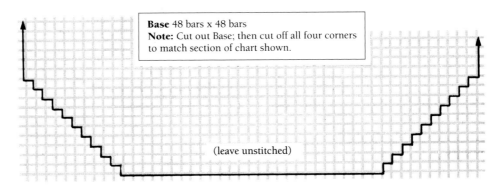

(leave unstitched)

193

Boudoir Clock

Materials

two sheets 7-mesh plastic canvas
1/4" - 3/8" clock movement
decorative clock hands approx 2" long (may be included
　　with the clock movement)
four 3/4" gold dome buttons
navy blue 6-strand embroidery floss
worsted-weight yarn:

white	60 yds	gold	2 yds
lt pink	5 yds	lt blue	2 yds
med pink	4 yds	royal blue	2 yds
dk pink	3 yds	green	5 yds
lt yellow	2 yds		

Instructions

Step 1: Draw outlines and cut out Front (with center hole for clock movement), Back, two Sides, two Top Flats, one Top Curve and Base. Cut out shaded square from Back piece. Cut out will be the Door to cover the Back opening.

Step 2: Stitch following charts; work all Continental first, then navy blue floss Backstitches and French Knots over previous stitching. For Back, fill in with white Continental.

Step 3: All overcasting and joining is done with white. Overcast small hole on Front, Back opening and Door edges and at the same time join Door to top edge of opening. Stitch four button "feet" on Base. If button has a shank, cut a "+" as shown on chart and pull button shank through securely.

Step 4: Join Side, Top Flat, Top Curve, Top Flat, Side and Base (see **Construction Diagram**). Join to beginning of first Side to make one continuous piece. Attach Front to Side/Top/Base unit matching straight edges. When joining curved edges extra Overcast Stitches will be necessary to cover the edge.

Step 5: Attach Back to clock unit matching sides and corners.

Step 6: Follow the manufacturer's instructions for attaching the clock movement parts in the correct order. To make the thickness needed for the 1/4" thick clock face, cut a piece of plastic canvas 3" - 4" square. Cut out a center hole the same size as the hole on the clock Front pattern. Push the clock shaft through the extra square of canvas first, then through the clock Front from the inside. Trim the nubs if necessary, but the shaft should be tight in the plastic canvas hole. If

using a clock movement designed for 3/8"-thick clock face, cut another 3" - 4" square with a center hole and add it behind the clock face. Add more squares for thickness if necessary. The dial fixing nut will hold the clock movement securely. Attach hands gently but snugly; insert battery and set clock with the rotary dial on the back of the movement case. **Note:** Measurement given for each pair of clock hands is the length of the longest (minute) hand.

Note: For added stability, fill a small plastic bag with beans, marbles, stones, etc., and set in base of clock.

Construction Diagram

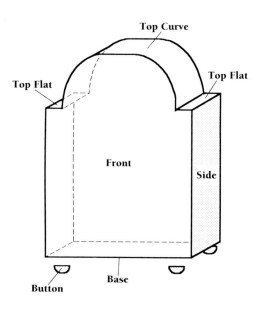

finished size: 7 3/4" tall x 5 5/8" wide x 2 3/8" deep

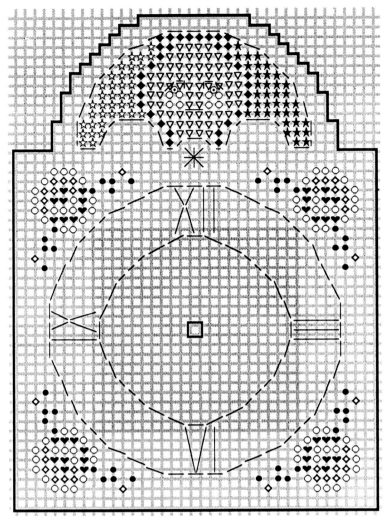

Front/Back 38 bars wide x 52 high (cut two)

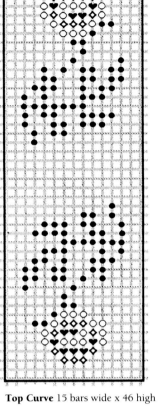

Top Curve 15 bars wide x 46 high

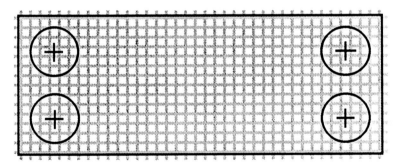

Base 38 bars wide x 15 high (unstitched)

Color Key

fill in white
- ○ = lt pnk
- ◇ = med pink
- ♥ = dk pink
- ▽ = lt yellow
- ☆ = gold
- ★ = lt blue
- ◆ = royal blue
- ⊙ = navy blue French Knot
- – = navy blue floss Backstitch
- ● = green

Top Flat 15 bars wide x 5 high
(make two)

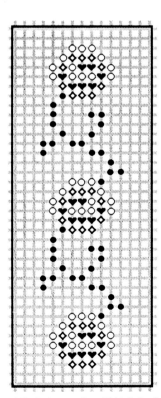

Side 15 bars wide x 38 high (make two)

Belt Bags

designed by Pat Diebold and Carol Wilson Mansfield

These little bags can be worn on a belt, on a chain around your neck, or in many other ways. They are perfect to hold a key, a tissue and a lipstick. Have the essentials always with you!

You Are Limited Only By Your Imagination!

There are many ways to suspend your bag. If you are using your Bag on a belt, you will need to use Back A (below). Thread the belt material through the slots and fasten. Some items that can be used as a belt are a woven belt with clasp (available in assorted colors at your fabric store), chain links, heavy wide ribbon, and regular buckle belts you may already have in your closet.

You can also use your Bag as a necklace or small purse by using Back B. Fasten metal jump rings (18mm diameter) to top edges of Sides, then thread the strap material through the rings. Ribbon, chain links, metallic or satin cording, and bead strands all can be used.

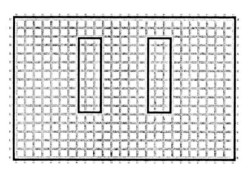

Back A 26 bars wide x 17 high

cut out outlined areas

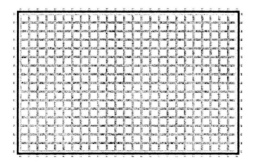

Back B 26 bars wide x 17 high

Bag Assembly

All of the Bags are constructed in the same way. The colors needed will be noted in the instructions for each individual project. Referring to **Construction Diagram**, make a strip as follows: join long straight edge of Flap to front edge of Top; join back edge of Top to top edge of Back; join bottom edge of Back to back edge of Bottom; and join front edge of Bottom to bottom edge of Front. Join side and bottom edges of Sides to side edges of Back, Bottom and Front, then overcast all remaining edges of Bag.

After Bag is assembled and all trims are in place, glue fuzzy Velcro™ dot to wrong side of Flap and glue hook half to corresponding area of Front.

Construction Diagram

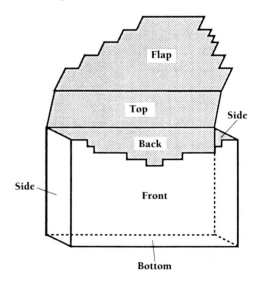

Southwest

Materials

1/2 sheet 7-mesh plastic canvas
silver button, 1/2" diameter
monofilament line and sewing needle
17 silver pony beads
4 brown suede strips, 12" long
2 silver jump rings, 18mm diameter
white Velcro™ dot, 5/8" diameter
tacky craft glue or hot glue
worsted weight yarn:

off-white	19 yds	lt purple	3 yds
peach	3 yds	brown	2 yds
blue-green	5 yds		

Instructions

Step 1: Draw outlines and cut out Front, Flap, two Top/Bottom, two Sides, and Back A or Back B from page 196.

Step 2: Stitch following charts. Fill in Back with off-white Continental. If using Back A, overcast edges of cut out areas using off-white. Using monofilament line and sewing needle, sew button to Flap where indicated on chart.

Step 3: Assemble Bag following instructions on page 196 using off-white. Place jump rings through bottom front corners of Bag. Following **Diagram** for each knot, fold each suede strip in half and knot two onto each jump ring. Thread silver beads onto suede strips at intervals and knot strips to hold in place. Cut ends of suede strips to desired lengths.

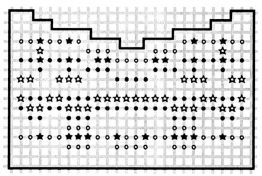

Front 26 bars wide x 17 high

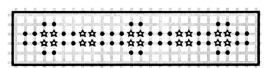

Top/Bottom 26 bars wide x 6 high (make 2)

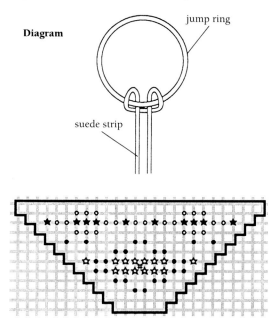

Diagram

jump ring

suede strip

Flap 26 bars wide x 12 high

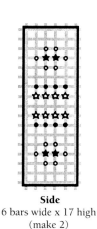

Side
6 bars wide x 17 high
(make 2)

Color Key

fill in off-white Continental
o = peach
● = blue-green
☆ = lt purple
★ = brown
♯ = button placement

197

Gift Surprise

Materials

1/2 sheet 7-mesh plastic canvas
black Velcro™ dot, 5/8" diameter
3 yds metallic yarn
tacky craft glue or hot glue
worsted weight yarn:

red	6 yds
green	9 yds
blue	20 yds

Instructions

Step 1: Draw outlines and cut out Front, Flap, Bow, two Top/Bottom, two Sides, and Back A or Back B from page 196.

Step 2: Stitch following charts. Be sure to stitch top portion of Bow on reverse side as indicated on chart. Fill in Back with blue Continental. If using Back A, overcast edges of cut out areas using blue. Overcast all edges of Bow using green.

Step 3: Assemble Bag following instructions on page 196. Use red, green, and blue to match previous stitching for all joining, then use blue for overcasting. Bend side tips of Bow to unstitched bars indicated on chart. Using green, tack side tips and unstitched bars to Flap at ribbon intersection.

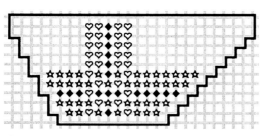

Flap 26 bars wide x 12 high

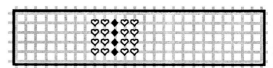

Front 26 bars wide x 17 high

Side
6 bars wide x 17 high
(make 2)

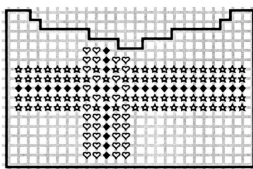

Top/Bottom 26 bars wide x 6 high (make 2)

Color Key

   fill in blue Continental
☆ = red
♡ = green
♦ = metallic gold
● = unstitched bar for joining

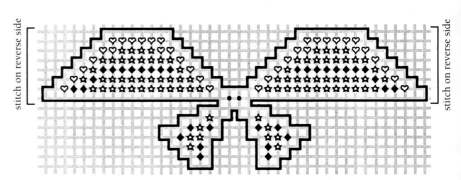

stitch on reverse side

Bow 40 bars wide x 15 high

Coin Bag

Materials

1/2 sheet 7-mesh plastic canvas
9 gold coins with hole in top, 1/2" diameter
9 black seed beads
3 yds metallic gold yarn
monofilament line and sewing needle
black Velcro™ dot, 5/8" diameter
tacky craft glue or hot glue
worsted weight yarn:

dk pink	4 yds
blue	4 yds
purple	3 yds
black	20 yds

Instructions

Step 1: Draw outlines and cut out Front, Flap, Top, Bottom, two Sides, and Back A or Back B from page 196.

Step 2: Stitch following charts. Work Backstitches last, over previous stitching. Fill in Back with black Continental. If using Back A, overcast edges of cut out areas using black.

Step 3: Assemble Bag following instructions on page 196 using black. Use monofilament line and sewing needle to sew beads and coins to edges of Flap where indicated on chart. Go down through bead, through coin, and back up through bead.

Color Key

fill in black Continental
o = dk pink
♡ = blue
★ = purple
⟋ = metallic gold Straight Stitch
＃ = bead and coin placement

Top 26 bars wide x 6 high

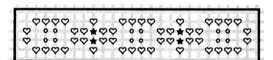

Bottom 26 bars wide x 6 high

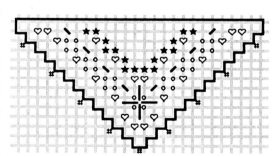

Flap 26 bars wide x 14 high

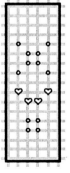

Side
6 bars wide x 17 high
(make 2)

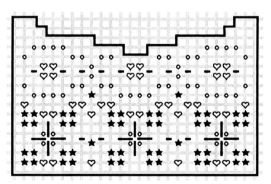

Front 26 bars wide x 17 high

~Ribbons and Lace Jewelry Boxes~

designed by Carol Wilson Mansfield

Use plastic canvas to craft these charming, feminine designs, suitable for the prettiest bedroom retreat. These boxes come in three sizes, and can be lined with a coordinating fabric if you wish. They are an elegant way to store your prettiest accessories safely.

Materials *(for set of three boxes)*

3 sheets 7-mesh plastic canvas
2 lace medallions, 2 1/2" diameter
2 yds 1/4" wide ribbon, mixture of colors
6 ribbon roses, 3/4" across
tacky craft glue or thread for sewing decorations
cardboard and fabric for lining see Step 6 (optional)
worsted weight yarn:

cream	95 yds
pink	40 yds
lavender	35 yds
blue	25 yds
green	20 yds

Instructions

Step 1: For each box, cut two Top/Bottom pieces, two Sides and two Front/Back pieces. Bottom piece is left unstitched.

Step 2: Stitch following charts. Overcast three edges of Top piece with cream, leave back edge for joining to box.

Step 3: Join Front, Back, Sides and Bottom of box with cream. Overcast edge of box, joining back edge to back edge of Top piece by overcasting through both pieces of canvas.

Step 4: Decorating Large and Medium Boxes: Center lace medallion at front of Top; glue on ribbon roses and ribbon loops. Leave one ribbon long enough to tie. Glue matching ribbon for tying to center edge of Bottom. Tie to close.

Step 5: Decorating Tiny Box: Glue on ribbon rose and ribbon loops to center front of Top. Leave one long ribbon for tying; glue matching ribbon to center edge of Bottom. Tie to close.

Step 6: Lining Boxes (optional): Cut cardboard rectangles to fit four sides, bottom end top of box. Trim them so they fit easily, not tightly. Cut fabric 1" larger on all sides than each cardboard rectangle. With fabric face down center

cardboard and glue fabric around four sides of the back of the cardboard (**Fig 1**). Stretch fabric so it is smooth and tight. If padded lining is desired, cut a layer of batting for each rectangle and glue between fabric and cardboard. Glue the lining pieces into the box; cover seams with narrow cording if desired.

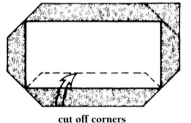

Fig 1

cut off corners

TINY BOX

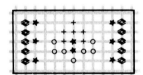

Front/Back 13 bars wide x 7 high
(make two)

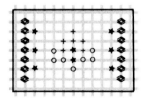

Top/Bottom 13 bars wide x 9 high
(cut two, leave one unstitched)

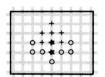

Side 9 bars wide x 7 high
(make two)

MEDIUM BOX

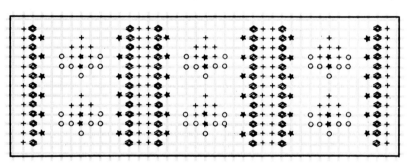

Front/Back 41 bars wide x 15 high (make two)

Color Key

fill in cream
+ = pink
★ = lavender
✿ = blue
○ = green

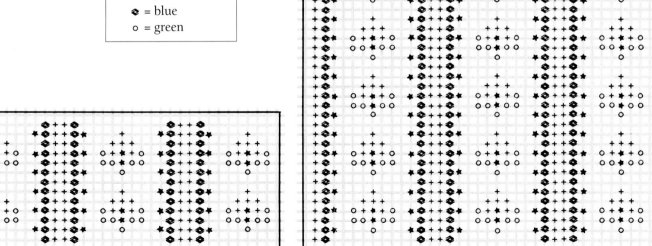

Side 33 bars wide x 15 high (make two)

Top/Bottom 41 bars wide x 33 high (cut two, leave one unstitched)

charts continued

LARGE BOX

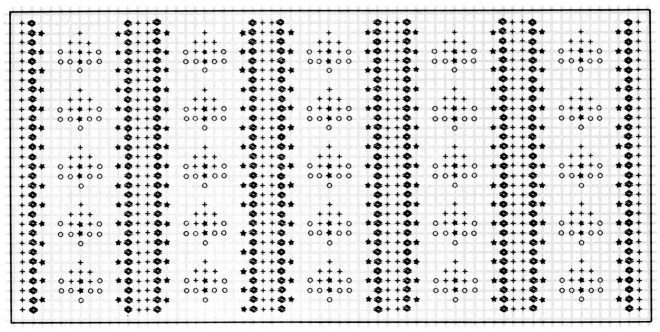

Top/Bottom 67 bars wide x 33 high (cut two, leave one unstitched)

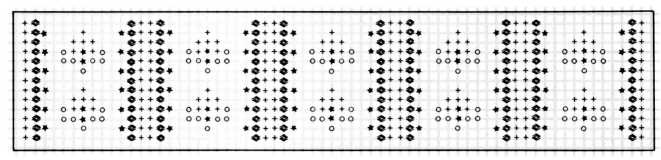

Front/Back 67 bars wide x 15 high (make two)

Side 33 bars wide x 15 high (make two)
Use same chart as Side for Medium Box

Color Key
    fill in cream
+ = pink
★ = lavender
❧ = blue
○ = green

Home Sewing

Home Sewing

Almost all of us know the basics of sewing. You just thread a needle, put it into the fabric and then pull it out again.

But being able to translate that simple skill into beautiful quilts, delightful wallhangings, superb decorating for our homes, or wonderful toys turns a kindergarten game into a real art.

In this section you'll find some of our favorite home sewing projects, and since quilting is our all-time favorite sewing project, we've included lots of wonderful quilts.

One of the reasons we love quilting so much is that right from the start, your very first project won't end up worn or unused or stuffed into the back of a drawer. No, your very first quilting project can end up keeping someone warm. In addition, there is a tradition that quiltmakers purposely put a mistake in their quilts because only God was perfect. So if you make a terrible mistake in a quilt project, you have a choice. You can spend time ripping out and starting over, or you can leave the mistake and say you put it there on purpose.

Quilting

Choosing the Fabric

Whether you choose to make your quilt using the traditional method or the new faster methods, you must start by choosing your fabric.

Old time quilts were traditionally made of 100% cotton, and this is still the fabric that experienced quilters prefer.

Cotton has a number of properties that make it especially suitable for patchwork. You will find less distortion with cotton fabric which means that your carefully cut small pieces will fit together more easily. If you make a mistake and find a puckered area, a quilt made of 100% cotton often can be ironed flat with a steam iron. In addition, the needle moves through cotton with ease as opposed to some synthetics. If you are piecing a quilt by hand, or if you are hand quilting, this is an extremely valuable quality.

Instructions for each of our quilts will tell you how much fabric to purchase. Our fabric requirements tend to be rather ample; you may be able to conserve fabric by cutting more carefully.

Many quiltmakers today are omitting the prewashing of fabric to purposely give quilts the puckered look of an antique quilt after it has been washed. This is a fine idea if you are making a quilt which will be entered in a quilt competition or hung on a wall. However, if you are making a quilt that will need to live through many, many washings, you want to make sure that you eliminate any future problems right from the beginning.

Therefore, before you begin to work on your quilt, be sure to check that your fabric is colorfast and preshrunk (don't trust those manufacturer's labels). You can wash all of the fabric or you can merely test. Start by cutting a 2"-wide strip, cut crosswise, of each of the fabrics that you have selected for your quilt. To determine whether the fabric is colorfast, put each strip separately into a clean bowl of extremely hot water, or hold the fabric strip under hot running water. If your fabric bleeds a great deal, all is not necessarily lost. It might only be necessary to wash all of the fabric until all of the excess dye has washed out. Fabrics which continue to bleed after they have been washed several times should be eliminated.

To test for shrinkage, take each saturated strip and iron it dry with a hot iron. When the strip is completely dry, measure and compare it to your original measurements. The fabric industry allows about 2% shrinkage in cotton fabrics. That means that your 45" crosswise fabric should not lose more than 1". If all of your fabric strips shrink about the same amount, then you really have no problem. When you wash your finished quilt, you may achieve the puckered look of an antique quilt. If you do not want this look, you will have to wash and dry all of the fabric before beginning so that shrinkage is no longer a problem. If only one of your fabrics is shrinking more than the others, it will have to be washed and dried, or discarded.

Make sure that your fabric is absolutely square. If it is not you will have difficulty cutting square pieces. Fabric is woven with crosswise and lengthwise threads. Lengthwise threads should be parallel to the selvage (that's the finished edge along the sides; sometimes the fabric company prints its name along the selvage) and crosswise threads should be perpendicular to the selvage, **Fig 1**. If fabric is off-grain, you can straighten it. Pull gently on the true bias in the opposite direction to the off-grain edge, **Fig 2**. Continue doing this until crosswise threads are at a right angle to lengthwise threads.

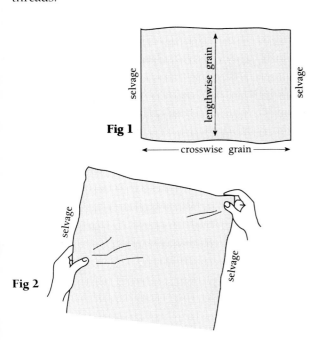

Traditional Piecing

In traditional piecing, each small patch of the quilt block is cut out and then sewn together.

Templates

In quilting, patterns used to cut out patches are called "templates." The patterns for the necessary templates for each quilt are given full size and appear with the specific quilt. To make templates, lay a piece of tracing paper over the pattern pieces in the book and carefully trace the pattern pieces. (Do not photocopy the pieces instead of tracing. Photocopy machines are not exact, and your pieces may not fit together.) Carefully glue your tracing onto heavy card-

board or plastic. Special plastic for making templates is available in quilt, craft or stationery stores. If you use a clear plastic, you can trace directly onto plastic and eliminate the gluing. Now, cut out the plastic or cardboard templates.

It is important that all templates be cut out carefully because if they are not accurate, the patchwork will not fit together. Use a pair of good-size sharp scissors (not the same scissors that you use to cut fabric), a single-edged razor blade or a craft knife. Be careful not to bend the corners of triangles.

> **Note:** The template patterns are printed without seam allowance. In quilting the traditional seam allowance is 1/4", and you must allow for these seam allowances when making your templates.

Cutting the Pieces

Cutting the fabric is one of the most important steps in making a patchwork block. You must be accurate in order to have the pattern fit smoothly.

Start by laying your laundered, freshly-ironed fabric on a smooth surface with wrong side up. Have all your supplies ready: scissors, rulers, sharp pencils, marking tools, templates, etc.

Whether you choose to piece by hand or machine, cut and piece a trial block first. This will give you a chance to double-check the pattern and to make certain that you like both design and colors.

Cutting for Hand Sewing

Lay the cardboard or plastic template on the wrong side of the fabric near top left edge of material (but not on selvage), placing it so that as many straight sides of pieces as possible are parallel to crosswise and lengthwise grain of fabric, **Fig 3**. Try to keep long side of triangles on the bias by placing short sides of triangles on straight of fabric. Trace around template. You can mark with a regular well-sharpened hard lead pencil (using a light color for dark fabrics and a regular pencil for light fabrics), but there are many quilt makers who use fabric marking pens available at quilt stores and departments. Test any marking materials to make certain that they will not run when wet.

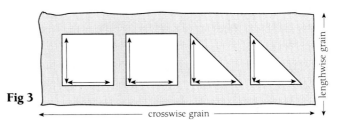

Hold your pencil or marker at an angle so that the point is against the side of the template. Measure 1/4" around this shape, and draw a line. This is the line you will cut on. Now you will see that the first line (where you traced your template) is your stitching line. If your cutting line is not perfectly accurate, it will not matter. Your stitching line, however, must be perfectly straight or true, or the pieces will not fit together correctly. In **Fig 4**, the broken line is the cutting line; the solid line is the seam line.

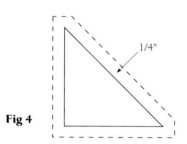

Fig 4

Continue moving template and tracing it on fabric the required number of times, moving from left to right and always keeping straight lines parallel with grain. You will save fabric if you have pieces share a common cutting line as in **Fig 5**, but if this is confusing leave a narrow border or margin around each piece. Use a sharp scissors and cut carefully.

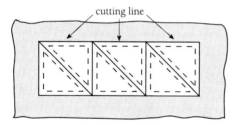

cutting line

Fig 5

Cutting for Machine Sewing

For machine piecing, an exact 1/4" seam allowance must be measured and marked. Lay the template on the fabric as described above for hand piecing and trace around it with the marking tool, if desired. Now measure the 1/4" seam allowance around this shape. Using a ruler, draw this second line **absolutely accurately**. This is the line that you cut on.

Sewing the Block

Before starting to sew a block, lay out all of the pieces that will be needed for that block. Always work with well-ironed fabric.

Sewing the Block by Machine

Machine piecing is done with the straight stitch foot and throat plate on the machine. Set your machine for about 10 stitches to the inch and use a size 14 needle. The traditional seam allowance in quilting is 1/4" so you are going to need some method to make sure that you sew with a perfect 1/4"

seam. If your machine has the 1/4" marked on the throat plate you are in luck. If not, measure 1/4" from your needle hole to the right side of the presser foot and place a piece of tape on the plate. Keep edge of your piece lined up with tape and you will be able to sew a perfect 1/4" seam.

Place two pieces together with right sides facing. Make certain that the top edges of both pieces are even. Pin; baste if desired.

You can construct blocks using the production line method. In this method, **Fig 6**, you do not begin and end your thread with each patch, but let thread run over a continuous chain of patches. When you have made a row of patches, snip them apart. Don't worry about threads coming undone. They will eventually be anchored by the cross seams.

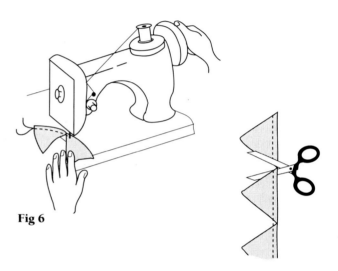

Fig 6

After you have joined two pieces together, press seams flat to one side, not open. Open seams will weaken the quilt. Generally seams can all be pressed in the same direction. But avoid pressing darker pieces so they fall under lighter pieces, since they may show through when the quilt is completed.

You may want to turn seam on top in one direction and seam on bottom in opposite direction, **Fig 7**. This will help to keep seams that are crossed with other seams from bunching at crossing points. You can clip away any excess fabric at these points if necessary. Just be sure to iron all seams before they are crossed with another seam. When crossing seams, be especially careful to match seam to seam.

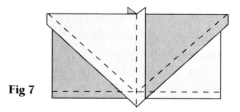

Fig 7

Sewing the Block by Hand

Place two pieces together with right sides facing, and place a pin through both pieces at each end of pencil line, **Fig 8**. Check the back to make sure that the pins are exactly on pencil lines. When sewing larger seams, place pins every 1 1/2", removing the pins as you sew past them. Always stitch on the sewing line, being careful not to stitch into the margins at the corners, **Fig 9**. Use a fairly short needle, #7 to #10 (#9 and #10 are the most popular) and no more than an 18" length of thread. Join pieces with short, simple running stitches, taking a few back stitches at the beginning and end of each seam rather than a knot. If the seam is very long, it is a good idea to make a few back stitches at various places along the seam. Take small, evenly spaced stitches and keep the seam as straight as possible along the pencil line. When you sew two bias edges together (as in sewing two triangles along the long side) try to keep the thread taut enough so that the edges do not stretch as you sew them. After you have joined the pieces, press the seams as described for machine sewing.

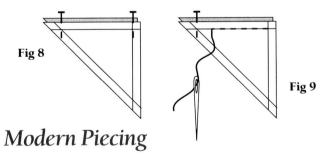

Fig 8

Fig 9

Modern Piecing

The introduction of the rotary cutter has literally revolutionized the art of quilt making. By using a cutter and its accompanying protective mat along with acrylic rulers, you can almost eliminate use of templates. In addition, time spent cutting and piecing can be literally cut in half.

The method usually begins with chain piecing strips and then cutting the strips into squares which are sewn together quickly to create the block.

Not every quilt can be made using these methods; for some quilts only part of the work can be done this way. If you are interested in trying this method, try the Nine-Patch Flower Garden on page 215. Some of the techniques which we have listed for the traditional method are still valuable for the modern method. For instance, the 1/4" seam allowance is always used, and pressing seams to one side is still viable.

Start by using the proper tools. You will need a rotary cutter along with its protective mat. Don't try to substitute anything for the mat; it won't work. The mat designed to accompany a rotary cutter is self-healing and it can't dull the cutter blade. There are several brands of cutters currently on the market. They all look a little bit like a pizza cutter with very, very sharp blades. In fact, the blades are so sharp that the cutters are sold with protective guards. This guard should only be removed when you are actually cutting fabric. If you drop your cutter without its guard or cut across a pin, you can dull the blade. A dull blade should be replaced immediately since it will not cut fabric correctly. To keep from hurting yourself as you cut with this extremely sharp instrument, remember one simple rule: **Always cut away from your body.**

In addition to the cutter and its accompanying mat, you will need a straight edge. There are many acrylic rulers currently on the market which are intended for use with the rotary cutter. The rulers usually have markings on the surface which will help in accurate cutting. For most of the cutting in this book, a ruler of about 6" x 24" will be sufficient. These acrylic rulers are printed with grids that are extremely helpful in accurate cutting.

Before you begin to cut your strips, you must make sure that your fabric is perfectly straight. It will be necessary to straighten the fabric along the edge where it was cut off the bolt, as this is seldom cut straight. Fold fabric in half, making sure selvages are even, then fold again, **Fig 10**. This means that you will be cutting through four layers at all times. You may want to press down the folds so that your fabric is easier to handle.

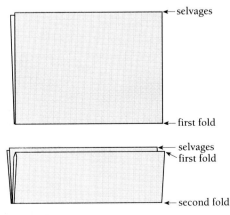

selvages
first fold

selvages
first fold

second fold

Fig 10

Carefully line up your fold line along one of the horizontal lines of your mat. Place your ruler along the edge of the fabric and cut off the raggedy edge, **Fig 11**. Once you have made this initial cut, you can use this straight edge to align your additional measurements. Place your ruler along the edge that you just straightened, lining up the correct measurement line on your ruler (for your size strip) with the straight edge of the fabric; begin cutting your strips, **Fig 12**.

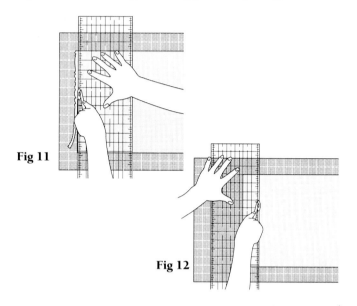

Fig 11

Fig 12

> **Hint:** Make the initial cut, **Fig 11** with your left hand and the succeeding cuts, **Fig 12**, with your right hand, assuming that you are right handed. The force of the cutter against the mat will compensate for any lack of power you have in your left hand.

In this method, the quilt begins with sewing strips of different colors together. Place the first two fabrics right sides together, matching edges. When you have sewn the first strips together, don't end your thread; just continue feeding the next two strips, **Fig 13**. This is called chain piecing. When you have made a continuous row of strips, snip them apart.

When you have finished sewing the first two strips, begin chain piecing the next color if it is required and then the next, **Fig 14**. After you have joined all the pieces together, press the

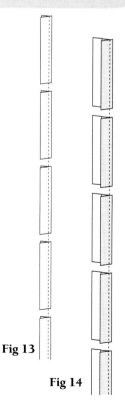

Fig 13

Fig 14

seams flat to one side, not open. Generally seams can be pressed in the same direction.

But avoid pressing darker pieces so they fall under light pieces since they may show through when the quilt is completed.

After you have sewn all of the strips, the individual quilt instructions will tell you how to cut the strips into squares and how to join the squares into blocks. Again be sure that you continue to press your seams to one side.

Blocking the Blocks

When you have completed a block, it must be "blocked" before it is joined to another block. The term "blocking" means keeping the edges straight on all sides of the quilt so it will be a perfect rectangle when finished. The term applies to the quilt's parts as well as to an entire quilt, so the blocking process is a continuous one from start to finish.

Place the completed block on the ironing board and pull the edges straight with your fingers. Cover the block with a damp cloth and steam with a warm iron (or use a steam iron). Iron the block perfectly flat with no puckers starting with the edges first and the center last. Move the iron as little as possible to keep the block from stretching.

Joining the Blocks

After you have pieced and blocked the required number of blocks for your quilt, lay them out to get the final effect before sewing them together.

Using the 1/4" seam allowance, join the blocks in horizontal or vertical rows. When rows are completed, join two rows together, matching seam lines. Then add additional rows.

> **Hint:** When crossing seams, be especially careful to match seam to seam. One learns to do this fairly accurately while sewing by feeling with the fingers. It helps if the lower seam is turned one way and the top seam the other, so press seams for odd numbered rows in one direction; even numbered in the other.

Adding Borders

Some of the quilts in this book have borders added. Although we give measurements for border strips, we recommend that before cutting your border strips, you measure the quilt top and cut your borders to the exact size. If you have made some mistakes in the piecing (for instance, if you made your blocks with a larger than 1/4" seam allowance) this will be the time to adjust your border measurements.

Using the 1/4" seam allowance, attach one side border to the right side of the quilt and one to the left. Then attach the top and bottom borders. Use the 1/4" seam allowance at all times. Repeat for additional borders.

Preparing the Quilt Top

Give the quilt top a final blocking, making sure all corners are square and all seams are pressed to one side.

We have made suggestions for quilting your quilt top, but you may wish to follow your own quilting plan. However you are planning to quilt your top, you will need to mark the quilting pattern before joining the top to the backing and batting.

If you prefer to tie your quilt, skip the next section on marking the quilting design.

Marking the Quilting Design

Mark all quilting lines on the right side of the fabric. For marking, use a hard lead pencil, chalk or other special quilt marking materials. If you quilt right on the marked lines, they will not show. Be sure to test any marking material to find one that works best for you.

A word of caution: Marking lines which are intended to disappear after quilting - either by exposure to air or with water - may become permanent when set with a hot iron. Therefore, don't iron your quilt top after you have marked your quilting pattern.

If you are quilting around shapes, you may not need to mark your line if you feel that you can accurately gauge the quilting line as you work. If you are quilting "in the ditch" of the seam (the space right in the seam), marking is not necessary. Other quilting patterns will need to be marked.

An easy way to mark an allover diamond quilting pattern is to begin in the lower right hand corner of the quilt top, measuring 3" up from the bottom right hand corner of the quilt, and make a mark. Make another similar mark along the bottom of the quilt 3" from the right hand corner. Join these two marks with a diagonal line. Starting at this bottom diagonal line, mark diagonal lines approximately 1 1/2" apart from the bottom right of the quilt to the top left. Using this same technique, draw intersecting diagonal lines across the quilt top from the top right of the quilt to the bottom left. The intersections will make the diamond-shaped quilting pattern across the quilt.

Attaching Batting and Backing

There are a number of different types of batting on the market. Very thin batting will require a great deal of quilting to hold it (quilting lines no more than 1" apart); very thick batting can be used only for tied quilts.

For most quilt projects, you are better off with a medium weight bonded polyester sheet batting. There are currently on the market battings recommended for machine quilting. If you are planning to machine quilt, you should investigate these battings.

We have indicated the amount of fabric required for the backing in each pattern. If you prefer another fabric, buy a backing fabric that is soft and loosely woven so that the quilting needle can pass through easily. Bed sheets are usually not good backing materials.

Since many of the quilts in this book are wider than fabric width, you may have to sew lengths together to make your quilt backing. Cut off selvages and seam pieces together carefully; iron seam open. This is the only time in making a quilt that seams should be pressed open. By seaming several lengths of fabric from the quilt top, an interesting pattern can be created on the back as seen in the photo below.

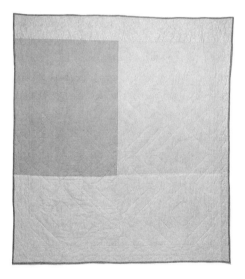

Cut batting and backing larger than the quilt top: about 2" wider than quilt top on all sides. Place backing, wrong side up, on flat surface. Place batting on top of this, matching outer edges.

Hint: Remove batting from its packaging a day in advance and open it out full size. This will help to get the batting to lie flat.

The layers of the quilt must be held together before quilting. There are two methods for doing this: thread basting and safety pin basting.

For thread basting: First, pin backing and batting together; then baste with long stitches, starting in the center and sewing toward the edges in a number of diagonal lines. Now center quilt top, right side up, on top of the batting. Baste the top to the batting and backing layers in the same manner.

For safety pin basting: This is a new method of preparing a quilt for quilting. Because you don't have to put your hand under the quilt as you do when you are thread basting, the quilt top does not move out of position. Layer the backing, batting and quilt top and pin through all three layers at once. Start pinning from the center and work out to the edges, placing the pins no more than 4" to 6" apart. Think of your quilt plan as you work and make certain that your pins avoid the prospective quilting lines. Choose rust proof pins that are size #1 or #2.

Hand Quilting

The actual quilting stitch is really a fairly simple one for anyone who has ever sewn. There are many books which attempt to teach the quilter how to make the proper stitch. It's something like teaching someone to swim with a swimming manual. You're never really going to learn unless you dive right into the water!

The stitch is just a very simple running stitch, but working through three layers at once may be a bit difficult at first. Use one of the short, fine needles especially designed for quilting (they are often called "betweens"), and 100% cotton quilting thread.

By the way, all quilters wear thimbles! If you have never used a thimble before, you are going to have to now. The thimble is worn on the middle finger of your right hand (or your left, if you are left-handed). The thimble is used to push the needle through the fabric as in **Fig 15**.

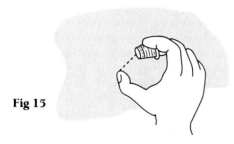

Fig 15

The quilting can be done in a traditional floor frame, but chances are you'll probably find a quilting hoop more convenient. Place hoop over middle of quilt, pull quilt slightly taut (not as stretched as for embroidery) and move extra fullness toward edges. Begin working in center and move extra fullness toward outer edges. As you work, you will find the quilting stitch has a tendency to push batting, and by working from center out you can gradually ease any excess fullness toward edges. If you wish, run quilting thread through beeswax to keep it from tangling.

Begin with an 18" length of thread with a knot in one end. Go into quilt through top about 1/2" from where you plan to begin quilting, and bring needle up to quilting line. Pull gently but firmly, and knot will slip through the batting where it will disappear. Now place left hand under hoop where needle should come through. With right hand, push needle vertically downward through layers of the quilt until it touches left hand.

If you are a beginner, you may need to pull needle through with left hand, and push it back upward to where it is received by right hand, close to last stitch. As you become more proficient, you will be able to do the whole operation with one hand, merely using the left hand to signal that the needle has penetrated the three layers. Some experienced quilters are able to put several stitches on the needle just as if they were sewing.

Make stitches as close together as you can; this is the real secret of beautiful quilting. The stitches should be evenly spaced, the same length on the front as on the back. When entire quilt has been quilted, lift it from frame or hoop and remove basting stitches.

Machine Quilting

You do not need a special machine for quilting. You can machine quilt with almost any home sewing machine. Just make sure that it is in good working order and that the presser foot is not set for too much pressure which can cause rippling. An even-feed foot is a good investment if you are going to machine quilt since it feeds the top and bottom layers through the machine evenly.

Use fine transparent nylon thread in the top and regular sewing thread in the bobbin.

In order to fit a large quilt under the arm of the sewing machine it will be necessary to fold the quilt so that it is manageable. If you are quilting in horizontal and vertical lines, you will make your first row of quilting along a center seam. Now starting at the sides, roll the quilt to within four to five inches of this center seam. Then, roll the quilt up from the bottom to within a few inches of where you want to begin sewing.

If you are quilting diagonally, your first row of quilting will go from one corner to the opposite corner. You will roll your quilt to within four to five inches of that first diagonal quilting line. Then roll the quilt up from bottom corner to within a few inches of where you will begin sewing.

With the rolled quilt in your lap, place the quilt so that you are in the right position to begin. Lower the presser foot and start. Make certain that you have a table on the other side of the machine to catch the completed work. Otherwise the weight of the quilt can cause a problem. Work from the center out, re-rolling the quilt as you work.

To **quilt-in-the-ditch** of a seam (this is actually stitching in the space between two pieces of fabric that have been sewn together), use your hands to pull the blocks or pieces apart and machine stitch right between the two pieces. Try to keep your stitching just to the side of the seam that does not have the bulk of the seam allowance under it. When you have finished stitching, the quilting will be practically hidden in the seam.

We have **straight line machine quilting** next to a seam (as in *Little Red Schoolhouse*). You may want to mark these quilting lines with a ruler. It may take a little practice to feel in control and keep the lines of quilting straight.

Free form machine quilting is done with a darning foot and the feed dogs down on your sewing machine. It can be used to quilt around a design or to quilt a motif. Mark your quilting design as described in Marking the Quilting Design on page 209. Free form machine quilting takes practice to master because you are controlling the quilt through the machine rather than the machine moving the quilt. With free form machine quilting you can quilt in any direction - up and down, side to side and even in circles without pivoting the quilt around the needle.

Tying the Quilt

Use knitting worsted weight yarn (washable of course), crochet thread, several strands of embroidery floss or other washable material.

Work from center of quilt out, adjusting any excess fullness of batting as you go. Thread an 18" length of yarn into a large-eyed needle. Do not knot! Take needle down from top through all three layers, leaving about 1" of yarn on right side. Bring needle back up from wrong side to right side about 1/8" from where needle first entered. Tie a firm knot, then cut, leaving both ends about 1/2" long. Make sufficient ties to keep three layers together.

Attaching the Binding

Place quilt on flat surface and carefully trim backing and batting 1/2" beyond quilt top edge. Measure quilt top and cut two 2"-wide binding strips the length of your quilt (for sides). Right sides together, sew one side strip to one side of quilt with 1/4" seam allowance (seam allowance should be measured from outer edge of quilt top fabric, not outer edge of batting/backing). Turn binding to back and turn under 1/4" on raw edge; slipstitch to backing. Do other side in same manner. For top and bottom edge binding strips, measure carefully adding 1/2" to each end; cut strips 2" wide. To eliminate raw edges at corners, turn the extra 1/2" to wrong side before stitching to top and bottom. Finish in same manner as sides.

Drunkard's Path Quilt

This quilt looks deceptively simple to piece. After all, there are only two pieces necessary to create the block. The quilter had better take care, however, and watch the layout very carefully when setting blocks in order not to lose her way when creating the twisting, turning pathway of the drunkard.

The quilt, measuring approximately 70" x 84", is made up of ninety-nine 7" pieced blocks set 9 across and 11 down. There are two blocks used to make the quilt: Block 1 and Block 2. **Fig 1** shows the layout of the quilt made with these blocks. The border is made with Blocks 3 and 4 which are actually half blocks. **Fig 2** shows the quilt with its borders. The corners are filled with quarter blocks called Block 5. The entire quilt is finished with a 1/4" binding of the blue fabric.

Fabric Requirements

3 1/4 yds light
3 1/2 yds dark

Cutting Requirements

	Block 1	Block 2	Block 3	Block 4	Block 5	for quilt
Template A dark		4		2	1	244
Template A light	4		2			244
Template B dark	4		2			244
Template B light		4		2	1	244

Number of Blocks

Block 1 (for quilt)	49
Block 2 (for quilt)	50
Block 3 (for borders)	22
Block 4 (for borders)	18
Block 5 (for corners)	4

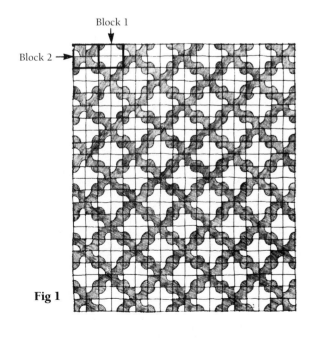

Fig 1

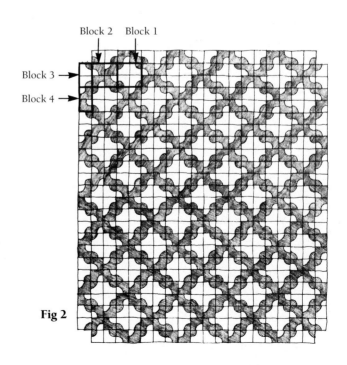

Fig 2

213

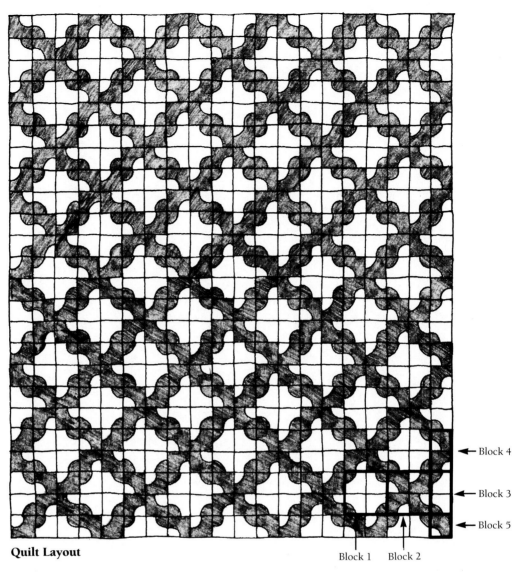

Quilt Layout

← Block 4

← Block 3

← Block 5

Block 1   Block 2

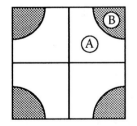

Block 1

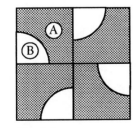

Block 2

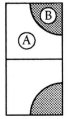

Block 3

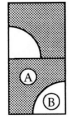

Block 4

Block 5

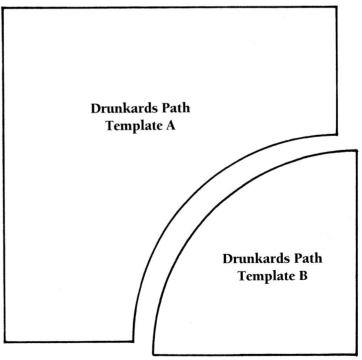

Drunkards Path Template A

Drunkards Path Template B

Allow for Seams When Cutting Fabric

214

Nine-Patch Flower Garden Quilt

designed by Rita Weiss

If you have ever wondered what to do with fabric with pre-printed blocks--called "cheater blocks"--why not plant a flower garden? If the blocks have sailboats on them, you could have a Nine-Patch Ocean; if you want a quilt for a young child, why not buy a juvenile animal print and have a Nine-Patch Zoo? Just use the same instructions and let your fabric determine your quilt title.

Size of Quilt Top

83 1/2" x 109"

Finished Size of Floral Block

9" x 9"

Finished Size of Nine-Patch Block

3 3/4" x 3 3/4"

Setting

The floral blocks are set five across and seven down with sashing created from strips of the gold print and the mauve plus the nine-patch blocks. The quilt is finished with borders of both the gold print and mauve.

Fabric Requirements

gold print: 3 1/2 yds (includes border cut crosswise and pieced)

mauve: 5 yds (includes border and binding cut crosswise and pieced)

floral block fabric: 4 yds*

backing: 6 1/2 yds

Fabric Note: Check the fabric to make sure that you will have enough printed fabric for the 35 blocks.

Cutting Requirements

Note: *Do not cut fabric borders before measuring pieced quilt top.*

thirty-five 9 1/2" x 9 1/2" floral squares

thirty-one 1 3/4" strips (cut crosswise), gold print

fifty 1 3/4" strips (cut crosswise), mauve

two 4 1/2" x 93 1/2" strips (for first side border), gold print

two 4 1/2" x 76" strips (for first top and bottom border), gold print

two 4 1/2" x 101 1/2" strips (for second side border), mauve

two 4 1/2" x 84" strips (for second top and bottom border), mauve

Instructions

1. For sashing strips, join 2 mauve strips to a gold strip, **Fig 1**. Repeat for a total of 21 pieced strips. Cut crosswise every 9 1/2" until you have 82 pieces, **Fig 2**.

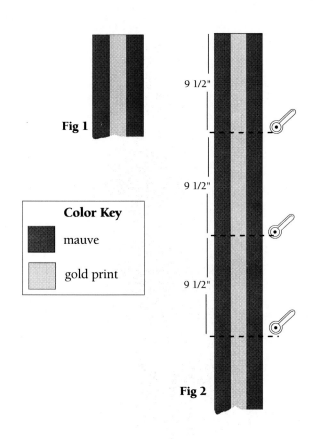

Fig 1

Color Key

■	mauve
□	gold print

9 1/2"

9 1/2"

9 1/2"

Fig 2

continued

2. For Nine-Patch blocks, sew 2 mauve strips to a gold strip to create pieced Strip A. Repeat for a total of 2 pieced Strip A. Then sew 2 gold strips to one mauve strip to create pieced Strip B, **Fig 3.** Repeat for a total of 4 pieced Strip B. Cut crosswise every 1 3/4", **Fig 4,** until you have 48 pieces of Strip A and 96 pieces of Strip B. Sew a Strip B piece on each side of a Strip A piece, **Fig 5,** until you have 48 Nine-Patch blocks.

Nine-Patch Block Diagram

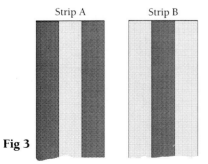

Strip A   Strip B

Fig 3

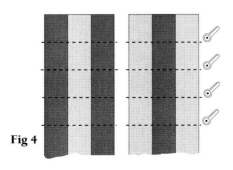

Fig 4

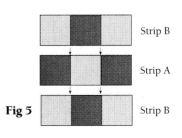

Strip B

Strip A

Strip B

Fig 5

3. For long sashing strips, join 8 Nine-Patch blocks to 7 sashing strips, **Fig 6.** Repeat for five more strips.

4. Join 7 floral blocks to 8 sashing strips as shown in **Fig 7**. You now have a vertical strip of 7 joined blocks. Make four more vertical strips.

5. Following quilt layout, join the vertical strips to the long sashing strips created in step 3 above.

6. Add gold print border to sides and then to top and bottom. Add mauve border to sides and then to top and bottom.

7. To finish quilt, follow finishing instructions beginning with Preparing the Quilt Top on page 209.

Quilting Suggestion

The photographed quilt was quilted in the ditch around the mauve strips and squares. The Quilting Template was used to mark the border. Do not add seam allowance when making Quilting Template.

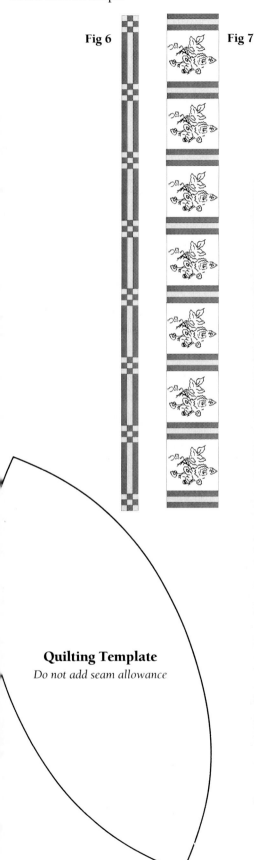

Fig 6   **Fig 7**

Quilting Template
Do not add seam allowance

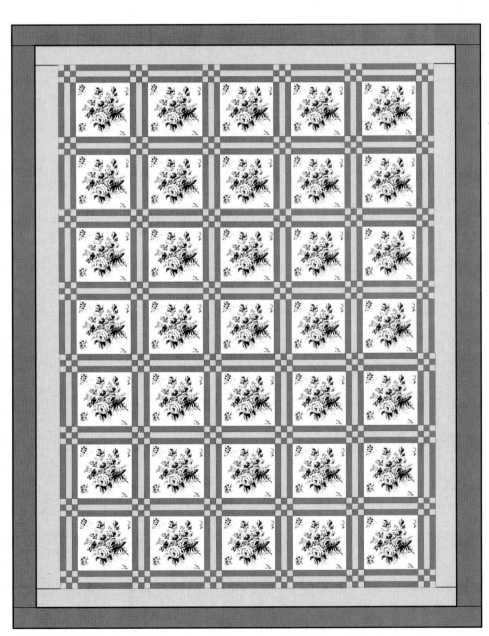

Quilt Layout

217

Double Irish Chain Quilt

We've never really known what the Irish have to do with this kind of quilt pattern, but these "chains" have been called "Irish" for about a hundred years. While this is a pattern that lends itself to the modern piecing methods, we show it here pieced as grandma would have made this quilt. Perhaps to really make it Irish, it would have to be created in shades of green instead of this lovely pink and white.

The quilt, measuring approximately 70" x 84", is made up of thirty Block 1 and twenty Block 2 set on point. The sides are created from eighteen Block 3 and the corners are created with four Block 4. The entire quilt is bound with a 1/2" binding of white fabric.

Fabric Requirements

2 1/4 yds pink
4 yds white
5 yds backing fabric

Cutting Requirements

	Block 1	Block 2	Block 3	Block 4	for quilt
Template A pink	12	4	1		458
Template A white	13				390
Template B white		4	2	1	120
Template C pink			2	2	44
Template D white		1			20
Template E white			1		18
Template F white				1	4

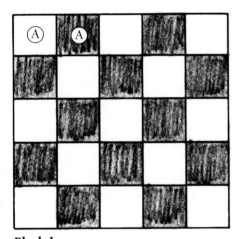

Block 1

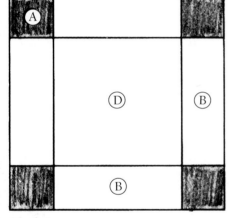

Block 2

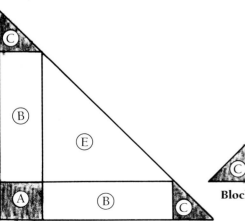

Block 3

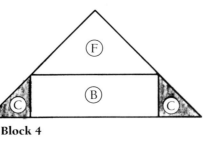

Block 4

Quilt Layout

Block 1   Block 2   Block 1   Block 3   Block 4

Block 3

Block 2

continued

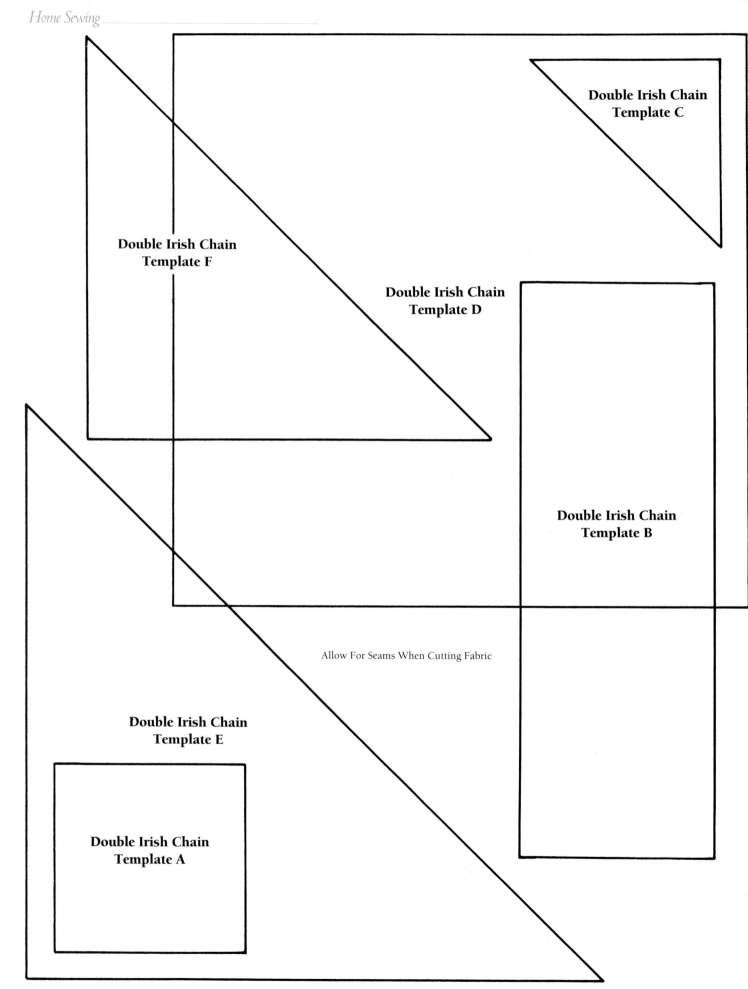

**Double Irish Chain
Template C**

**Double Irish Chain
Template F**

**Double Irish Chain
Template D**

**Double Irish Chain
Template B**

Allow For Seams When Cutting Fabric

**Double Irish Chain
Template E**

**Double Irish Chain
Template A**

The Basket Quilt

The appliquéd basket design was a popular motif in the beautiful album quilts of the nineteenth century. We salute that enterprising quiltmaker who designed a way to create a basket quilt by piecing rather than appliquéing. Perhaps, like many of us, she found piecing easy and appliqué taxing. The block is easy to piece with just a minimum of appliqué necessary to complete the pattern.

The quilt, measuring approximately 74 1/2" x 86 1/2", is made of forty-two 10" pieced blocks set six in width and seven in length with 2" pink strips set between the blocks. The quilt is finished with a 2" pink border and bound with 1/4" white binding all around.

Note: Each block is pieced first, **Fig 1**, and then the handle (Template F) is appliquéd on.

Fabric Requirements

12 1/2 yds white
5 yds pink

Cutting Requirements

		for a block	for quilt
Template A	white	1	42
Template B	white	1	42
Template C	pink	11	462
Template C	white	5	210
Template D	white	2	84
Template E	white	1	42
Template F	pink	1	42

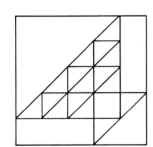

Fig 1

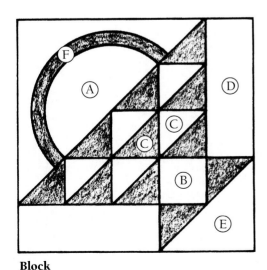

Block

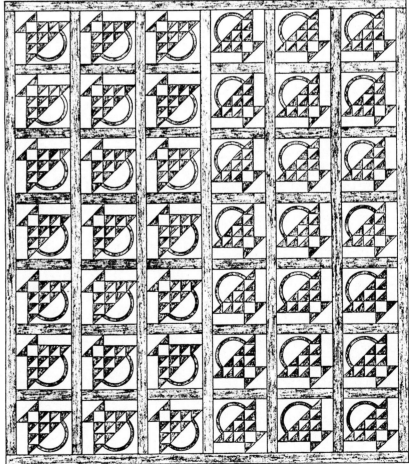

Quilt Layout

continued

221

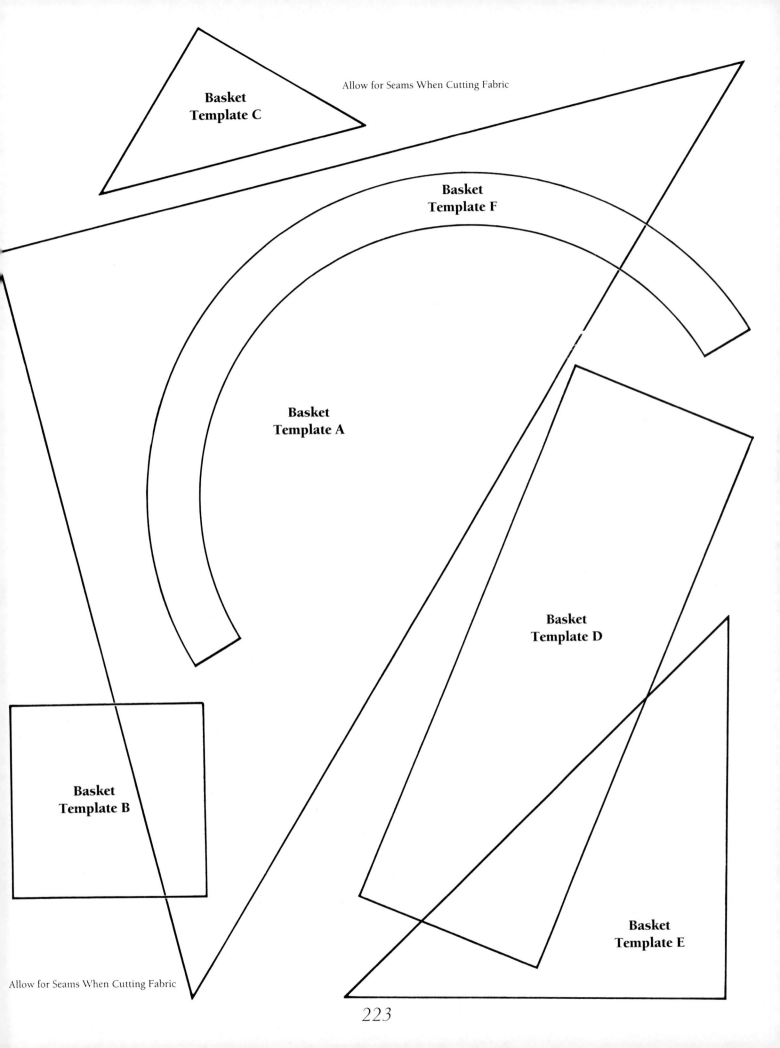

Allow for Seams When Cutting Fabric

**Basket
Template C**

**Basket
Template F**

**Basket
Template A**

**Basket
Template D**

**Basket
Template B**

**Basket
Template E**

Allow for Seams When Cutting Fabric

223

The Fan Quilt

This lovely quilt was designed and created by Florence McLaughlin Gray (1847-1938) in the last part of the nineteenth century. The beautiful fan patterns and the spectacular border make this quilt into a piece of art. By following the directions, you can re-create this antique quilt.

The quilt, measuring approximately 64" x 78" is made up of eighty 7 1/4" x 7 1/4" blocks set eight across and ten down. The fan is completed first and then appliquéd to a 7 3/4" x 7 3/4" square of gold fabric (finished size 7 1/4" x 7 1/4"). A border made up of Templates A & C is used around the four sides (see **Fig 1**) and a binding, made from the green fabric completes the quilt.

Fabric Requirements

1 1/2 yds green
2 1/4 yds assorted prints
4 1/2 yds gold
5 yds backing fabric

Cutting Requirements

		for a block	for quilt
Template A	green	1	80
Template B	assorted prints	8	640
Block	gold	1	80
Template A	(for border) green		66
Template C	(for border) gold		62

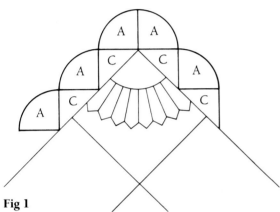

Fig 1

Quilt Layout

Block

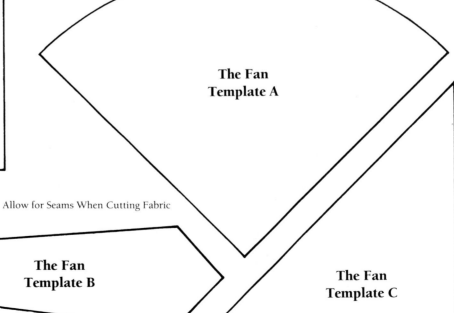

The Fan
Template A

Allow for Seams When Cutting Fabric

The Fan
Template B

The Fan
Template C

225

Ocean Waves Quilt

This is another quilt designed and pieced by Florence McLaughlin Gray, who made the lovely Fan Quilt on page 224. In addition to making quilts, Florence was an accomplished painter, and one look at this quilt and you know immediately that the quilter understood color and design. The striped pink and red fabrics are placed so expertly as to create not just a quilt but a striking graphic statement. Probably made about 100 years ago, this quilt remains fresh today and is reminiscent of a work of modern art.

The quilt, measuring approximately 72 1/2" x 80 1/2" is made up of sixteen 16" blocks and four half blocks, which measure 16" x 8". Two 2"-wide borders—one blue and one white—and a 1/4" pink seam binding finish the quilt.

Fabric Requirements

4 1/2 yds blue
3 yds assorted pinks
2 1/2 yds white
5 yds backing fabric

Cutting Requirements

		for a full block	for quilt
Template A	blue	48	864
Template A	assorted pinks	48	864
Template B	white	8	144
		for a half block	
Template A	blue	24	
Template A	assorted pinks	24	
Template B	white	4	

Quilt Layout

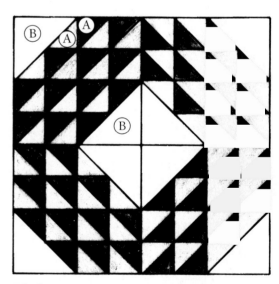

Block

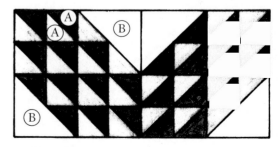

Half Block

Allow for Seams When Cutting Fabric

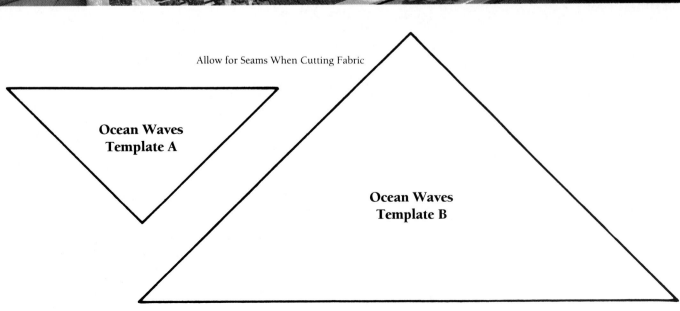

**Ocean Waves
Template A**

**Ocean Waves
Template B**

Crayons Crib Quilt

Little Red Schoolhouse Crib Quilt

Quilts for Little Ones

If there's one time when you want to make a quilt, it's when a little one arrives on the scene. Here are two delightful quilts to make for the little ones in your life. In case you have no little ones, these quilts make charming wall hangings.

Crayons Crib Quilt

designed by Rita Weiss

The bright colors used to make this traditional "Rail Fence" quilt make us think of those colorful crayons we played with as children. This is a very simple quilt to make and one that could probably be pieced in a weekend. We've given instructions for making this quilt by the traditional method using templates, but we've also given instructions for making this quilt with modern speed techniques.

Size of Block

9" x 9"

Size of Quilt

Approx 43 1/2" x 52 1/2"

Setting

The blocks are set 4 across and 5 down with a 3" border and a 3/4" binding.

Fabric Requirements

yellow, orange, purple, blue, green fabric: 1/2 yd each
red fabric: 3 1/4 yds (includes border, backing and binding)

Traditional Method

Cut the following:

Template A red, 20
Template A yellow, 20
Template A orange, 20
Template A purple, 20
Template A blue, 20
Template A green, 20

Side Borders:
Cut two red strips, each 3 1/2" x 45 1/2"

Top and Bottom Borders
Cut two red strips, each 3 1/2" x 42 1/2"

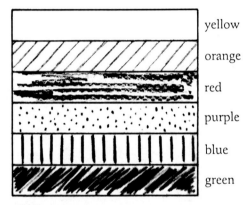

yellow
orange
red
purple
blue
green

Block Diagram

Instructions

1. Following the Block Diagram, make 20 blocks following the same color sequence in each block.

2. Following the Quilt Layout, join the blocks.

3. Add the red borders to sides and then to top and bottom.

4. To finish quilt, follow finishing instructions starting with Preparing the Quilt Top on page 209.

Modern Method

Cutting Requirements

five 2" strips (cut crosswise), red, yellow, orange, purple, blue and green
two 3 1/2" x 45 1/2" strips, red for side borders
two 3 1/2" x 42 1/2" strips, red for top and bottom borders.

continued

Instructions

1. Sew one strip of each color in the order shown in Block Diagram. Repeat with remaining strips until you have five strip-pieced fabrics.

2. Cut crosswise every 9 1/2", **Fig 1,** until you have 20 blocks.

3. Repeat steps 2 to 4 of Traditional Method to complete the quilt.

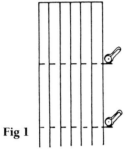

Fig 1

Quilting Suggestions

The photographed quilt was quilted in the ditch around each of the crayons.

Crayons Layout

Color Key	
□	yellow
▨	orange
▤	red
▦	purple
▥	blue
▨	green

Allow for Seams When Cutting Fabric

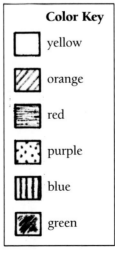

**Crayons
Template A**

Little Red Schoolhouse Crib Quilt

designed by Rita Weiss

Grandmother may very well have gone to a little red school-house that looked like the ones in this quilt. Perhaps that's why the quilt block has been around for such a long time. Most little tykes today will never go to such a charming little red schoolhouse; so why not keep the memory alive on a quilt? We used four different reds to create our schools; you may remember your schoolhouse as being only one shade of red.

Size of Block

9" x 9"

Size of Quilt

Approx 43 1/2" x 52 1/2"

Setting

The blocks are set 4 across and 5 down with a 1" border of the natural fabric and a 2" border of one of the red print fabrics. The quilt is finished with a 3/4" binding of the same red fabric as the border.

Fabric Requirements

red print 1, 2 and 4: 3/4 yd
red print 3: 2 1/2 yds
   (includes border, backing and binding)
natural: 1 1/2 yds

Traditional Method

Cut the following:

	for block	for quilt
Template A red print 1	2	10
Template A red print 2	2	10
Template A red print 3	2	10
Template A red print 4	2	10
Template B natural	1	20
Template C red print 1	1	5
Template C red print 2	1	5
Template C red print 3	1	5
Template C red print 4	1	5
Template D red print 1	2	10
Template D red print 2	2	10
Template D red print 3	2	10
Template D red print 4	2	10

	for block	for quilt
Template D natural	1	20
Template E red print 1	3	15
Template E red print 2	3	15
Template E red print 3	3	15
Template E red print 4	3	15
Template E natural	2	40
Template F natural	1	20
Template G natural	1	20
Template H red print 1	1	5
Template H red print 2	1	5
Template H red print 3	1	5
Template H red print 4	1	5
Template I red print 1	1	5
Template I red print 2	1	5
Template I red print 3	1	5
Template I red print 4	1	5
Template J natural	1	20
Template K natural	1	20
Template L natural	1	20
Template M red print 1	2	10
Template M red print 2	2	10
Template M red print 3	2	10
Template M red print 4	2	10
Template N natural	1	20
Template O natural	1	20

First Border:

Cut 2 natural strips each 1 1/2" x 45 1/2" for sides

Cut 2 natural strips each 1 1/2" x 38 1/2" for top and bottom

continued

Second Border

Cut 2 red print 3 strips each 2 1/2" x 47 1/2" for sides

Cut 2 red print 3 strips each 2 1/2" x 45 1/2" for top and bottom

Instructions

1. Make five blocks of each of the four red prints following the Block Diagram.

2. Join the blocks following the Quilt Layout, and placing the red print schools as shown in **Fig 1**.

3. Add the natural borders and then the borders made from the red print 3 fabric.

4. To finish quilt, follow instructions in Quiltmaking How-to, starting with Preparing the Quilt Top on page 209.

Quilting Suggestion

Quilt around the windows, doors, and roofs of each schoolhouse as shown in **Fig 2**.

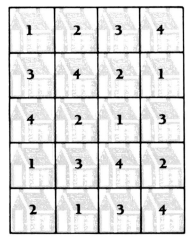

Fig 1

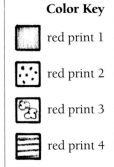

Fig 2

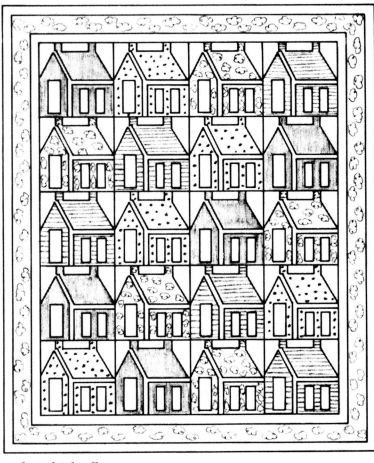

Little Red Schoolhouse Layout

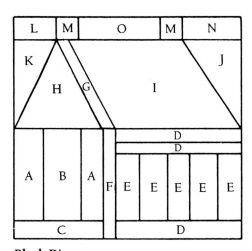

Block Diagram

Color Key

red print 1

red print 2

red print 3

red print 4

232

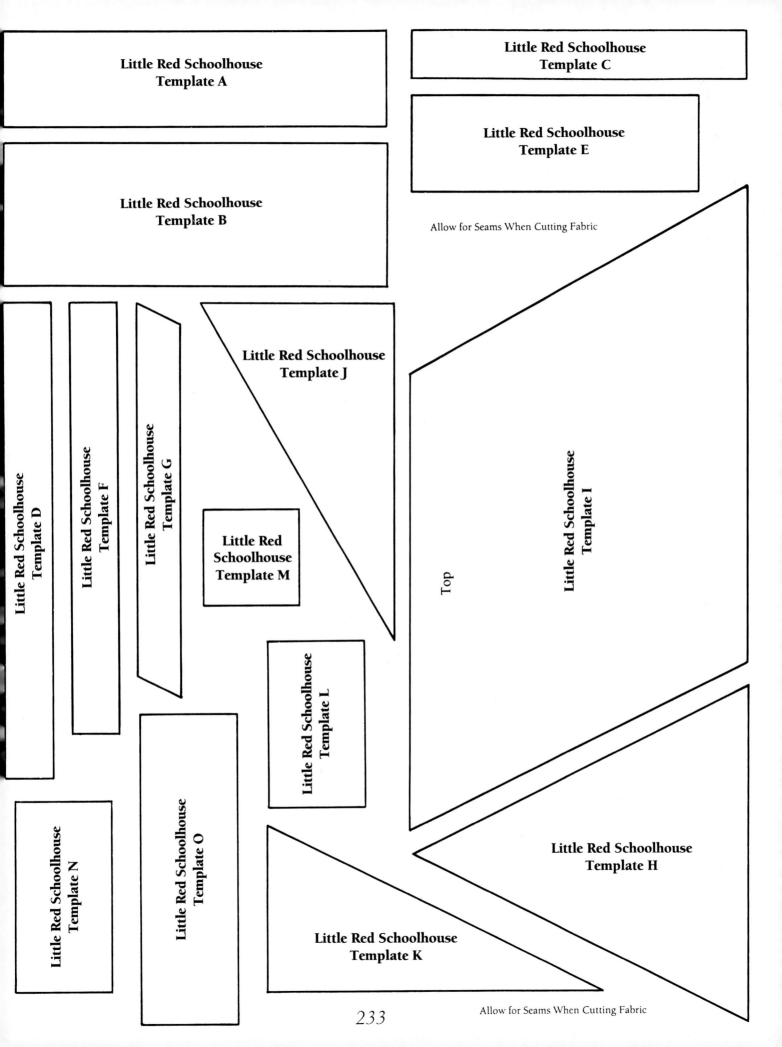

Little Red Schoolhouse
Template A

Little Red Schoolhouse
Template C

Little Red Schoolhouse
Template B

Little Red Schoolhouse
Template E

Allow for Seams When Cutting Fabric

Little Red Schoolhouse
Template D

Little Red Schoolhouse
Template F

Little Red Schoolhouse
Template G

Little Red Schoolhouse
Template J

Little Red
Schoolhouse
Template M

Top

Little Red Schoolhouse
Template I

Little Red Schoolhouse
Template L

Little Red Schoolhouse
Template N

Little Red Schoolhouse
Template O

Little Red Schoolhouse
Template K

Little Red Schoolhouse
Template H

233

Allow for Seams When Cutting Fabric

Tableskirts and Toppers

designed by Donna Babylon

Covering a small table with a beautiful fabric is an inexpensive and effective solution to many decorating problems. These tables—whether you purchase a new one or use an existing one—come in a variety of sizes and provide the perfect place to show off a special photograph or a bouquet of flowers. Use your table as a night stand, or place it in a sitting area to enjoy during those special moments. When you read these directions, you may think "this is a lot of math." Don't let it scare you, Just follow the directions, and you'll be delighted with the results.

The Tableskirt

1. Measure diameter of the table. Write measurement here _____ .

2. Measure drop length desired (the distance from table top edge to floor), add 1", and multiply this number by 2. Write measurement here _____ .

3. Add diameter of the table to number found in step #2. This is diameter of the tableskirt. Write measurement here _____ .

4. Divide diameter of tableskirt by width of fabric you are using. Round this number up to next highest whole number. This will give you the number of panels needed to make your tableskirt.

5. Multiply number of panels by diameter of tableskirt. This gives you amount of fabric in inches. Write amount here _____ .

6. Divide by 36" to determine number of yards needed. Round number up to nearest 1/4 yd increment. A little extra fabric is always a safe measure. **Note:** If your fabric has a definite repeat pattern or motif, add repeat distance to each panel. Write measurement here_____ .

Example:
The diameter of table used in our photographs is 20". The distance from table edge to floor is 25 3/4". Using formula above, the calculations are:

1. 20

2. 25 3/4" + 1 = 26 3/4" x 2 = 53 1/2"

3. 53 1/2" + 20" = 73 1/2"

4. 73 1/2" ÷ 44 = 1.67 (round up to 2)

5. 2 x 73 1/2" = 147"

6. 147" ÷ 36" = 4.08 (4 1/8 yds)

Cutting and Piecing Panels

Tableskirts are constructed from a large square of fabric. Most fabrics need to be seamed together to form a piece of cloth large enough to cover the table. However, a tableskirt is never seamed in the middle. You have to do a little bit of "creative piecing" to hide the seams in the sides. Motifs in printed fabrics should match, since the seams will be seen.

1. For two panels: Cut number of panels needed to make your size of tableskirt. These panels should be equal in size. The easiest way to do this is to fold your fabric in half on the crosswise grain. The selvages will be directly on top of each other. Cut along this fold line. Press to remove any creases from fabric.

2. Cut one of the two panels in half lengthwise, **Fig 1.**

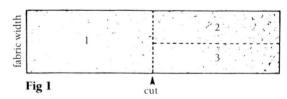

Fig 1

3. Place one half panel right sides together to one side of whole panel, matching design motifs if necessary, **Fig 2.** Stitch, using 1/2" seam allowance. Repeat for other side. Trim off selvages and press seams open.

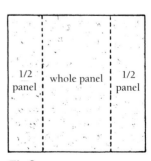

Fig 2

*Basic Round Topper
with Decorative Option #3*

*Basic Square Topper
with Decorative Option #5*

*Basic Round Topper
with Decorative Option #1*

continued

4. For three panels: Divide entire length of your fabric by 3. Cut three panels using this measurement. Press to remove any creases from the fabric.

5. Place two panels right sides together, matching design motifs, if necessary. Stitch, using side 1/2" seam allowance. Repeat for other panel. Trim off selvages and press seams open.

Finishing Tableskirt

1. On floor or large work surface, fold pieced cloth in half with right sides together, matching seams, **Fig 3**. Fold again into quarters, **Fig 4**. Make sure edges are even and the fabric is smooth; pin randomly to secure fabric in place.

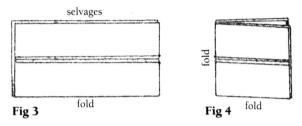

Fig 3   fold   **Fig 4**   fold

2. Divide diameter of tableskirt (from step #4 on page 234), in half. Example: 73 1/2" ÷ 2 = 36 3/4". This is the radius of the tableskirt.

3. Measure radius distance from folded corner, or "pivot point." Mark in 1" increments with a water soluble fabric pen. You have drawn a quarter circle, **Fig 5**. Cut through all layers using the line as a guide.

4. Working in small sections, press raw edge of circle under 1" to wrong side, **Fig 6**. The hem of a circular tableskirt is on the bias. To ensure a smooth hemline, let majority of tableskirt rest in a chair that is placed near ironing board while you press.

5. Press raw edge under again until it meets crease, **Fig 7**. You have now formed a 1/2" hem. Stitch along folded edge. Press entire tablecloth.

Toppers

Choose a contrasting solid or coordinating print fabric when creating the toppers. Even the toppers can be embellished! Let your imagination be your guide.

Basic Square Topper

1. Determine size of the square needed. For a basic square, add at least 20" to diameter of the table. For example, a table with a 20" diameter will need a 40" square. This will give you a 9" drop on all four sides (the square has a 1" seam allowance). For a more dramatic look, you may want the square to be larger.

2. Depending on the size of the square, you may or may not have to piece fabric to get the desired size. Check chart below to see the largest size square that can be made from a width of fabric. You may have to trim some of the excess fabric away to get an exact square.

> 1 1/4 yds of 44" fabric will give you up to a 44" square
> 1 3/8 yds of 48" fabric will give you up to a 48" square
> 1 1/2 yds of 54" fabric will give you up to a 54" square
> 1 3/4 yds of 60" fabric will give you up to a 60" square
> 2 1/2 yds of 90" fabric will give you up to a 90" square

3. If you have to piece your fabric, follow the same formula as for tableskirt to determine number of panels and how to piece fabric to make it large enough.

4. Press raw edges 1" toward wrong side of fabric on opposite sides of square. Tuck and press raw edges into the crease, creating a 1/2" hem, **Fig 8**; pin to hold. Repeat process for opposite two sides, taking care to make sure all raw edges of fabric are concealed, especially at corners, **Fig 9**.

5. Stitch along inside fold line around edges. When you come to a corner, place needle in down position, raise presser foot, and pivot fabric. Put presser foot down and continue stitching, **Fig 10**.

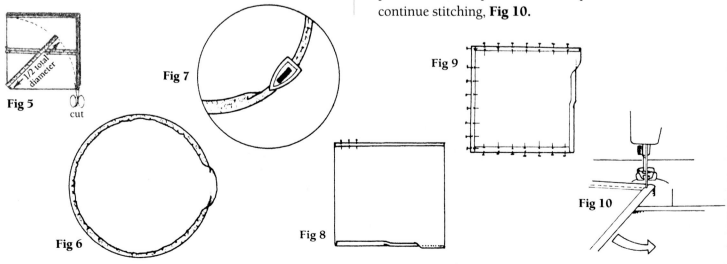

Fig 5   cut   **Fig 7**   **Fig 9**   **Fig 10**   **Fig 8**   **Fig 6**

Decorative Option #1

Tie corners of topper with a coordinating ribbon, **Fig 11.**

Decorative Option #2

Select coordinating ribbon(s) and arrange attractively, perhaps criss-crossing from edge to edge of topper, **Fig 12.**

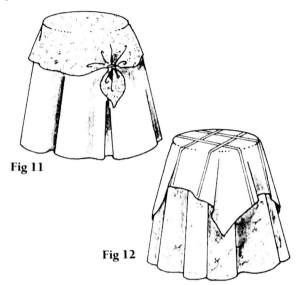

Fig 11

Fig 12

Decorative Option #3

Sew a lace edging along edge of topper, **Fig 13.**

Decorative Option #4

Make two square toppers from different fabrics and place them catty-cornered on table. One or both may be embellished with ribbons or lace edging, **Fig 14.**

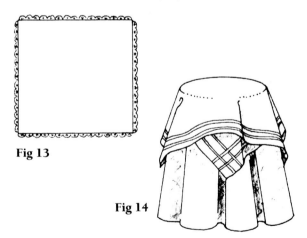

Fig 13

Fig 14

Decorative Option #5

(shown in photo on page 235)

Add a coordinating stripe along edges.

Basic Round Topper

A basic round topper is constructed exactly like its longer counterpart. It can be as long as you want, but a good guideline for a pleasing proportion is 1/3 or 2/3 the drop length. For example, 25 3/4" ÷ 3 = 8 1/2" or, rounded up to next whole number, 9". Two thirds the distance is 18".

Decorative Option #1

(shown in **Fig 15** and photo on page 235)

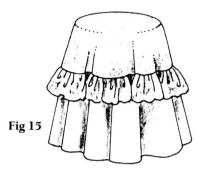

Fig 15

Ruffles add the softest of finishes for a round topper and can be made in a matching, contrasting or coordinating fabric. The ruffle is considered part of overall drop length. The ruffle can be any width, but a nice width is 4" finished. Yardage for the ruffle is figured separately. First you have to determine the size of the topper.

Topper Yardage

1. Determine overall drop length of topper. Subtract finished width of ruffle. Write measurement here_____.

2. Add 1/2" to the above measurement and multiply by 2. Write measurement here _____.

3. Add diameter of table. This will give you diameter of topper. Write measurement here _____.

4. Divide diameter of topper by width of fabric to be used. Round number up to next highest whole number. This will give you number of panels needed to make your tableskirt. Write number here _____.

5. Multiply number of panels by diameter of topper. This will give you amount of fabric in inches. Write amount here _____.

6. Divide number found in step #5 by 36" to determine number of yards needed. Round number to nearest 1/4 yd increment. Write number here _____.

Example:

The diameter of the table used in the photographs is 20". The desired drop length of the topper is 10". The finished length of the ruffle is 4". Using these numbers, apply them to the above formula.

1. 10" - 4" = 6"

2. (6" + 1/2") x 2 = 13"

3. 13" + 20" = 33"

4. 33" ÷ 44" = .75 (round up to 1)

237

continued

5. 1 x 33" = 33"

6. 33" ÷ 36" = .91 or 1 yd

Ruffle Yardage

1. Determine circumference of topper. This can be done by multiplying the figure in step #3 in the Topper Yardage section by 3.14. Write measurement here _____.

2. Multiply circumference by 2 1/2. Write measurement here _____.

3. Divide by width of fabric you are using. Round up to next highest whole number. This will tell you how many strips are needed for the ruffle. Write number here _____.

4. Determine finished width of ruffle. Multiply finished width by 2 and add 1". For example, if you want 4" finished ruffles: 4 x 2 = 8 + 1 = 9. This is the cut width of the ruffle strips. Write width here _____.

5. Multiply cut width of strips by number of strips needed. Write number here _____.

6. Divide this number by 36" to determine amount of fabric you need. Write yards needed here _____.

Example:
Continuing with same numbers as before, the formula would be:

1. 33" x 3.14 = 104"

2. 104" x 2 1/2 = 260"

3. 260" ÷ 44 = 5.9 (round up to 6")

4. 4"(finished width) x 2 = 8 + 1 = 9"

5. 9" x 6" = 54"

6. 54" ÷ 36" = 1 1/2 yds

Constructing Topper with Ruffle

1. Make topper exactly the same as for tableskirt, except do not hem.

2. Cut number of strips for ruffle. Form one long strip by placing strips right sides together, end to end. Stitch short ends using 1/2" seam allowance; press seams open. Stitch last two ends together, forming one large circle; press seam open.

3. Fold tube wrong sides together, matching raw edges. The ruffle will be "softer" if folded edge is not pressed into a sharp crease.

4. Divide topper and ruffle into quarters. Mark with a safety pin placed in a perpendicular position.

5. Set your machine to longest and widest zigzag stitch.

6. Place unwaxed dental floss or small cording 1/2" from raw edges of ruffle. Leave about a 5" tail of cording for gathering. Begin to stitch, being careful not to catch cording in stitching. After you have stitched several inches, leave needle in down position and gently pull cord to gather ruffle. Continue in this manner, stopping every 10" to 15" to gather the ruffle.

7. Pin ruffle right sides together to topper, matching safety pins. Adjust gathers to fit between markings. Be sure that all gathers are distributed evenly.

8. Stitch through all thicknesses, using a 1/2" seam allowance. If you are pleased with distribution of gathers, remove cording or floss. If not, remove the stitches from the section you need to readjust, redistribute gathers and finish stitching.

9. Trim seam to 1/4" and finish with a zigzag or overcast stitch. Press seam toward topper.

Decorative Option #2
Add pre-gathered, purchased lace trim over fabric ruffle from Basic Round Topper - Decorative Option #1. Use circumference measurement and divide by 36" to determine how much lace to purchase. Baste both lace and ruffle together and treat as one.

Decorative Option #3 (shown in photo on page 235):
The basic round topper can be even more decorative by making topper "balloon" or "pouf" around circumference of table. The balloon topper is made exactly like the basic round topper. However, a special two-cord shirring tape (available in drapery departments) is used to gather topper into poufs. The amount of shirring tape needed depends on number of poufs you want, and the depth of the poufs, **Fig 16.**

Fig 16

238

1. The number of poufs is a personal choice. Usually, topper is divided into fourths, sixths or eighths. To determine number of poufs you prefer, place topper over tableskirt and pin some test poufs in place. Also determine how deep you want poufs to be. Make note of this measurement here.

2. Fold topper into quarters, sixths or eighths, depending on number of poufs you decided on. Press a crease where each of the poufs will be.

3. Multiply depth of each pouf by number of divisions to determine amount of two-cord shirring tape to purchase. Cut shirring cords into appropriate lengths.

4. Knot cords at one end and fold over raw edges at the same end. Place this end at the hem line directly over the creases.

5. Secure tape to topper by stitching tape in place along both sides of the tape, **Fig 17.**

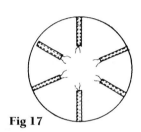

Fig 17

6. Poufs are created when cords are pulled and the fabric gathers. Tie cords securely. Do not cut off excess cord in case you want to wash the topper in the future—just hide them in the poufs.

7. For a fun and decorative touch, add a bow, rosette, or bouquet of dried flowers at each of the divisions.

Decorative Option #4
This is really a combination of Decorative Options #1 and #3. The topper will have a ruffle, and it will also be gathered into delicate poufs, **Fig 18.**

Fig 18

239

The Bearry Brothers

designed by Nora Fran Dilks

There's magic in a teddy bear. He's just some fabric, a little embroidery, some stuffing. But put those simple ingredients together, and he's an object for loving. A completed teddy bear--whether he's made by an expert or someone who can't quite get both ears the same size--dares the world not to love him. And in a battle between a helpless human and a teddy bear, the bear will always win. Before beginning to make our Bearry brothers, Blue Bearry and Razz Bearry, be sure to read the general hints on teddy bear making.

Razz Bearry

Blue Bearry

General Hints on Teddy Bear Making

1. For fabric bears, use tightly woven fabric, such as a good 100% cotton. Loosely woven fabrics cannot be stuffed sufficiently, and the bear will not hold his shape.

2. All fabric requirements are based on 44" - 45" wide fabric.

3. All seam allowances are 1/4". This will avoid extra trimming and clipping of seam allowances.

4. All the pattern pieces appear full size on pages 246-248. Lay a piece of tracing paper over the pattern and carefully trace the pattern including the markings. (Do not photocopy the pieces instead of tracing them. Photocopy machines are not exact.)

Stuffings

Stuff your bear firmly! The bears will not hold their shapes unless they are firmly stuffed. Overstuff rather than understuff. Here are some special hints on stuffing:

1. Stuff small areas or details, such as paws, with small amounts or little clumps of stuffing.

2. Carefully position stuffing into all areas of the bear in order to avoid lumps and under-stuffed areas.

3. Fluff up each clump or cluster of fiberfill before inserting into bear. This will help avoid a lumpy looking bear.

4. As you stuff, mold the bear with your hands to obtain a good shape and help avoid the "lumpies."

Embroidery

Here are some simple embroidery stitches which are used for creating bear faces:

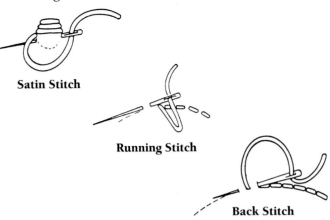

Satin Stitch

Running Stitch

Back Stitch

Attaching Button Eyes

All eyes are sewn on after bear has been completed. Thread a long needle with a sturdy, heavy-duty thread such as Buttonhole Twist or Button and Carpet thread. Thread should match bear fabric.

1. Do not knot thread. Sink thread into bear about 1" from where eye attaches.

2. Bring needle up to spot where eye should be placed, allowing several inches of thread to extend out from where stitch entered body. Secure thread by stitching several small stitches on top of each other at point where eye attaches (the stitches will be covered by the eye). Clip off extending thread.

3. Stitch through button and then into bear to secure eye to body. Repeat 5 or 6 times.

4. Secure thread by stitching several small stitches on top of each other. Make sure that these small stitches will be covered by button.

5. Sink threaded needle down into bear and bring needle up through body about 1" away from eye. Clip off end of thread that extends from body. Be sure to clip this close enough so that it does not show.

Blue Bearry

Size

Approximately 14" tall

Fabric

1/2 yd blue and white cotton print (for Blue Bearry's body)

Optional: 6" x 36" piece cotton print (for Blue Bearry's bow)

Notions

Two 1/2" blue ball or half-ball buttons (for Blue Bearry's eyes)

Blue embroidery floss

Sewing thread

Heavy-duty thread (for Blue Bearry's eyes)

Polyester fiberfill

Blue Bearry's Body

1. Following layout in **Fig 1,** and using pattern pieces for Bear (pages 246-248), cut out required pieces. You should have: 1 Body Back, 2 body Fronts, 1 Seat, 2 Legs, 2 Ear Fronts, 2 Ear Backs, 1 Snout, 1 Head Back, 1 Head Front, 2 Foot Bottoms.

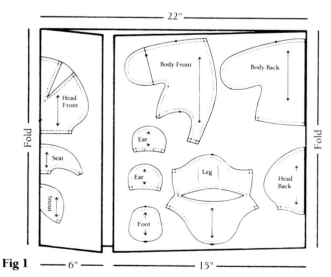

Fig 1

2. Transfer necessary markings.

3. Right sides together, stitch two Body Fronts along front seam **Fig 2.**

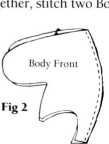

Body Front

Fig 2

4. Run a row of gathering stitches along edge marked "ease" on Seat. Pull in stitches slightly until Seat matches lower edge of Body Back. Stitch Body Back and Seat together, matching center backs, **Fig 3.**

5. Right sides together, match Body Front to Body Back. Pin side seams together and join only to underarm dot, **Fig 4.** **Note:** If arms are completely stitched together at this point it is difficult to set in legs.

6. Right sides together, match back and front crotch seams. Pin and then join, **Fig 5.**

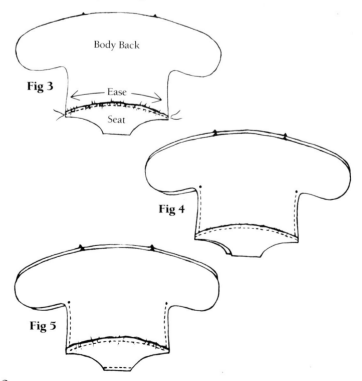

Body Back

Fig 3
Ease
Seat

Fig 4

Fig 5

7. Right sides together, fold Legs in half matching dart openings. Stitch dart closed along sewing line. Cut out dart opening, **Fig 6**.

8. Run a row of gathering stitches along curved front edge of foot marked "ease," **Fig 7**.

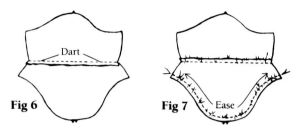

Fig 6

Fig 7

9. Right sides together, fold leg in half lengthwise, matching center back seam. Join this seam, **Fig 8**.

10. Fit Foot Bottom into circular opening at leg bottom matching single notches on Foot Bottom to seam of leg. Baste and then sew. **Note:** Wider end of Foot Bottom matches toe end of leg, **Fig 9**.

11. Baste Leg into leg opening matching notch on top of curve of front leg to notch on Body Front, **Fig 10**. Stitch together. By carefully matching notches, legs will automatically face front. Edge of leg marked "outside" should match up to side seam of body.

12. Repeat steps 7 to 11 for second Leg.

13. After legs are set into body (and while body is still inside out), finish stitching front and back arms together. Stitch to notches on neckline edge, **Fig 11**.

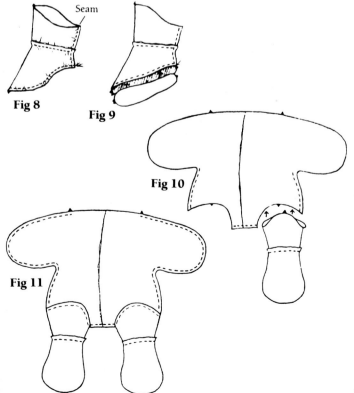

Fig 8

Fig 9

Fig 10

Fig 11

14. Turn right side out and stuff through opening. Stitch opening closed by hand.

Blue Bearry's Head

1. Stitch pleats in Ear Fronts, **Fig 12**.

2. Right sides together, join Ear Backs to Ear Fronts, leaving bottom edge open, **Fig 13.** Turn right side out. Baste bottom edge of ear closed.

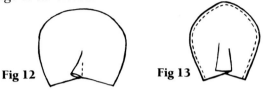

Fig 12

Fig 13

3. Seam darts together on Head Front, **Fig 14.** Baste ear to right side of Head Front with pleat side of ear against face. Ear is placed along top edge of head, starting at dart and extending along side toward neck edge, **Fig 15.**

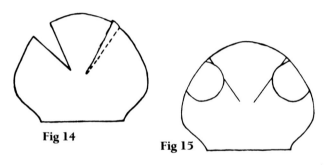

Fig 14

Fig 15

4. Right sides together (and with ears sandwiched between), baste Head Front and Head Back together. Stitch allowing neck edge to remain open. Turn right side out. Stuff.

5. Center head on body, making sure that Head Front (with darts) is facing same direction as Body Front. Pin head securely to body, anchoring head to body by pulling front and back edge of head over shoulders. Head opening will cup over shoulders. Stitch head to body with small, invisible hand stitches, **Fig 16.**

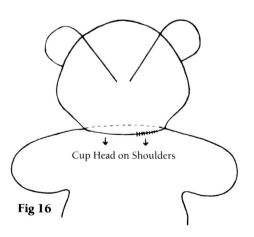

Cup Head on Shoulders

Fig 16

continued

243

Blue Bearry's Face

1. Seam dart in snout, **Fig 17.**

2. Turn under 1/4" all around snout and baste or pin down.

3. Position snout to front of face over point that resulted from stitching two large darts on Head Front. Seam on snout will face down. When you feel snout is in correct spot, giving your bear proper look and character, pin in place, **Fig 18.**

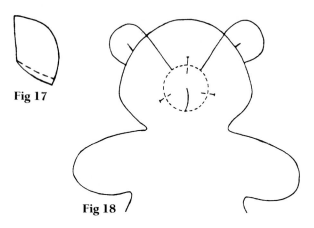

Fig 17

Fig 18

4. Attach snout to face with small, invisible stitches, stuffing snout as you work.

5. Attach eyes following instructions on page 241. The buttons are placed above snout between darts, **Fig 19.**

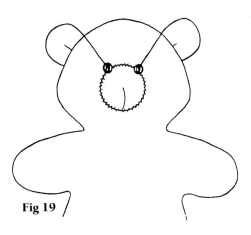

Fig 19

6. Embroider nose with Satin Stitch and mouth with Back Stitch. Mouth is embroidered along seam line of snout, **Fig 20.**

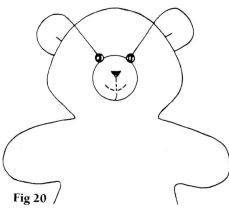

Fig 20

Blue Bearry's Bow (Optional)

1. If necessary, piece fabric to achieve desired length.

2. Fold in half right sides together. With 1/4" seam allowance, stitch along short ends and down long edge, leaving an opening for turning, **Fig 21.** Cut corners on diagonal if desired.

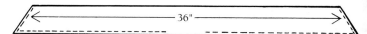

Fig 21

3. Turn inside out. Slip stitch opening.

4. Tie bow around Blue Bearry's neck.

Razz Bearry

Size

Approximately 14" tall

Fabric

1/2 yd raspberry cotton print (for Razz Bearry's body)

7" x 12" piece solid raspberry cotton (for contrasting paws, feet and ears)

Optional: 6" x 36" piece cotton print (for Razz Bearry's bow)

Notions

Two 1/2" blue ball or half-ball buttons (for Razz Bearry's eyes)

Blue embroidery floss

Sewing thread

Heavy-duty thread (for Razz Bearry's eyes)

Polyester fiberfill

Razz Bearry's Body

1. Following layout in **Figs 22 and 23,** and using pattern pieces for Bear (pages 246-248), cut out required pieces. From the raspberry print, you should have: 1 Body Back, 2 Body Fronts (cut along line for contrasting paw), 1 Seat, 2 Legs, 2 Ear Backs, 1 Snout, 1 Head Back, 1 Head Front. From raspberry solid fabric you should have: 2 Ear Fronts, 2 Contrasting Paws, 2 Foot Bottoms.

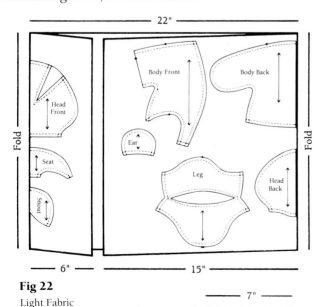

Fig 22
Light Fabric

Fig 23
Dark Fabric

2. Join contrasting Paws to Body Fronts as indicated on pattern, **Fig 24**.

3. Follow instructions for Blue Bearry, using contrasting Foot Bottom.

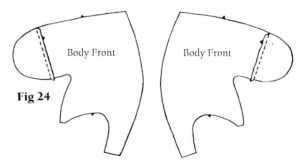

Fig 24

Razz Bearry's Head

Follow instructions for Blue Bearry's head.

Razz Bearry's Face

Follow instructions for Blue Bearry's face.

Razz Bearry's Bow (optional)

Follow instructions for Blue Bearry's bow.

continued

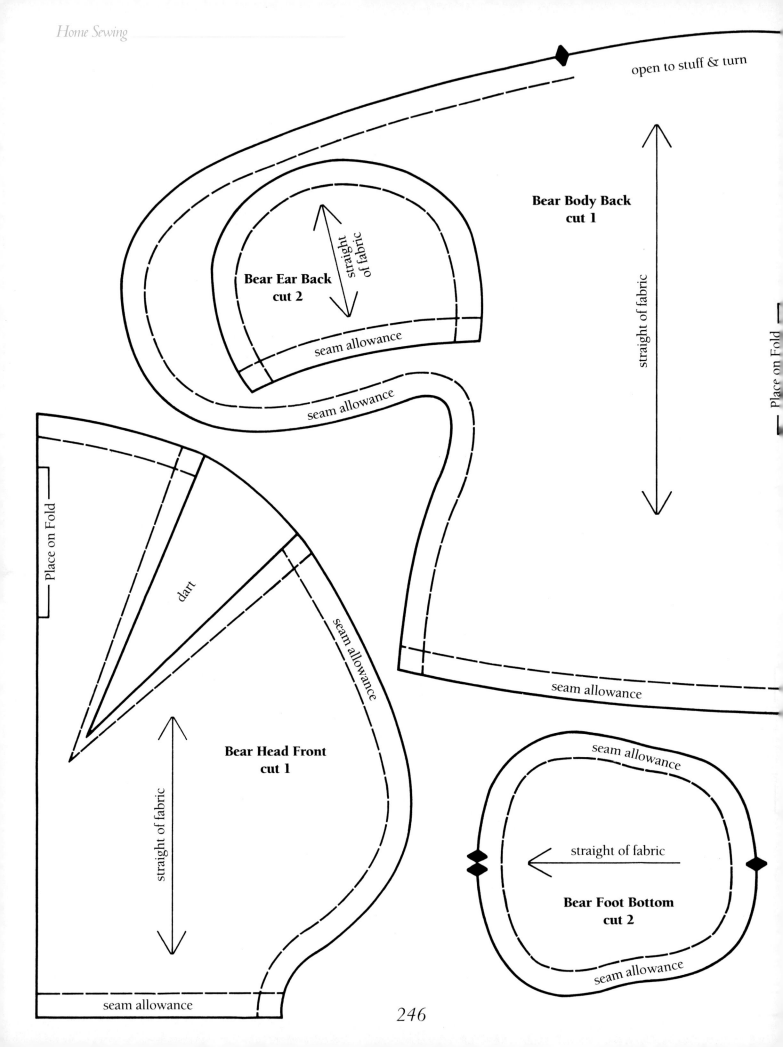

open to stuff & turn

**Bear Body Back
cut 1**

straight of fabric

Place on Fold

**Bear Ear Back
cut 2**

straight of fabric

seam allowance

seam allowance

seam allowance

Place on Fold

dart

seam allowance

**Bear Head Front
cut 1**

straight of fabric

seam allowance

seam allowance

straight of fabric

**Bear Foot Bottom
cut 2**

seam allowance

seam allowance

246

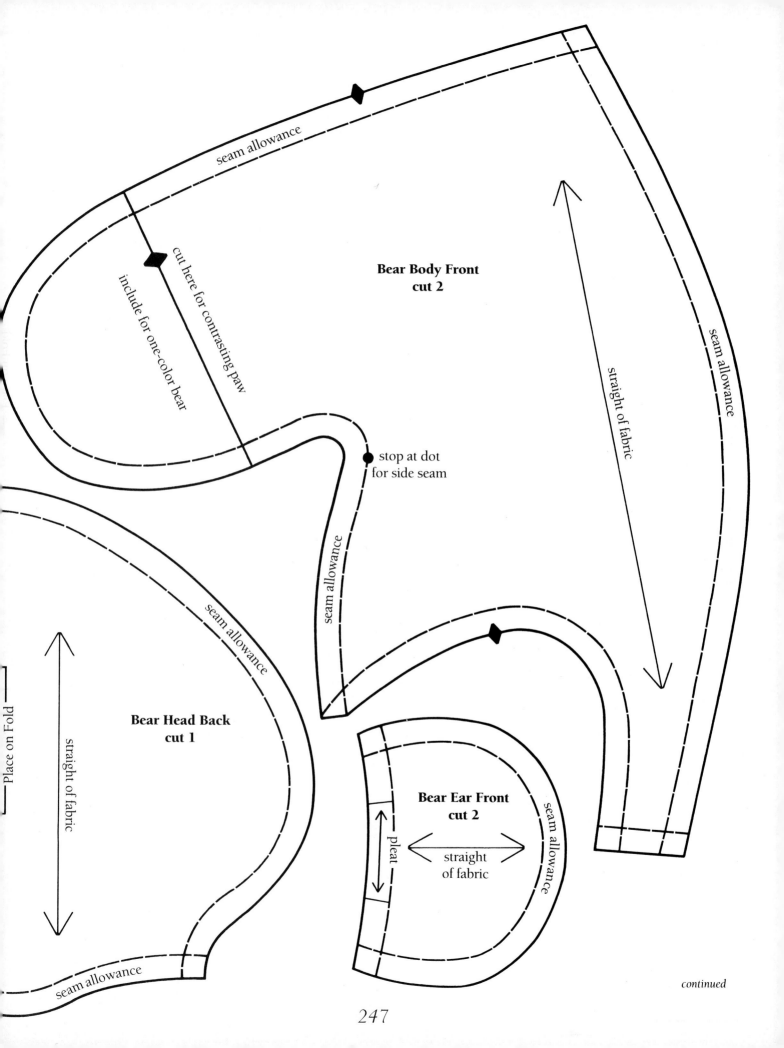

seam allowance

cut here for contrasting paw

include for one-color bear

**Bear Body Front
cut 2**

straight of fabric

seam allowance

stop at dot
for side seam

seam allowance

seam allowance

Place on Fold

straight of fabric

**Bear Head Back
cut 1**

seam allowance

pleat

**Bear Ear Front
cut 2**

straight
of fabric

seam allowance

seam allowance

continued

247

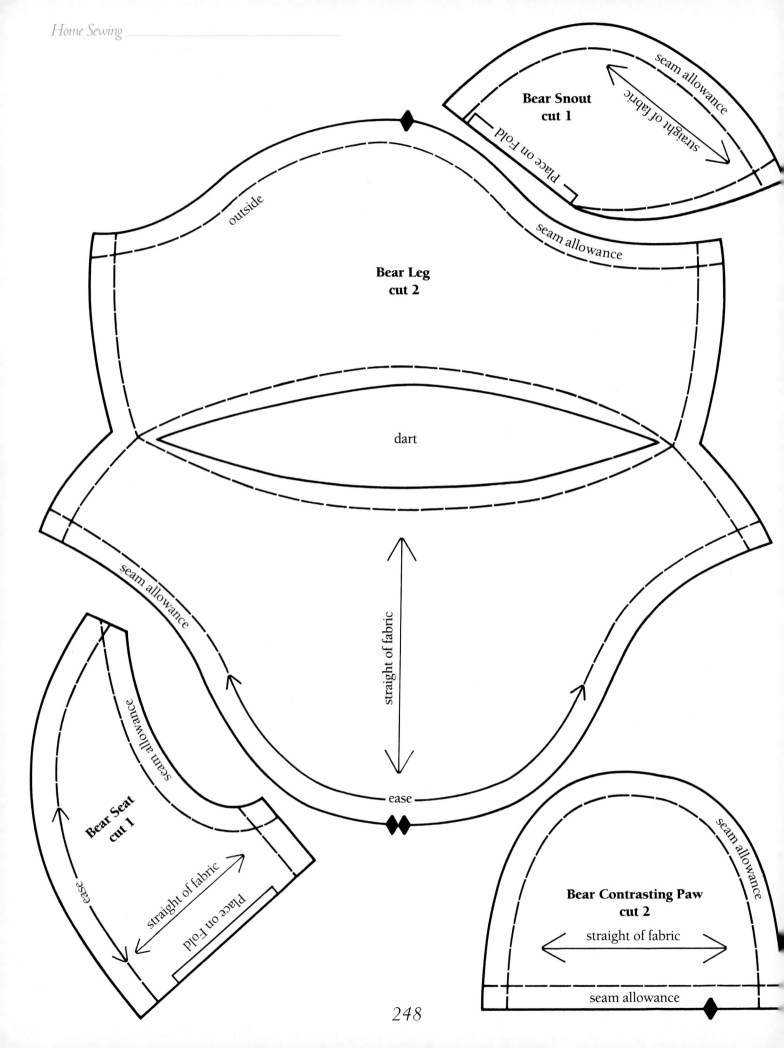

Bear Snout
cut 1

seam allowance

straight of fabric

Place on Fold

outside

Bear Leg
cut 2

seam allowance

dart

straight of fabric

ease

seam allowance

seam allowance

Bear Seat
cut 1

ease

straight of fabric

Place on Fold

Bear Contrasting Paw
cut 2

straight of fabric

seam allowance

seam allowance